Six Approaches to Child Rearing

Models from Psychological Theory

D. Eugene Mead

Brigham Young University Press

to Stanley and Mildred,

Vilate,

Sherrill,

Stanley, Marcia, and Christine

Library of Congress Cataloging in Publication Data

Mead, Donald Eugene, 1934-
　　Six approaches to child rearing.

　　Includes bibliographical references and index.
　　1. Children—Management.　　2. Child psychology.
I. Title.
HQ772.M39　　　　　649'.1　　　　76-19040
ISBN 0-8425-0327-7 pbk.

Library of Congress Catalog Card Number: 76-19040
International Standard Book Number: 0-8425-0327-7 (paperback)
Brigham Young University Press, Provo, Utah 84602
© 1976 by Brigham Young University Press. All rights reserved
Printed in the United States of America
76 3.5M 18300

Table of Contents

Acknowledgments

The author is indebted to a great many people, but probably most to my teacher Oscar C. Christensen, who first helped me understand how to be helpful to families. I am indebted also to Barbara Vance who suggested the need for this text and who gave me continuous encouragement in its development. Thanks are owed to Farrell W. Lewis, Darnell Zollinger, and A. Lynn Scoresby for reading selected parts of the text and giving valuable criticisms. I especially thank the many students in Child Development and Family Relationships 312 (Principles of Child Guidance): their questions helped shape this book. The support of J. Joel Moss, my friend and Chairman of the Child Development and Family Relationships Department at Brigham Young University, is gratefully acknowledged. And a special thanks and my admiration to the girls in the typing pool who typed on various sections of this text, and especially to Karen Brooksby and Kristine Allen, who typed the final drafts of the manuscript.

D. Eugene Mead

Guidance and Development

Parents everywhere and from all walks of life seem to want about the same things for their children. Researchers have found that both European and American parents want their children to be honest, happy, considerate, obedient, dependable, well mannered, and self-controlled (Kohn, 1959; Pearlin and Kohn, 1966). Other parents might mention spontaneity and creativity, success, independence, courage, or willingness to stand up for themselves and their convictions. It is impossible to make a definitive list. However, parents would be wise to establish for themselves the list of skills and values they wish their children to develop. With the ends clearly in mind, parents can more easily select a model for child rearing and guidance: by choosing the right model, parents can help determine the kind of children they have around them and the kind of adults those children will become.

Socialization

Parents are charged with the responsibility for socializing the young. *Socialization* is the process of acquiring the skills, knowledge, and values which will enable the individual to participate successfully in any phase of human interaction (Goslin, 1969). Socialization is a lifelong process. We are all being constantly socialized as we move from group to group and assume new roles. Although socialization occurs outside the family as well as within it, parents are most responsible for socialization of the children, especially in the early years. The model the parents choose for child rearing may therefore make an important difference in how successful their children come to be.

Parents receive the responsibility for socializing their children from religious institutions, government bodies, and their informal peer groups. However, parents themselves have been only informally socialized to assume such responsibilities (Hill and Aldous, 1969). What little training parents have in guidance and discipline comes largely from their own experience. They are limited to the observations they have made of their own parents and the parents of their peers. Their observation has been further limited by their subjective point of view as participants, for good or bad, in the very action they have been expected to observe; besides which their observations were made while they themselves were immature. All this means that parents learn their roles through on-the-job training.

This book surveys six approaches to child rearing and discipline that have been derived from psychological theories and models of human personality and behavior. A single formal theory of child rearing does not exist. Over the years psychological theories of personality, child development, and learning have been applied to problems of discipline and guidance in the classroom and at home. The theory chapters in this book attempt to bridge the gap between theory and practice by focusing on aspects of the theories which pertain to guidance and discipline problems and by attempting to relate general principles to specific applications.

Guidance

Guidance is the more or less deliberate child-rearing strategy parents use to get the type of children they want to have. It has been said that each new generation of children is a barbarian invasion. Children are born with no culture, no conception of the world of other people, no language, and no morality (Parsons, note 1). Children must learn all these things and more as they go along, and the techniques, methods, and tactics parents use to help a child acquire skills, knowledge, and values they believe he needs in life are their guidance practices.

Guidance practices may be deliberate or accidental; they may be the result of conscious deliberate efforts on the part of the parents or they may be the result of implicit rules and concepts which the parents have never openly discussed. It seems likely that the more parents make their guidance practices explicit and specific the more successfully they will guide their children; yet though parents can increase their skill in guidance techniques, children will not all turn out to be exactly what their parents had in mind. Why not? However much parents agree in their ideals for children (Kohn, 1959), they are usually confused about how to translate those ideals into action.

Part of the confusion stems from the fact that parents often do not know their own values (Kohlberg, 1964). For example, parents often find it hard to decide whether to stop the child right now from doing whatever he is doing or to let the child make decisions about that type of behavior on his own. While blue-collar parents more frequently want children to be obedient to authority and middle-class parents often want children to act from principle and conscience, most parents are confused about which technique to use and when to use it.

Confusion about which technique to employ continues even when parents are relatively sure of what they want to teach. A technique which works at age five may not work at age twelve. What works for boys often does not work for girls. To make matters worse, methods that stop a child right now from doing an act may not help the child develop a conscience that will serve to control behavior in the future. And a technique that brings stealing to an end probably will not keep a child from talking back or otherwise disobeying.

Kohlberg (1964) has suggested that some parents are so unsure of themselves and what they should teach that they are not even sure if they should try to teach their children moral values at all. Some feel that they should merely provide a happy home and trust that the child will develop morality all on his own. Berkowitz (1964) is rather emphatic against this attitude: "Parents who want their children to strive for excellence and to be responsible and law-abiding citizens must take an active part in training their children" (p. 95). If Berkowitz is correct, we must work our way out of the confusion and try to give our children guidance.

Our ability as parents to provide guidance may be limited by our own skills and personal learning history. Brim (1959) suggests that our ability to act deliberately and rationally varies with the child and the situation. With some children we can have a perfectly reasonable conversation on almost any subject. With other children we find ourselves unable to carry on a sensible discussion on any subject. Our ability to provide guidance also varies with the subject matter. Some people who are quite capable of teaching money management find themselves completely unable to discuss the facts and emotions associated with sexual behavior or aggressive acts. As parents we need to recognize our own limitations and improve our skills or seek assistance in areas where we are deficient.

To make up for lack of specific skills parents have traditionally turned to other family members for assistance. Parents also turn to schools, churches, and youth groups for supplementary education for their children. It is important to recognize, however, that agencies outside the home, no matter how carefully selected, will shape children differently than the parents. Our guidance techniques do not result in "perfect" children partly because the process of socialization takes place both in the home and outside of it.

As the child develops physically he becomes more and more mobile in the community. He takes part in more and varied groups. Inputs from Sunday school, kindergarten, the neighborhood gang, and other groups influence the child's behavior. Inasmuch as the new behavior deviates from behavior prized and valued by the parents it results in children who differ from the parents' "ideal." Outside groups, and especially peer groups, come to have more and more control over the child's behavior as he grows up, until external groups assume almost complete control of the adult's behavior. Since this is so, parents who are concerned about inner-directed children and adults may need to work especially hard at establishing internal controls to counteract, as far as possible, the external influences.

Besides the parents and external influences there is a third source of variation in the child's behavior: the child himself. Children influence the guidance process too, as most parents will attest. Changes which occur in the child create changes in the parents. Socialization is never a one-way process. Changes in the child can come from growth, learning, or the child's responses to himself. (The child's response to himself is sometimes referred to as his *self-concept*, his goals, or his *personality*.) When such changes occur in the child's behavior, parents' reactions may accelerate the change, slow it down, or in some other way alter it. However, parents can rarely change it completely.

Changes related to physical growth rarely dictate specific changes in human behavior. Our genetic inheritance appears to establish characteristic activity levels which remain relatively constant throughout our lifetime. More importantly, changes caused by growth allow other behavior changes. For example, when a child learns to walk he has a greater field of activity and new perspectives—which create a new set of problems for parents to face. Another example: puberty brings on increased interest in the opposite sex, new feelings and emotions, and changing expectations from peers. In both cases parents must help the child set new limits and establish ways of coping with new situations and changed expectations. Changes due to the child's growth often require changes in the parents' guidance techniques.

The child's learning is probably the greatest single source of changes in the child's behavior. Most of what we think of as biologically determined behavior changes rapidly under the influence of learning. The child's natural capacity to adapt to changes in his environment leads to behavioral changes which are not always welcomed by the parents. It is more than a joke to say we spend the first two years teaching a child to talk and the rest of his life trying to get him to be quiet. Because we can never control all his learning, the child is bound to turn out differently than his parents had hoped or planned.

The child's behavior may also be the result of his self-concept. Thus the child's decision to act or not act may be influenced by learning, growth, and his own personal evaluation of how this choice will fit into his goals. Any or all of these processes—growth, learning, or personal evaluation—lead to new responses on the part of the child. Who ever said parenting was going to be easy?

Discipline

The fact that the child is an active participant in the guidance process brings the adult socializer and the child into conflict from time to time (Becker, 1964; Brown, 1965; Goslin, 1969; Kohlberg, 1964). When conflict occurs parents and teachers often apply external controls in order to gain compliance. The external controls often take the form of punishment. Any event which deprives the child of rights, privileges, or accustomed rewards, or which is aversive, can be considered punishing. The meaning of discipline is "to teach or train." However, the frequent association of the word with punishment has caused most parents (and children) to associate the term *discipline* with punishment. Thus, when most parents think of disciplining their children they automatically think of punishing them.

Discipline, according to Aronfreed (1968) and Medinnus and Johnson (1967) may be defined as attempts to bring external control over children. Thus discipline includes *both* positive and negative responses on the part of the adult (Aronfreed, 1968; Becker, 1964; Brim, 1959; Kohlberg, 1964). Reward, praise, and encouragement are used to discipline children, besides physical punishment, shouting, and scolding. While discipline is but one part of the child guidance process (Becker, 1964; Gordon, 1970b) it appears to be the part which causes most parents and teachers the greatest concern.

It is important to recognize that both discipline and affectional relationships have similar consequences for the child (Becker, 1964). The learning that takes place at the time of the child's transgressions cannot be separated entirely from the base of positive affection established at other times in adult-child interactions (Aronfreed, 1968). Dreikurs (1968) and others (Madsen and Madsen, 1972) have pointed out that we cannot really teach anyone with whom we are not on friendly terms. Our discipline and guidance are more effective when we have established and are maintaining a friendly relationship with the child. Almost all parental behavior which is observed by the child shapes or influences the child's behavior in some way.

Although children are subject to many influences in the process of socialization, for most children the influence of their parents is probably the greatest single factor. Because of this, parents should work to develop the skills they need in order to rear children who will make the greatest possible contribution to their culture. The development or adoption of a useful theory of child guidance is one way parents may improve their child-rearing skills.

Using Theory in Child Rearing and Guidance

Wherever and whenever parents or teachers get together the conversation eventually turns to questions of guidance and discipline. The almost universal question seems to be "Why do children act that way and what can be done about it?" Parents and teachers engaged in daily interaction with children feel that their struggle is unique and that a solution is badly needed. However, the problem usually fits into a class of problems common to other children at a certain stage in similar circumstances. While the reason this child hits or hides or steals may be peculiar to him, and while his acts are done in his own unique manner, there will still be enough similarity between the causes, the behavior, and the effects on others for his parents to find help from a more general case.

As far as we can group problems faced by children and parents into categories and find potential solutions for those problem categories we can derive some principles for child guidance. Over the years such principles have been derived informally and passed on by word of mouth to young parents. Parents, grandparents, uncles, and aunts have all contributed to the new parents' "theory" of child guidance. From time to time these rules and principles were written down as part of religious teachings or in the laws of political units. The purpose of these principles is, of course, to help parents and others to act appropriately in response to children's behavior. Today, in our mobile and technological world, experts often take the role of extended family members. However, their function is still the same: to provide principles and axioms by which parents may appropriately match the behavior of their children.

Many parents and future parents blanch at the mention of theory and ask, "Why theory? Why not just tell us what to do when the baby won't stop crying, or Janet has trouble making friends in third grade, or Richard takes up with a group we suspect of experimenting with drugs?"

Good theory, if understood and put to use, is really very practical. If each problem encountered by a parent were truly unique then each problem would require a singular solution. Fortunately this is not usually the case. When problems fall into classes or patterns, then solutions which have been found to work well with that class of problems stand a high chance of working with this specific problem. Theory brings together the general principles which may be used to derive a solution for a special case.

The purpose of theory development is to produce laws, propositions, axioms, and corollaries general enough to cover a number of specific cases (Burr, 1973). Theory may show how events in nature are related to each other, and indicate any regularities in occurrence which may be predicted with some level of certainty. If the statements of a theory are correct, and no other influences are operating at the time, then we should be able to predict specific events from the general case described by the theory. For example, if we know that reinforcement or reward following a behavior increases the probability of that behavior being repeated, we may apply this general principle in specific cases. If we wish a child to share more with other children, we can wait until he shares something with another child and then arrange for a reward. If we do this frequently, we may expect to see sharing increase. Theory helps us go from the general to the specific. It helps us to act more effectively in response to circumstances (Skinner, 1957) presented by our children and their problems.

There are several steps a parent might use to apply theory (Burr, Mead, and Rollins, 1973). These steps correspond to the four steps in the experimental method: observation, hypothesis-making, testing, and evaluation (Yates, 1975).

Careful observation of the child's behavior is a must for parents as well as the scientist. If we are to be effective in our child guidance techniques we need to observe carefully the child's current behavior, as he is right now. This means setting aside any feelings we have had as a response to behavior in the past and taking time to get to know the child here and now. It is important that we consider our goals and values and determine which behaviors it is important to increase as well as which behaviors we wish to decrease.

Careful observation includes recording behavior frequencies. By counting the number of times the child comes into the house crying and observing the circumstances which precede (such as not getting his way with others) and which follow (such as cookies and conversation with mother) we may find the cause of the behavior and its seriousness. By continuing to record our observations during corrective action we can notice when the behavior changes. As we see the behavior changing on our record we can tell how effective our guidance is.

Following our observation and recording of the child's behavior we are ready to start using theory. We must reason from the specific behaviors of the child back to the general principles found in the theory. One might begin by asking, "What class of behaviors does the behavior of this child fit into?" If we see the child hitting, kicking, and biting, it is fairly easy to fit the behavior into the category of aggressive behaviors. It is sometimes more difficult when the child does not participate with others or sits quietly through much of the day. Should we consider the behavior as shyness or withdrawal, sulkiness or thoughtfulness, introversion or contemplation? Often careful observation of the entire situation is necessary before we can decide where the behavior fits.

However, we must be careful not to suppose that to name the problem is to solve it. Identifying the behavior too often results in nothing more productive than labeling a child. When labels, such as lazy, aggressive, mean, and jolly, are attached to a child there are unfortunate side effects. First, parents may not move to help the child solve the problem because they come to believe he *is* the labeled behavior; for example, if parents assume the child does not do things because he *is* "lazy," they may give up because they feel there is nothing they can do. Second, there is the danger in the application of labels that the child himself may come to believe that he *is* that way. Once he believes that he *is*, for example, lazy, he will respond according to the label instead of trying to change.

The purpose of assigning the child's behavior to a class of behaviors is to identify an applicable theoretical principle with its tested solutions. This allows the parents to apply a solution more confidently than if they had to work out a solution by trial and error. Diagnosis of the problem should therefore lead to parents making an educated guess—a hypothesis—about ways to change the child's behavior.

Forming a hypothesis sets up a miniature experiment. When a child frequently hits, bites, pushes, takes toys away from others, and demands that the others do just what he asks, his parents may decide that his behavior is more than normal assertive responses—more than just standing up for his rights. After determining the problem, the parents see what solution their theory* suggests: this solution becomes their educated guess, and they are ready to test it.

During the testing stage the parents try the solution and observe the results, continuing to record the data. Behavior does not change immediately, of course. While children occasionally learn on the first try, most changes require repetition for improvement to take place. Parents should look for progress, not perfection.

After a reasonable amount of testing the results are evaluated. If the results are as predicted in our hypothesis the theory is verified. If not, the parents may need to go back to the first step and doublecheck their work. Were they observing the complete sequence associated with the behavior? Did they properly classify it? Should they modify their hypothesis? Did they apply the proper treatment? Did they give the treatment enough time to really work? If the parents answer *yes* to these questions then they may need to revise the theory or get a new one. (Failure of a theory to get the results we wish is not an indictment of the theory. Naturally a theory which continually fails to get us the results we seek should be discarded. However, it should only be set aside for a new and better theory.)

Theory may be useful to us in our attempts to guide and discipline our children in at least two more ways. The theory should indicate some of the long- and short-range outcomes of particular parental practices: it should tell us what kind of adults our children might become because of a particular pattern of discipline, besides what the children would be like while under the regimen. Theory can also help us as parents to prevent problems before they occur, besides helping us solve what has already gone wrong.

The theories reviewed in the second and third sections of this book provide a variety of principles for effective parenting. The widely variant approaches presented in the text show that there is no "right" way to rear children. Families consist of individuals with different heredities and learning histories. Parents and children must continuously adjust to each other's needs. However, because parents have both a legal and moral responsibility to guide their children, they must decide together how to work for the optimum development of their children. This book provides information to help parents make intelligent choices.

Your Personal Guidance Theory

All of us have some principles that guide our actions when we deal with children. Taken together, these principles are an informal theory of child guidance.

Some of this informal theory may be based on tradition and folklore. And while we cannot and should not ignore the collected wisdom of our cultural heritage it should be noted that folklore and tradition are often contradictory and sometimes counter to scientifically established fact. Contradictions in folklore include such sayings as "Spare the rod and spoil the child" and "You can catch more flys with honey than with vinegar." While both sayings may have some validity it is difficult to know when and under what circumstances to apply the honey or the rod. Certainly the sayings themselves do not help in making a decision concerning the right time and place to reward or punish a child; in fact, research (Skinner, 1953) suggests that excessive punishment has a high probability of being counterproductive in teaching the child appropriate behavior. (Further examples of folklore not squaring with the facts may be found in LeMaster's [1970, pp. 17-31] very interesting chapter on the folklore of parenthood.)

Personal experience is a far more important source of parents' informal theory of child guidance and discipline. The methods used by our parents and other adults who were important to us in our youth remain deeply impressed upon us. When as parents we are puzzled by the behavior of one of our children, our first response is often similar to the action our parents took with us. We react with behaviors which are familiar and routine.

A third source of information for our personal guidance theory is advice from the professionals. Books, magazines, and the family physician all supply suggestions and advice which we add to our personal experience as best we can. We can make better use of the advice of theorists if we have a grasp of the nature of theory and some ideas about how to apply it.

Organization of the Book

The three chapters in Part One deal with theories included primarily for their historic interest and the part they have played in child guidance and discipline over the past fifty years: Chapter Two describes psychoanalytic theory as applied to child rearing and discipline, Chapter Three explores developmental theory, and Chapter Four contains the socio-teleological approach.

Part Two includes three theories that are currently receiving considerable attention in the scientific community: Chapter Five is the cognitive developmental approach, Chapter Six presents the phenomenological-existential approach, and Chapter Seven contains the behavioral view as applied to guidance and discipline.

No theory has been developed just for child rearing. This text applies the principles and propositions of the various theories much as an engineer applies the theories of the physical sciences. To apply a theory properly it is important

---

*The theories found in this book (and elsewhere) vary widely on what they assume are the causes of aggression or any other behavior. Therefore, they also vary greatly in the methods recommended to bring about a change. To avoid confusion it is recommended that parents pick a theory which is comfortable to them and that they stick with it unless it proves unworkable.

to understand its underlying assumptions. This book examines each theory's assumptions concerning the nature of man, the nature of children, and the relationship of the individual to the group.

The Nature of Man

All the theories included in this work assume that man is a biological organism which has evolved through the long ages into his present physical form. The theories disagree markedly, however, upon the extent to which man's biological inheritance determines current behavior. Some theories claim that most of our behavior is determined by our genetic inheritance, while others state that our behavior is primarily the result of our experience with the environment. Over the years the question of how much of our behavior is determined by heredity and how much by environment has come and gone and come again. A far more practical question may be how *both* influence behavior. If we could understand how and when heredity and environment influence behavior we would have a better chance of understanding if and how we can change a child's behavior.

The Nature of Children

None of the theories reviewed here assume, as did some 18th-century writers (Bardis, 1964), that children are merely small adults born knowing good from evil, who misbehave out of perversity. Modern theorists see children as immature organisms, though they differ on the nature and extent to which immaturity influences behavior. For some theorists certain behaviors cannot emerge until appropriate levels of development have been attained through growth. For other theorists the important differences occur, not as the result of growth, but as the result of the time it takes for growth to occur. This is essentially the heredity versus environment argument applied to child growth and development.

The question is an important one for parents. The position one takes on this issue may influence how, when, and even *if* we try to influence the behaviors of our children. If we assume, for example, that all two-and-a-half-year-olds are terrible and unmanageable due to growth patterns, then we may logically choose to ignore the behavior until further growth occurs and the child matures out of the behavior. Our behavior might be markedly different if we assume that terrible and unmanageable behavior is learned and can therefore be changed.

The Relationship of the Individual to the Group

The question of whether the group exists for the individual or the individual for the group is at least as old as written history (Frank and Meserole, 1965). Some theories focus on the importance of the individual apart from the group, while others suggest that group feelings are inherent and essential to the very nature of man. The position taken by parents on this issue may have a bearing upon their child-rearing practices. If parents wish to work toward developing children who are good team members they may not follow the same principles as those who want their children to be independent thinkers.

Other Dimensions and Issues

As Millon (1967) has pointed out, "Different theories ask different questions, use different procedures, and focus on different types of data." As a result, there appears to be no way of directly comparing each dimension of each of the theories. This book develops each aspect of the various theories which appears to have relevance for child rearing and discipline, and important similarities and differences between theories will be pointed out.

A Word of Caution about Eclecticism

The reader should be aware that presenting a number of points of view as equally plausible approaches to child rearing may create problems. Some writers feel that exposure to a number of theories will lead to a "healthy eclecticism" (Brim, 1959). However, others feel that the result may be "a vapid eclecticism, with [the parents assuming] the general formula, 'There's much to be said on all sides' " (Hilgard, 1956). The latter approach may lead to confusion or a general apathy. To avoid such an outcome it seems reasonable to suggest that parents-in-training accept one approach and attempt to learn it well enough to apply its principles and methods easily and comfortably. In accepting a particular approach care must be taken not to assume a rigidly dogmatic and bigoted position which would prevent understanding the truths that may be found in other models.

Part One

In this section, three theories are reviewed which have been influential in the child-rearing practices of the United States over the past fifty years. Undoubtedly the most well-known and widely held theory of human behavior in Western culture has been that of psychoanalysis. Freud's theories of human behavior have been deeply influential in our thinking about child rearing and discipline. The excitement and controversy generated by psychoanalysis have given rise to a great deal of research, most of which has been found not to support the basic assumptions and tenets of the theory (Eysenck and Wilson, 1973; Kline, 1972). In science this signals the end of the usefulness of the approach (Kuhn, 1970). The psychoanalytic approach is included here, first because it is so widely known and followed that it may continue to be a part of child-rearing conversation, if not practice, for some time; and second because it has come to play an important part in much of our literature, art, theatre, and even law.

Developmental theory has also played an important role in child-rearing practices in this country during the first half of this century. Gesell's work was widely known and disseminated by two of his students, Ilg and Ames, who published a syndicated column in many newspapers giving guidance to parents. The developmental approach was also widely used in preschool programs throughout the United States. Despite its popularity with the public, the theory has not generated recent excitement in the scientific community. Tied as it is to the facts of physical growth and development, its usefulness in predicting behavior has been extremely limited. And since much of modern psychology and biology is focused upon behavior, Gesell's form of developmental theory has lost much of its momentum. As in the case of psychoanalysis, developmental theory's widespread use merits it a place here to help parents and students orient what *has been* to what *is*.

The third theory included in Part One is the socio-teleological theory, first developed by Adler and successfully elaborated by Dreikurs in the United States. Less well known than the two methods described above, the socio-teleological approach has nonetheless been influential in bringing a focus upon the entire family as the unit of study with child rearing and discipline. Socio-teleological theory has developed a rich store of practical methods for parents, but has been less successful in developing research to test its underlying assumptions and principles. Many of the practical methods utilized by the socio-teleological approach may be more easily and clearly explained by other theoretical models—especially behavioral learning theory. When this happens, scientists tend to utilize the theory which explains the phenomena most easily. It is worthwhile to include the socio-teleological approach because it has developed so many helpful methods and because it is useful to see how the principles of one theory relate to others.

Students and parents who are concerned primarily with contemporary theories and how they are applied to child-rearing may wish to attend only briefly to the

11

theories described in Part One. They may even choose to go directly to Part Two and return to Part One only for reference. However, many parents and students will find the material in Part One useful and therefore rewarding.

The Psychoanalytic Approach 2

Chronologically, Sigmund Freud's psychoanalytic theory antedates all other comprehensive theories of personality (Ford and Urban, 1963). Not only has Freud's theory of human personality been on the scene longer than any other theory, but it has also been of great influence in twentieth-century Western thought. Psychoanalysis has influenced the fields of entertainment, art, literature, and law. It has also been widely used as a basis for child guidance and discipline. Psychoanalysis has probably been the most influential theory of personality during the first half of the twentieth century.

Freud began his career in medicine as a neurologist. In his attempt to understand hysteria and neurosis, Freud used a technique which he and Breuer termed the "cathartic method" (Brill, 1938). The cathartic method consists of allowing the patient to talk out his emotional responses concerning some real or imagined traumatic event in his past. After experiencing some disappointment in the use of hypnosis as a means of eliciting the cathartic talk, Freud hit upon the method of *free association*. Freud (1938) saw free association as a method of "observing" repressed or forgotten events which were conceived to be the cause of the neurotic or hysteric symptoms. The associations were not, therefore, free, but were determined by the repressed material in the patient's unconscious mental system. The material which was produced in free association had to be analyzed and interpreted. It is from this process that Freud developed the term *psychoanalysis*.

The method of free association was both the source of Freud's success and his weakness. As a method of observation it served to elicit from the patient a great deal of verbal material which could be subjected to analysis and interpretation by Freud and other analysts. They were not interested in analyzing the patient's free associative verbal behavior. If they had been they might have had an excellent tool. What they wanted to do was look into the patient's unconscious mental activity, much as an astronomer looks into the heavens with a telescope to observe otherwise invisible stars. Free association was for Freud the psychoanalyst's telescope. Unfortunately, for a number of reasons it proved a rather unreliable instrument.

The unreliability of the observations made through free association were built in almost from the first. To begin with, they were made in the physician's office. The tradition of privacy as part of the doctor-patient relationship is almost sacred tradition. Therefore, the scientific method of having two or more observers record the same event was not possible. This surrounded the psychoanalytic session in a mystic aura, and made research difficult, if not impossible. And to make matters even worse, the unconscious processes described by Freud, such as the conflict between the instinctive id forces and the learned ego structures which we shall discuss at length later, can only be inferred from analysis of the free association data. This would not be a problem if the observations always produced the same results; but they do not. And without a basis of observable facts, two or more analysts may differ on the meaning of the causes of a given behavior, without much chance of eventual agreement. How to get reliable data then becomes the issue: how to standardize observation.

Analysts hit upon the method of the "training analysis" as the answer. If the analyst is trained to see exactly as other analysts see, then he will make reliable observations. Starting with Freud as the authority (a position which he readily accepted; Freud, 1938, p. 933), other analysts were expected to undergo an extended training analysis, usually lasting two or more years. The purpose of the training analysis is to make the new psychoanalyst a reliable and standardized observer of the unconscious mental processes. Unfortunately, the unreliability of free association is compounded by just this process (Eysenck and Wilson, 1973). The time and expense of the training analysis is too great to be undergone more than once in the lifetime of most analysts. Over their lifetimes analysts tend to drift away from their original standardized observation methods, and so cannot be expected to remain reliable indefinitely.

Although Freud's (1938) most important theoretical studies are based on data he acquired through observation of his patients' free associations, it should be possible to test, by the usual methods of science, the propositions and concepts that he elaborated (Eysenck and Wilson, 1973). We shall review some of that evidence at the end of the chapter; but first we shall look at the components of the theory which seem most pertinent to child rearing and discipline. Only the briefest summary of the most salient factors of Freud's theorizing can be presented here.

The Psychoanalytic View of the Nature of Man

Freud was trained in the physics and biology of his day, and so applied the scientific principles of that time to his understanding of the nature of man and human behavior.

The physics of Freud's day viewed the physical world in terms of balance and imbalance (Fromm, 1947). It was a closed system which attempted to maintain homeostasis. *Homeostasis* means that whenever there is an imbalance created in some way, countering forces attempt to force the system back into a balanced state. Freud (1938) applied the homeostatic principle to his view of personality. He saw human behavior as an attempt to maintain a balance within the psychic or mental energy system.

A stimulus that creates an imbalance, such as a sudden hunger or pain, is unpleasant to the individual, and may produce feelings of anxiety. Anxiety at its most extreme is a feeling of helplessness, dread, or powerlessness in the face of an unknown threat to survival. The individual, in response to those feelings, attempts to remove the unpleasant feeling in order to reinstate the balance and its associated feelings of comfort and pleasantness. One may attempt to remove the imbalance by doing away with the feelings. One may try to wish away the feelings, or he may try to do something about the situation which is creating the feelings. But however it is accomplished, the psychic energy system must come back to a new level of balance. According to Freud, man is always reacting to stimulus events, whether internal or external. Internal events that cause imbalance are changes in physical states, such as hunger or thirst. External events that cause imbalance are changes in the environment, such as a new person or a threat. Whatever the source of imbalance, man is continually striving to gain the pleasure of the balanced state.

Freud was also influenced by the biology of his day. Freud saw man's basic drives as being biological: the drive for individual survival, and the drive for survival of the species (Freud, 1938, 1961; Hartmann, 1967). In order for the individual to survive he must learn to defend himself from outside threats and attacks. This can be, and is for Freud, both physical and psychological defense. The drive for survival of the individual is an aggressive drive. The species can survive, however, only by procreation, and so the second major drive of mankind is the sexual drive, which promotes group survival.

To Freud, therefore, man is a dynamic energy system which attempts to maintain a balance within the system, and to solve the problems created by the two basic biological drives—aggression and sex. According to Freud the processes which have evolved for solving the problems of imbalance are the id, ego, and superego.

The Id. Man inherits the two basic drives, the sexual drive and the aggressive drive. At first these drives are not separate from each other. The sex drive and the aggressive drive are, for Freud, undifferentiated, a single source of energy available to the newborn infant for survival. This early primitive source of energy for survival Freud labeled the *libido*. The libidinal energy is under the control of the id.

The id is the inherited biological mental apparatus for dealing with the psychological survival of the child. The id knows nothing of reality* or rationality. The id responds to external or internal environmental disturbances with attempts to return the physical and psychological state to an immediate new state of balance. As was stated above, returning to a balanced state is experienced by the individual as pleasurable. Since the id attempts to always create a balanced state, without considering reality, the id is said to operate on the *pleasure principle*.

In attempting to reduce the tension created by a disturbance to the system the id can only create an image of something which might reduce or remove the source of tension. If the individual is cold the id wishes for warmth. If the wish is unsatisfactory in solving the problem and reducing the feeling of being cold, the individual may become frustrated and angry. If the unsatisfactory condition, in this case being cold, continues, the experience may produce a great deal of anxiety. The id can focus on either aggressive or sexual energies to restore balance. If the id focuses upon aggressive aspects, the individual may become aggressive and hostile in his general approach to life. If, on the other hand, the id focuses on sexual feelings, the individual may seek a sensuous solution to his problem. To win "warmth" from others he may act in a passive, helpless, and dependent manner. Thus his wish for warmth, if coupled with trauma and anxiety, may lead the individual to either assertive aggressive wishes or passive dependent wishes.

Obviously none of the solutions given above is very satisfactory over time. The individual who is cold must find a way to increase his body temperature: he must seek and find a source of additional warmth. One must learn to differentiate between the wish to be warm and sources of warmth in the world of objective reality.

The Ego. While the id knows only the subjective world of wishes, the ego is the part of the mind which comes to know and deal with the world of objective reality. The id attempts to solve problems by the pleasure principle, seeking immediate gratification. The ego, however, can delay tension release until an appropriate object or time appears. The ego utilizes the *reality principle* to solve problems which have created an imbalance in the psychic system. By the indi-

---

*Freud's term *reality* corresponds to the term *environment* in several of the other theories (developmental, Chapter Three; cognitive developmental, Chapter Four; and behavioral, Chapter Seven) and to the concept of the phenomenal field in existential-phenomenological theory, Chapter Six.

vidual finding a blanket or moving near a real (not imagined) fire the wish for warmth is satisfied in reality and not by a wish.

In time the ego becomes the gatekeeper of the personality. The ego utilizes rational and realistic processes to select, order, and organize the energy of the individual to best satisfy his basic drives. Survival may best be served by delaying satisfaction of sexual urges, for example, in a society which severely punishes individuals who openly display sexual behaviors. The ego works to satisfy the basic drives through testing reality and organizing the individual's drives in accord with the perceived reality. The ego is and remains a servant of the id. The ego derives its psychic energy from the id. The same primary motivating forces, sex and aggression, drive the ego and the id.

The Superego. Part of the reality of the objective world, as the child comes to know it, are the rules and values of society. The child first encounters these rules in his interaction with his parents. Parents reward acceptable behaviors and punish unacceptable behaviors. Over time the child builds an internal set of values and principles similar to those taught by his parents. (The process by which the child takes in his or her parents' values and especially those values associated with individual sex roles is explained in more detail below in the discussion of the latency period and the Oedipal complex.) It is the function of the superego to use the values and rules imposed upon the child by society to check the id's indiscriminate pleasure seeking.

The superego consists of two subsystems, the *conscience* and the *ego-ideal*. The conscience becomes the internal punishing agent. To obtain the parents' love the child avoids doing those things for which the parents have punished him.

Furthermore, the child will strive to do perfectly those things he has been rewarded for doing and upon which he sees his parents placing great value and importance. The ego-ideal is the source of the child's efforts to reach perfection (A. Freud, 1935; 1968).

If the child's superego is not too demanding in terms of punishment (guilt feelings) and striving for perfection the child can effectively substitute self-control for parental control. An overly punitive conscience may direct so much of the aggressive energy upon the individual himself that he constantly defeats himself. An overdeveloped ego-ideal, on the other hand, may also prove self-defeating in that the individual demands such a high level of performance that it becomes impossible to achieve. Failure to reach perfection may then be seen by the individual as total failure as a person, and he may give up altogether.

The superego is a modified portion of the ego which has derived its energy from the id. The superego, therefore, serves as a function of the id and is integrated with it. Unlike the ego, which attempts to delay the impulses, the superego attempts to block unacceptable impulses completely. It does this by substituting moralistic goals for realistic goals and by diverting energies from primitive impulses to idealistic and perfectionistic goals (A. Freud, 1968). Nonetheless, the three processes—id, ego, and superego—work together for the survival of the individual and the species.

In sum, Freud conceived of man as a biological organism under the influence of two basic instinctive drives, sex and aggression. These drives are said to be in conflict with culturally imposed demands in the form of ethical and religious prohibitions on behavior. Freud conceptualized the id as the basic structure of mental activity in man. The id consists of sexual and aggressive energy. In order to gratify the basic wishes associated with the id impulses and achieve the pleasure of a return to a balanced or homeostatic state, the id releases part of its energy to deal with reality. The ego is that part of the mental system which has contact with reality in the service of the id. Neurosis results when the ego is unable to effectively contain and channel the id impulses (Brill, 1938). The superego forms from the ego as a result of the child's assuming the rules and prohibitions of civilization as his own rules and prohibitions. The superego is the source of conscience and ego-ideals or the striving for perfection. The three parts of the mental system—the id, ego, and superego—all function to insure the survival of the individual and the species.

The Psychoanalytic View of the Nature of Children

According to Freudian psychology, children are born without a concept of reality and without knowledge of values and principles. The newborn child is all id. The infant seeks immediate and complete satisfaction of all his biological urges in a primitive organismic way; this is the pleasure principle. The infant is completely arational. When he is hungry he wishes to be fed, when he is wet he wants immediately to be dry, and when he is asleep he does not wish to be awakened.

Throughout early childhood the child sees everything that happens in the world as connected to himself, his wishes, his feelings, and his experiences. The child is truly egocentric in that he sees himself as the center of all the world. Anna Freud (1968) likens this to the adult's dream and daydream world in which the dreamer is always the center of the action. It is normal for the child to remain egocentric throughout the preschool years. By five or six the child usually outgrows this way of looking at the world and begins to identify with other people's points-of-view, especially his parents'.

Because the infant is all id and has yet to develop an ego, the child is under the complete control of his basic biological drives. He is not capable of rationally approaching a problem. The child can only approach a problem emotionally. His behavior is governed by his fears, wishes, and impulses. He cannot wait for satisfaction, or delay rewards. Unlike an adult who has developed a reasonable ego, the child views the world in terms of here and now; he is unable to take a long-range view of events. It is important for parents and others involved in guiding the child during the preschool years to be aware of the child's egocentric and emotional approach to the world. Such an awareness should lead to a more sympathetic and understanding response to the child's behavior and should prevent us from demanding behavior from the child which he is not capable of performing.

Psychosexual Stages. In addition to the general description of childhood given above, Freud's writings (1938) suggest that children must go through four critical stages of psychosexual development on their way to becoming adults. Three of these stages, the oral, anal, and phallic, are centered around particular physical areas and the pleasurable sensations associated with them. The fourth stage is known as the latency stage and is characterized by the lessened importance of stimulation to the three erogenous zones.

The child's personality is formed by how he learns to handle the feelings which occur during his growth through the developmental stages. The child's patterns of interaction with others, especially parents, during the psychosexual stages determine all his future patterns of interaction (Freud, 1938). Since the psychosexual stages are so important for the developing child's personality, we shall review each in turn.

According to Freud, the most sensitive area of the body for the infant is the area of the mouth. Most of the infant's gratification or pleasure is associated with activities focused in and around the mouth. The fact that the mouth or *oral zone* is the source of satisfaction for the infant led Freud to label this stage of the child's life the *oral stage*. During the oral stage the child's sexual drive is centered first upon eating. The pleasure derived from sucking and from taking food into the mouth and swallowing it is associated with later tendencies for the adult to take pleasure in taking in information or acquiring possessions.

The infant also forms his first close relationship with another human being during this time. It is primarily in the act of feeding that the child receives the cuddling and affection which shape his tendencies toward being a warm and friendly or fearful and suspicious adult. In the mother's arms the child also comes to realize a feeling of dependence. Without mother, all life might cease. If the child becomes anxious about the possible loss of mother as a source of his satisfaction, a dependent, helpless, passive personality may develop.

Toward the end of the first year the child begins to have teeth. Biting and chewing gives the child a new way to meet the problems and challenges of his world. According to Freud, biting is one of the first active ways the child has of expressing his aggressive tendencies. In the adult this tendency may be expressed through "biting" argument and sarcasm. Sadistic tendencies may be developed during this final phase of the oral stage.

The second year of life sees a shift for the developing child from the oral zone as the most sensitive to the *anal zone*. The child's attention shifts from the pleasure he derives from ingesting food to the pleasure he derives from controlling his bowel and bladder. The pressure of feces or urine creates tensions and passing them produces a release of tension which is pleasant. The attempts on the part of the parents to get a child to control his movements is one of the first sets of limitations imposed upon the instinctive biological drives and the pleasure associated with tension release. The pleasure of passing one's feces must be delayed and undertaken at the proper place and time. Freud felt that the way the parents handled this training period, coming as it does at a time when the child is very young, would have a great effect upon the child's later personality characteristics.

Harsh and restrictive methods of toilet training may bring on rebellion from the young child. His fight against his parents may come by holding back his feces. If he continues this pattern of fighting into his adult life, he may develop an obstinate and stingy approach to dealing with others. Another way the child can fight back at this time is to void his bowel at the most inappropriate times. Freud felt that a response of this type was the prototype of the destructive, hostile personality. However, if parents help the child to master control of the bowels without inducing undue amounts of anxiety, the child may come to see himself as one who is creative and productive.

By the third or fourth year the child discovers himself sexually. The penis or clitoris becomes the center of the child's pleasurable feelings. Also during this period children usually discover that boys have penises and girls do not. The pleasurable feelings associated with the genitals in the three- and four-year-old is part of the important development of the child in the *phallic stage*. Far more important, as far as Freud was concerned, is the important relationships the child works out between himself and his parents.

According to psychoanalytic theory the discovery that some children have penises and that others do not takes place at a time when the boy is beginning to have strong, even sexual, feelings for his mother (Freud, 1938). This is in addition to the strong dependency feelings developed for mother in the oral stage. The boy begins to see himself as a rival for his mother's affection with his father. However, since father is larger and more powerful it would be dangerous to oppose him. The child's primitive thinking leads him to fear that if father becomes extremely angry he may remove the child's offending organ, his penis, and leave him in the same condition as his sister. This fear of castration leads the boy to repress his sexual desire for his mother and to identify with his father. It is the working out of his sexual feelings toward his mother that sets the stage for the male child's later relationships with members of the opposite sex. Further, in working out the hostile feelings the boy has toward his "rival" father, the child establishes patterns of relating to authority figures in life. In taking his father's role the child *identifies* with powerful male figures. Freud labeled the conflict with father over the male child's love for his mother the *Oedipal conflict*.

Obviously the girl's pattern is somewhat different. Like the boy, she has had a strong dependency relationship with the mother from the oral stage. However, Freud postulated that upon discovering that she does not have a penis her primitive thinking leads her to assume that her developing feelings for her father have caused her mother to remove her penis. This feeling that mother has castrated her weakens her ties to mother and strengthens her ties to father. Father has the valued organ and may share it with her. The hopelessness of the situation causes the girl to attempt to resolve the problem by repressing her incestuous feelings toward father and also her hostile thoughts about mother. Here the girl *identifies* with mother, thus assuming female roles and patterns. As with the boy, how the daughter learns to handle these conflicts determines her later relationships with members of the opposite sex and with authority figures.

It seems strange and farfetched to us to hear the child's behavior described in this way. How did Freud come to such conclusions? After hours of listening to his neurotic patients describe, in free association, their fears of their parents or of sex and their secret sexual dreams and wishes Freud began to ask himself what all this talk had in common. He concluded that the secret desire for the opposite-sexed parent, the fear of the powerful but necessary adults, and the tremendous struggle to resolve these conflicting feelings is a universal human experience. Why then don't we all remember it? Because of repression, of course. The shameful thoughts are forced back into the unconscious, lost to recall but able to influence behavior by producing symptoms.

The Oedipal struggle is seen by Freud (1938) as necessary for the child to overcome his powerful sexual and aggressive instincts. Fearing actual violence and/or loss of parental love the child gives up and represses his infantile attempts at self-gratification. The child finds himself caught between two powerful sets of forces, his own instinctive desire for immediate gratification of his sexual aggressive urges and the need for his parents' love and support. The oedipal conflict is Freud's explanation of this internal battle.

A satisfactory outcome of the Oedipal conflict results in an adult who can and does direct his normal sexual and aggressive drives toward healthy sexual outlets, such as child rearing and productive work which serves the good of others as well as of himself. Failure to reach a satisfactory conclusion may result in an adult who is dominated by his instinctive sexual and aggressive drives, forever infantile and perverse, with little or no regard for the needs of others. On the other hand, should the child become overly submissive to his fears and the demands of his parents, as he perceives them, he may become a fearful, dependent, and withdrawn adult. He may always wait for direction from some powerful authority figure, unable or fearful of initiating action. Naturally, the outcomes are far more complex than this, and for some they are far more severe.

Whether successful in our Oedipal fight or not, Freud (1938) felt that for all of us the price of coming through the conflict is a lifetime of struggle. The battle is never completely won. The superego is the internal representative of the parents, left as an outpost to protect against further unwarranted outbreaks of the primitive instincts contained in the id.

Freud felt that after about age six the child has resolved many of the conflicts and problems related to the struggle to gain control over the pleasurable feelings associated with the erogenous zones, and he enters a period of *latency*. Between age six and puberty, the sexual energies are at a low ebb. With the onset of puberty the sexual drive returns with full biological urgency. If the previous stages went rather well, the chances are good that the child will learn to relate to members of the opposite sex in a positive and healthy way. The outcome is an adult who can treat members of the opposite sex as persons rather than as objects to be used and manipulated for his own selfish sexual pleasure. The normal, healthy adult turns his sexual energies to procreation and creative, productive activities.

Freud (1938) felt that the child's experiences in the first five or six years of life were critical in determining the adult personality. This is so, he felt, because the memory traces within the mind can never be fully lost to the individual. Therefore, through the unconscious id processes the earliest experiences continue to have an influence in all that the individual becomes. In moments of anxiety or stress the responses learned in the developmental stages will come out (Wolberg, 1967).

Repressed childhood fears and experiences continually influence the individual to act today as he did when he was a child. This is particularly likely to occur when we are confronted by situations which are similar to, or bear some symbolic relationship to, events which produced a great deal of anxiety during childhood (Wolberg, 1967). In such circumstances we often respond with defenses similar to those we used in childhood, without consideration for the reality needs of the present. The result is an intrapsychic balance attained at the expense of a reality relationship.

Parents should probably help the young child solve his fears and impulses through objects and people in the real world, rather than by fantasies. Parents should maintain a relationship with the child which allows them to understand the nature of the child's fears and his attempts to match his internal responses to the real events.

In summary, Freud sees the child as markedly different from adults. Children are biologically immature beings who must pass through several developmental stages on their way toward adulthood. Each of the stages of sexual development centers around a particular erogenous zone. The way a child learns to adjust to his feelings associated with that zone determines much of his adult personality.

The Relationship of the Individual to the Group

According to Freud (1961), we are all egoistic individuals. The pleasure principle drives us all to seek personal happiness. However, early in our lives we discover that we depend upon others and that some forms of happiness can only come about through our cooperation with others. The process of identifying with others causes us to turn some of our aggressive feelings back upon ourselves in the form of the superego. We use the superego to invoke guilt feelings whenever we think of performing acts which we anticipate may lead to punishment. Thus dependence, the need for cooperation, and the fear of punishment combine to force some reduction of our pleasure-seeking activities. Freud (1961) felt that guilt is part of the price we pay to live together with others in a civilized way.

Civilization is the result of the continual struggle within each of us between our erotic and aggressive urges and our learned moral, ethical, and religious practices. It is the struggle between the id and the ego (Freud, 1938). Civilization comes when our need to love grows to include all people. However, since our sexual and aggressive urges are very strong it costs us a great deal to keep them firmly in check. Violence of all sorts results from inability to maintain absolute control over the instinctive drives.

The inhibiting ethical and moral standards are seen as counter to the pleasure seeking of the individual. Neurotic behavior on the part of the individual can result from an overly punitive superego, which punishes him for mere desires. The excessive guilt can be the result of wishes to transgress sexual taboos or wishes to harm others through aggression. The superego acts to inhibit sexual and aggressive acts without regard for the instinctive basis for these behaviors. Nor does the superego, which is not in contact with reality, assess the difficulties presented by the external environment. In this way the superego acts as the agent of society in maintaining civilized behavior. The overly punitive society may induce some individuals to respond neurotically, just as does the overly punitive superego.

In the end, Freud was rather pessimistic as to whether man's love instinct would win out over his aggressive instinct. The individual's struggle to gain mastery over these two powerful forces is the basis for all human behavior. The struggle of love over aggression is also the struggle of civilization.

As parents we act as guides and referees in the child's struggles with the basic drives of sex and hostility and the demands of reality. Therefore, parents are society's representatives as the child gives birth to civilization all over again in each generation of mankind. Parents represent the group or social organization with its rules and regulations for *group* survival. The child's behavior is that of the totally egocentric id, bent on pleasure or self-satisfaction at any cost. When parents act to limit the egocentric demands of the id the cost to the child is some fear of loss of the parents' love, and/or guilt. If parents are overly harsh and punitive, the child develops an overly harsh and punitive superego. The result is neurotic behavior when similar or symbolically similar events occur later in life. To avoid this the parents may warmly and lovingly refuse to allow the child to satisfy the id wishes in unacceptable ways, while helping him to find acceptable ways to demonstrate his feelings. For example, rather than striking out in anger at a younger sibling, the child may be taught to express his hostility by striking a punching toy of some type. In this way the child can learn to displace (*see* page 22) his anger in a civilized manner.*

The needs of the social group are met in psychoanalytic theory by the child's slowly developing a functional ego and superego. The costs, Freud suggests (1961), are always high. We all pay for the development of an ego and superego by developing some irrational fears and some irrational guilt. Nonetheless, parents can and must help the child to accept the needs of others, deal with delayed gratification, and thus fit more or less smoothly into the civilized society of adults.

Other Dimensions and Issues

Other important dimensions of Freudian theory which apply to child rearing are the ways the ego relates the instincts to external realities. After a discussion of the development and operation of the ego defenses, or defense mechanisms, we will consider some of the ways the neo-Freudians have extended Freud's work in the area of what is now known as ego-psychology.

Ego functions. According to psychoanalytic theory, almost all learning takes place as a function of the ego. In infancy the process of thinking is limited to images present in the id. These images are of short duration and have no connection with reality. In the first year of life the child's egocentric, subjective view of the world begins to change to include a more "objective" view. The child learns

---

*While psychoanalysts might recommend this method, existential-phenomenological theorists (Chapter Six) are more inclined to help the child talk about his feelings of anger and frustration in his interaction with his sibling. Behaviorists (Chapter Seven) would more likely recommend rewarding behavior which is incompatible with hitting.

to direct his instinctive libidinal energies to include outside realities. Part of that first reality, the world of objects, includes the child's parents—especially his mother. Freud refers to the child's focusing of psychic energy upon an object to satisfy an instinctive wish as *object-cathexis*. As we have noted, a wish may be fulfilled by creating an image of something to fulfill the wish or by discovering something external to the id which is satisfying. Successful object-cathexis is necessary, therefore, to construct the ego and firmly base it on reality. As object-cathexis occurs, more and more of the psychic energy gets used for the testing of reality. The child's attention to and awareness of objective events is tied to the satisfaction of instinctual drives and wishes (pleasure). If events in the object world are associated with pleasurable feelings, the child is likely to return to those objects when that wish occurs again. Thus, if the nipple resolves the wish for food, the child seeks the nipple again when hungry.*

The process of object-cathexis or attachment can change many times. Therefore, if the nipple ceases to satisfy the same biological urge, the instinct that led the child to seek the nipple will now lead the child to seek another object which will satisfy the instinct. A single object may serve to satisfy several instincts at one time. The nipple, to continue our previous example, may satisfy the need for hunger and also the need for cuddling, the need for dependence, and the need for contact comfort. In modern terminology the nipple becomes a generalized reinforcer or reward system (cf. Chapter Seven).

The shifting of satisfaction from one object to another has been labeled *displacement*. Each individual engages in a unique series of displacements which satisfies his instinctive wishes in his own unique way. The infinite variety and diversity of human personalities is due to the individual's ability to displace satisfaction of pleasure from one object to another. The basic aim of the instincts remains constant, and that aim is satisfaction. Thus while the basic drives of sex and aggression remain the same, because of displacement the means of their satisfaction may change markedly over a lifetime.

A special variety of displacement is *sublimation*. Any displacement which leads to behavior or achievement for the good of society is said to be a sublimation of the instinctual energy. Thus the artist who diverts libidinal energy into his painting or music is said to have sublimated his drives into his art. In fact, most of our tender, affectionate, and sympathetic responses are sublimations of the original aggressive and sexual instincts (Freud, 1938; Brill, 1938).

The child learns as a result of his unending search for satisfaction of the instincts. It is impossible for the child to have all his wishes fulfilled. As soon as one instinctive wish or drive is satisfied another makes its wants known. Thus the child or adult is continually striving to satisfy his id impulses, to return the system to balance—but as long as he lives he will be constantly seeking.

Defense mechanisms. Since the id can never be completely satisfied it is inevitable that from time to time the ego will find the demands of the id, the superego, and external reality too great to cope with directly. In such cases extreme amounts of anxiety may be generated. The ego is then forced to take special measures to return the system to a balance. It does so by means of the defense mechanisms. Defense mechanisms remain unconscious except under unusual circumstances, and because of their operation at an unconscious level they distort reality.

One such defense mechanism is *fixation* (Freud, 1938). In the process of growing through the psychosexual stages, the process of changing cathexis from

---

*The process is similar to the effects of reinforcement described in behavioral theory (Chapter Seven); however, the explanation of why it occurs differs markedly.

one stage to another may cause too much stress. As a result the child may be flooded with anxiety. In such a case it is possible to form an overly strong cathexis of attachment within a stage, and psychosexual growth becomes permanently or temporarily arrested. This is one explanation of the dependent personality. Having grown overly dependent upon parental support and guidance, the child refuses to give up his infantile oral behaviors, *fixates* in the oral stage, and fails to move on to greater independence through control over his bowel and bladder. In time, of course, he does move on—but the trauma encountered during this period of fixation may lead to a permanent weakness in this area.

Another defense learned by the ego is *regression*. In the case of regression the child finds his present situation too stressful and so retreats into a stage of development which previously served to satisfy his instinctive needs. The three-year-old who finds his mother's attention taken away by a newborn sibling may retreat into pants wetting, thumb sucking, and drinking from the baby's bottle. Adult regressions may be to stages in which a person experienced a fixation as a child. Thus an adult under great stress may suddenly exhibit overly dependent behavior.

Repression is possibly the most important defense mechanism. In dealing with frightening or extremely unpleasant events, a person can run away, physically removing himself from the unpleasant situation (*see also* the discussion of avoidance and withdrawal in Chapter Seven). But if the anxiety-producing event is a wish or feeling, physical flight is of little use. Rather than continuing to suffer with the anxiety, the ego may force the painful thought into the unconscious, thus removing it from the immediate awareness of the individual. Running away through repression always costs something in terms of psychic energy (Freud, 1938, 1961; Wolberg, 1967). The result is likely to be neurotic symptoms which serve to indicate the presence of the painful thought no matter how deeply it is buried in the unconscious. Freud felt that repression was the most important of the defense mechanisms because of the devious ways it forced the individual to deal with his anxiety.

Projection is the process of blaming a feared or unpleasant thought or wish on another person or object. Rather than accept his own clumsiness, a person may smash the chair upon which he stubbed his toe "for getting in the way." Scapegoating is a form of projection used by individuals or groups against another group or a member of another group: "the enemy is hateful" rather than "I am full of hate."

A *reaction formation* involves substituting the anxiety-producing thought or feeling with its opposite. One of the most common occurrences of reaction formation is the replacing of hate with love. If for some reason the individual feels it would be too dangerous to express his hostile and aggressive feelings, he may unconsciously protest his love for the other party. Freud (1938) felt that slips of the tongue, for instance, were examples of the true (unconscious) feelings coming out. Thus the unconsciously hostile lover may say, "I hate you, my dear—oh, I really intended to say I *love* you."

The ego uses the defense mechanisms to deal with the multiple demands of the id, reality, and the superego. The defense mechanisms appear to be learned patterns for coping with these varying demands. The frequency and intensity with which a child uses defense mechanisms instead of reality testing to cope with a problem is a partial measure of the child's mental health. Therefore, it is important that parents and others responsible for the child help him to learn to utilize reality testing to resolve problems. This can be accomplished in part by protecting the child from being overly stimulated, especially by fear- and anxiety-provoking events (A. Freud, 1968). In this way parents can act as the child's auxiliary ego.

Conscious, rational thought is the servant of the ego in helping individuals gain control over the wishes of the id, and so over their own feelings and behavior. Verbal learning—words—become the essence of thinking. Parents can be of aid to their children by helping them to verbalize their feelings (*see also* Chapter Six). As the child learns to verbalize both internal and external feelings and events he will gain greater ego control. To the extent that the ego can learn to deal accurately with reality, instead of attempting to satisfy the instinctive wishes by fantasy and defensive maneuvers, the child will learn to be a rational adult. But since the ego is a function of the id, this can never fully occur. To some extent people are always subject to their primitive emotions (Freud, 1961).

Neo-Freudians. Freud's work was largely confined to the nature and dynamics of biological and instinctual factors in man. The id functions described above are largely events believed to occur inside the organism, having little to do with external environmental conditions. More recent students of psychoanalysis, such as Sullivan (1953) and Erikson (1963), have attempted to relate the basic concepts developed by Freud to social and environmental events.

Erikson's (1963) work seems particularly relevant to child rearing. Erikson has tried to show how society uses the basic instinctive structure of the developing child to create the types of individuals desired by the social group.

During the child's long period of dependence, the parents and others responsible for the socialization of the child take the inherent rudimentary instincts of the child and guide and give meaning to them according to the traditions of the particular society they belong to. According to Erikson (1963), each culture structures the inherent division between the sexes and the basic biology of the individual into a whole which is meaningful to the particular society and functional for the individual ego. This is accomplished, according to Erikson, by exploiting the anxiety associated with the normal fears encountered in overcoming each of the developmental crises: the "eight stages of man."

For Erikson (1963), the eight stages of man are an extension of Freud's schedule of psychosexual development, and are called the *psychosocial stages* of development. (A similar explanation for cognitive development is found in Chapter Five as proposed by Piaget and his students.) Erikson suggests that they represent critical steps in the adjustment of the individual ego to the demands of society. Each suggests the need for a favorable ratio of the positive factors over the negative factors of psychosocial adaptation; for example, of basic trust over basic mistrust. The child is prepared biologically to make a "decisive encounter with his environment" during each stage of psychosocial development. The social group responds to the child's assertions with characteristic patterns of training and coercion, which contributes to the child's personality in such a way that he takes on a part of the social or national character.

It should be recognized that Erikson's eight stages of man extend beyond childhood and adolescence. This is important, he says, for in order to understand either childhood or society we must understand how society helps the individual overcome the inescapable conflicts of childhood. It is the function of culture, as Erikson sees it, to promise some form of security, identity, and integrity as reward to the ego for accepting the rules, regulations, and values of society. (In Chapter Seven Skinner offers a similar argument on behalf of the behaviorists, but insists on different mechanisms for the accomplishment of these ends.) Erikson concludes that "in thus reinforcing the values by which the ego exists societies create the only condition under which human growth is possible" (1963, p. 277).

To Erikson, human growth means growth of the ego functions. By focusing on the fears and anxieties associated with each stage of development, and by providing a collective answer, society helps the individual meet and overcome the challenges. For example, organized religion helps resolve the crisis of the sense of trust versus the sense of evil by exemplifying and cultivating trust and by exploiting the sense of evil to prohibit unwanted behaviors. The more fully the society, often through the agency of the parents, helps the individual overcome each of the crisis periods exemplified by the eight stages of man, the more the individual ego becomes integrated into that society. It is in this sense that the individual comes to identify partially or fully with his culture.

Erikson points out that society consists of people, and that people are continually in the process of becoming parents. Parents continue to have some of the infantile traits which they in turn are trying to help their children overcome. Therefore, as parents and teachers we must be continually alert to the superstitions which we learned in our own stages of psychosocial development. With time and effort the vast array of superstitions created by our fears and anxieties may be altered, and a more supportive approach to child rearing and teaching can be substituted.

Application of Psychoanalytic Theory to Child Rearing

How can psychoanalytic theory be applied so that parents may achieve the type of children they desire? What does psychoanalytic theory suggest parents should do to prevent problems from occurring, and what can be done once they happen?

To begin with, psychoanalytic theory was designed to explain neurotic and psychotic behavior. It was based upon the verbal behavior of adult patients in free association. Freud analyzed all this talk in an attempt to determine the underlying causes, and his conclusions form the basis of psychoanalytic theory. What is observed in psychoanalytic procedures is the patient's patterns of verbal behavior in that special condition known as free association, and the patient's reports of his dreams. The problem for parents and others who would like to make practical application of the theory is how to connect the abstract formulations of the theory to the everyday behavior of children. To be of most help the theory should specify certain acts or behaviors on the part of the parent which, if applied, will bring about certain desired results. What, for example, should parents do to prevent their children from becoming neurotic or psychotic?

What causes neurotic behavior? According to Freud, the cause is repressed wishes emanating from the id which escape the ego's defenses and appear as symptoms. And the cure? Analysis of the free association material related to the symptoms to determine the unconscious desire that causes the neurotic behavior. During the course of the analysis the patients often form an intense emotional attachment to the therapist. Freud called this a *transference* of the patient's emotional attachment to his parents. If the therapist handled this well, much as a good parent would, with patience and understanding and without punishment, the patient often came to see that he need not feel so guilty about the behavior or feelings he associated with the symptom.

Two points might be made about this situation. First, the therapist, unlike the parent, is not confronted by the actual behavior, only the patient's report of the behavior. And while the patient may be expressing hostile and violent feelings about the parent, or even about the therapist as a substitute for the parent in the case of transference, the situation is clearly not the same.

Second, it is assumed that the patient's talk about feelings and behaviors which took place at some time in the past will change here-and-now behavior. Present talk about present behavior appears to be closely related, but it is nowhere as certain that the *subject* of the present talk is directly related; it is only assumed to be so in psychoanalytic theory. The problem for parents and other practitioners is to determine if parental response to behaviors described by the psychoanalytic theorists will have a long-term effect upon the child's, and later the adult's, behavior.

Assuming that events described by the psychoanalytic theorists—development of the ego and superego and the psychosexual stages—can be observed by parents, what should they do about them? Although we have already pointed out some of the answers in the general description of these concepts given earlier, we will touch upon each briefly to apply them to child rearing.

Parental Actions

The id is comprised of the basic instincts of sex and aggression, and is, therefore, part of our human inheritance. The child's behavior, for good or for bad, has its beginnings from within. The powerful, self-serving drives within the id cannot be changed, only redirected and controlled, first by external controls established by the parents and others, and later to some extent by the individual himself. Therefore, the only thing parents can do about these basic internal forces is to understand them and how they function. This understanding could possibly then be used to direct and control the expression of the child's instinctive urges when he is young and to help him develop his own controls for later life.

We are now ready to look at some ways parents may direct their children's instinctive urges toward productive and social practices. As the neo-Freudians have pointed out, these are primarily ego functions. Parents, in the early stages of the child's growth, assume the role of the child's alter ego while his ego is developing through growth and experience (A. Freud, 1935; 1968).

Moral Behavior

Honesty. Honesty, along with other forms of moral behavior including consideration, manners, and self-control, appears to be a product of the development of the ego and the superego. Prior to the development of the superego, parents should not expect children to have a self-regulating set of behaviors. If the prelatency child steals, tells lies, and in other ways breaks faith with his parents and community he is undoubtedly responding to some basic instinctive process. This does not mean parents should ignore this behavior. The child will not develop a conscience without developing a sense of guilt. And he will not develop a sense of guilt if his behavior goes unpunished (Fraiberg, 1959; A. Freud, 1935, 1968).

The punishment should "fit the crime,"—should be appropriate for the age of the child, and should not continue too long. Fraiberg (1959) states that what is meant by fitting the crime to the punishment is that the punishment should be relevant, from the child's point of view, to the misbehavior. It is important that the child be made aware of the connection between what he did and the punishment. The goal is to develop a sense of guilt which will act to inhibit the behavior when the child is in a similar situation in the future. What is wanted is for the child to incorporate the parents' values as part of his superego.

According to psychoanalytic theory, the child will only accept the parental values as his own, where these are in opposition to the instincts, if he fears punishment from the parents or loss of their love. Therefore, for parents to be effective in the transmission of their values they must establish a substantial basis of love. Erikson (1963) and Sullivan (1953) suggest that the development of the sense of trust or love begins in the relationship of the child to those who mother him. Those who mother the child need to respond to his individual needs in a warm, sensitive, and consistent way, teaching the child that there is meaning or purpose in their behavior. Trust seems to be born by demonstrations of caring. Faith in self comes about from faith in others to care and to do what is needed.

Although the child will continue to need demonstrations of trust throughout his life in order to maintain his integrated identity with his community (Erikson, 1963), he will in his second and third years of life turn from the development of a sense of trust to the development of a sense of autonomy. Parents will continue to develop the child's moral and ethical sense in this period of training by helping the child learn how to control his need to hold on and let go. Parents in this period of the child's development need to be firm but reassuring—firm in protecting the child from his own failure to recognize when to hold on to things and people, and when to let go, and reassuring in that they grant him the right to choose. (For an extended discussion on how to use choices as a teaching method see Chapter Four.)

The goal is to help the child gain "a sense of self-control without loss of self-esteem" (Erikson, 1963). Parents can achieve this by allowing the child to have his way within the established adult order demanded by the situation, while establishing the right for others to have rights and choices in the situation as well. Erikson suggests that this is the basis of the principles of law and order in later adult life.

Some time following the stage when the child learns to control and allow others to control, he begins to deal with the crisis of initiative. Initiative, according to Erikson (1963), is the capacity to plan an undertaking and follow through on it. The danger here is that the child's actions may carry him beyond his capacity for self-direction. He may act overly aggressive and cause hurt or damage beyond what he had anticipated, which may cause excessive guilt. Parents must act to help him check his exuberance short of permanent damage, whether the damage be psychological or physical. This is the genital or phallic stage of development, during which the child must learn to overcome his infantile wish for complete possession of his parents. In this period he begins the transition into becoming a parent, so far as he accepts the values of his parents—and therefore of his society—and begins to use them to guide his own and later others' behavior. He must learn to use part of his instinctive energies to observe his own behavior, direct himself in his actions, and, when necessary, correct his behavior through the administration of self-punishment (Erikson, 1963).

Parents may help in these developments by encouraging the child to judge himself fairly and evaluate his efforts realistically, rather than rigidly demanding perfection. Parents need to guard against overcontrol on the part of the child, both toward his own behavior and the behavior of others. Here the parents need to help the child guide his initiative rather than prohibit it. Once the child gains a fair degree of mastery in guiding his instinctive needs and directing his own inner set of checks and balances in the superego, he will have a fair set of moral principles helping him to be honest—to avoid stealing and other forms of antisocial behavior. The process may be far from complete at this stage in his development, but if a successful platform has been constructed in cooperation with his parents, the child should be able to make good progress as he enters the wider life of the community.

Preparation for a productive life. Parents not only want their children to be moral, in the sense of being honest, dependable, well-mannered, and self-controlled; they also want their children to be happy, and in most societies this means being successful in some productive way.

According to Erikson (1963), the child develops a sense of industry during the latency period. He develops the ability to gain recognition from others through the products of his hands and mind. In this period of his development he begins to master the technology of his culture. He develops skill in the use of tools, including reading, writing, and mathematics; fishing and hunting tools; the art of agriculture; or herding, depending on what skills he will need in his society for survival of himself and others.

Freud (1938) has suggested that the development of productive work is the outcome of the process of sublimation. Parents and others direct the instinctive drives away from the child himself and his self-satisfaction and toward socially acceptable work. This is a difficult process with its roots in the Oedipal crisis. Therefore, there is likely to be residual resentment against the parents which continues into this period of development. Parents may expect to find themselves in conflict with the child from time to time as they are working against the powerful instincts.

Erikson (1963) has pointed out that it is important that parents and teachers help the child develop a cooperative approach. And even more, parents need to help their children succeed and be successful so they may be open to new ideas and the development of new skills. It is important, says Erikson, that the child not develop a restricted and limited view of himself and his work. It is important that the individual see how his work contributes to the good of all, making it worthwhile and necessary.

As the child moves into adolescence he faces not only a crisis of productivity, but also a crisis of identity. The test is to identify the relationship between what he feels he is himself and how he is viewed by others. The identity crisis is a crisis of fitting together the child's self-concept with the perceptions of others and the world of work, which is another source of identity.

Erikson (1963) cautions that the danger here is role confusion. The child has doubts about his sexual nature and abilities. He has doubts about his ability to make a successful contribution in a career. And he has doubts about making a place in his peer group. The reaction to all this may be one of over-identification. He may give himself too completely to the group and fail to accept others who are not part of the "in group." Erikson suggests that it is necessary for parents to be understanding of this intolerance, as it is in part a defense against a sense of loss of identity. Parents should not, at the same time, condone or participate in this prejudiced intolerance.

It is during this period of transition from the moral and moralistic thinking of youth to the ethical thinking of adulthood that the adolescent tests out many of the values, creeds, and rituals which define the ideology of his society. Parents need to help their adolescent youth feel that leadership will bring out the best in themselves, and that the best in people will be drawn out by the rule of the best (Erikson, 1963). This is the process of moving from the follower position of childhood to the leader position of adulthood. Good adults know when and how to follow and when and how to take the lead. Failure to develop these skills may cause the individual to want always to be the leader, or to always want someone else to tell him what to do.

Development of a sense of ethics. Erikson (1963) suggests that once the young adult has established a sense of his own identity he is ready to risk it in a total relationship with another person. This is the crisis of intimacy. At this point the individual makes deep commitments to others and to affiliations of all kinds. These commitments require deep and significant sacrifices and compromises of self with others. Erikson quotes Freud as saying that a healthy normal person must be able to "work" and to "love." In this stage the individual learns what it is to really love, sexually and unselfishly.

Out of the stages of identity and intimacy the individual forges a sense of ethical behavior. He comes to see that his fate is involved in the fate of others, that his success in life is dependent upon others, and that theirs is dependent upon him. Therefore, human life, human production, and the needs of others are important in their own right. He can begin to take actions based on the rule of the common good rather than for the avoidance of punishment or out of fear that his parents and others might not approve. (*See* Chapter Five for an extended discussion of moral development from the point of view of the cognitive-developmental theorists.) The development of a sense of being needed as well as needing others leads to a new developmental crisis, according to Erikson: the crisis of generativity.

The stage of generativity is basically a period of development in which the individual reaches much of his creative and productive stride. Willingness to take on the responsibility for children and for one's other productions in life indicates, suggests Erikson, that one has faith in and a belief in life and the future, that society has meaning and value, and that one has a trust in the goodness or rightness of the community. Adults who have those feelings about their social group are the best ones to rear children. This is because they are capable of providing the type of mothering, discussed earlier, that gives the child a sense of trust. If the parents feel life has meaning and value, the child is likely to feel that way, too.

Erikson (1963) concludes the eight stages of man with a final crisis: the crisis of ego integrity. For individuals who have been productive, have taken care of things and people, and have accepted the successes and failures which are a part of life there comes a period of ego integration which allows them to look at life and declare it "good." Such individuals do not fear death, for they feel that they have given their best and it has been worthwhile. Those who have not reached a satisfactory level of integration may feel despair and wish to have time to start over to be productive.

Ego integrity is an emotional unity which contains the ultimate in trust. It is knowing that others will accept the person's contribution and count it worthy. This can only come about if he has a sense of community that allows him to feel he has truly contributed. Parents who have lived such a life leave a priceless heritage to their children. For when the youth, in looking to such adults, can feel the meaning and value of life, they do not despair of making a useful contribution as well.

Criticisms of the Psychoanalytic Approach

We have already encountered several difficulties with the psychoanalytic approach. In the beginning we commented that the goal of psychoanalysis, to research the unconscious, causes difficulties. Because the basic phenomenon is and must remain unobservable, the usual methods of scientific study do not apply. As long as the unconscious processes may only be inferred, the usual rules of observation, verification, and replication cannot be applied. This makes it difficult for parents, too. Since the child's mental life, which is considered to be the source of many of his problems, cannot be observed and directly influenced, parents are put in a difficult, if not impossible, position. How can they tell if their efforts are being helpful or harmful? Often, it seems, they cannot. Their efforts are limited, therefore, to the conscious ego processes.

But what is known of those conscious processes? Through the years considerable research has been conducted to test the relationships suggested by psychoanalytic theory. We have not the space, nor is this the place, to review this extensive body of literature. The interested reader is referred to three excellent reviews which we will merely summarize here along with several other more limited reviews: Eysenck and Wilson (1973), Kline (1972), and Zigler and Child (1973).

Developmental stages. Psychoanalytic theory suggests that psychosexual development establishes certain long-term personality patterns. For example, the methods parents use in the transition stages of early childhood—weaning, toilet training, and early sex education including handling of the Oedipal conflict—are said to influence the child's behavior and his adult personality. What evidence for this can be found?

While research has not given a completely clear and unequivocal answer, there seems to be little evidence that weaning and early feeding patterns have a lasting impact upon the child. Kline (1972), one of the most sympathetic of the reviewers, concludes that there is little support for the concept of an oral personality. Zigler and Child (1973) feel that there is some slight support for such traits but agree with all the other reviewers (Caldwell, 1964; Eysenck and Wilson, 1973; Kline, 1972) that there is almost no evidence to tie oral character traits in adults to feeding and weaning practices in childhood.

One of the most frequently mentioned relationships associated with the oral stage is the dependency relationship. Again reviewers appear almost unanimous in their agreement that there appears to be no connection between feeding and weaning practices and later dependent behavior (Caldwell, 1964; Maccoby and Masters, 1970; Yarrow, Campbell, and Burton, 1968). Dependent behavior seems to be a function of several factors—sex, age, and parental practices.

Younger children show more evidence of dependent behavior than do older children (Maccoby and Masters, 1970). Dependence may be in part a maturational factor, or it may be that we expect and therefore encourage dependent behavior in younger children more than we do in older children.

Sex is also a relevant factor in dependency (Kagen, 1964; Maccoby and Masters, 1970). In general the reviews agree that boys are less dependent than girls. This factor is complicated, however, when interactions with age and parental practices are taken into account. For example, Maccoby and Masters (1970) report that girls who are highly protected by their parents in the first three years of life tend to become adults who avoid stressful situations, though protection of daughters from three to ten years of age is not related to withdrawal in adult women. Kagen (1964) suggests, however, that passive six- to ten-year-old females tend to become passive adults. And Maccoby and Masters (1970) find that infancy socialization practices do not consistently predict dependency at preschool age. It appears that girls at all ages are more dependent than boys, but that sex alone does not predict dependency.

Parental practices appear to play an important role in the dependency of children. Overall it appears that parental warmth (Becker, 1964; Yarrow, et al., 1968) and restrictiveness (Becker, 1964; Campbell, 1964; Maccoby and Masters, 1970) contribute to dependent behavior in children. It appears that a warm, controlling relationship is likely to reward and punish in such a way that dependent behavior is maintained and increased in children (Maccoby and Masters, 1970; Yarrow, et al., 1968).

We can summarize this discussion of dependency by stating that it appears more in younger children than in older children, is found in girls more than in boys, and seems to be related to warm, restrictive parental practices rather than feeding or weaning practices as predicted by psychoanalytic theory. In fact, the warmth factor may be seen as going directly against Freudian theory, although the restrictive aspects do not. In all, the facts seem to fit the behavioral explanation (Chapter Seven) somewhat better than the psychoanalytic. Thus, when dependency relationships are reinforced, as in young children and females, they tend to be in evidence and to persist. When these behaviors are not reinforced, as in older children, especially males, they tend to drop out.

Review of the literature on anal characteristics reveals a somewhat different picture. Here reviewers generally agree that the personality characteristics

usually associated with anal character—orderliness, obstinacy, and parsimony—
do seem to occur together (Kline, 1972; Zigler and Child, 1973). However, no
direct connection between toilet training practices and these characteristics has
been found (Eysenck and Wilson, 1973; Kline, 1972; Zigler and Child, 1973).
There appears to be a connection between parental practices and these traits,
inasmuch as parents who exhibit this "obsessive-compulsive" syndrome often
have children who behave in similar ways. Caldwell (1964) and Zigler and Child
(1973) conclude that parents, especially mothers, are in a position to teach these
behaviors, a fact which would fit closely with the behavioral approach (Chapter
Seven). It can be concluded that Freud (1938) was correct about the trait, but
not about its etiology (Kline, 1972).

The reviewers are not in agreement about the research related to the Oedipal
conflict and the related concepts of castration complex and penis envy. Kline
(1972) feels that the studies he has reviewed generally support psychoanalytic
theory in this area. Eysenck and Wilson (1973) and Zigler and Child (1973) are
less convinced. The latter scholars feel that the studies reported fail to achieve
sufficient rigor and leave so many questions unanswered that one could not
conclude on the basis of this evidence that fears of castration, or other childhood fears of parents, are related to later sexual behaviors in any clearcut way.
Zigler and Child (1973) present much evidence that supports learning theory
explanations rather than psychoanalytic, although they argue that even this
evidence is tenuous. Further research into the nature of childhood sexuality and
the relationship of sexual learning in childhood to later sexual behavior (Zigler
and Child, 1973) is needed before any helpful suggestions to parents can be
authoritatively given.

What can be concluded from the reviews of the empirical literature relative to
psychoanalytic theory? Kline (1972), despite his obvious sympathy, concludes
that the emphasis given by psychoanalysis to feeding and toilet training cannot
be justified (p. 94). Therefore, the concern over oral and anal characters is
unnecessary. Eysenck and Wilson (1973) suggest that scientific theories are never
disproved. They simply become irrelevant and are discarded when they fail to
prove useful. Should they consistently fail to make successful predictions about
experimental outcomes, they are cast aside in favor of theories which do predict
with some degree of frequency. Eysenck and Wilson (1973) state that psychoanalytic theory "has consistently failed over the years to produce positive evidence of its predictive powers; thus it is in a highly vulnerable position" (p.
393).

Because of its widespread usage in popular literature, drama, and other entertainment fields, psychoanalysis is likely to continue to be part of our intellectual
world for some time to come (Eysenck and Wilson, 1973). However, the scientific usefulness of the theory is, as pointed out above, in serious question. The
same factors which limit its usefulness for science also limit its usefulness in
child rearing and guidance. Lack of specificity and inability of the theory to
connect to observable and therefore manipulable factors make it difficult, if not
impossible, for parents to apply the theory with any assurance of success.

The Developmental-
Maturational Approach

3

One of the most widely used approaches to child guidance in the United States over the past fifty years has been the developmental-maturational theory developed by Dr. Arnold Gesell. Gesell's training and work as a pediatrician led him to have an interest in the growth and development of normal children. Dr. Gesell and his students carefully studied the record of hundreds of infants and children at the Yale Clinic of Child Development. From these studies they developed their well-known ages-and-stages approach to child guidance. The key to Dr. Gesell's developmental-maturational theory is the concept of growth or development (Gesell uses the two terms interchangeably). Gesell views the child as a unitary whole: all of him is growing, his body, his mind, and his personality. For Gesell, all growth is the result of the child's genetic inheritance, the end product of man's long evolutionary history.

The Developmental-Maturational View of the Nature of Man

Gesell and his associates assume that man is first and foremost a biological organism. As such, man is living, growing protoplasm subject to all the laws of growth found in any living organism (Gesell and Ilg, 1949). Man's most fundamental ability is his ability to grow. Tissues, organs, and behavior are all subject to identical laws of development (Gesell and Amatruda, 1945).

The role of growth. Growth is a process of progressive differentiation and organization. Organization can be seen as the integration and stabilization of basic behavior patterns (Gesell and Amatruda, 1941). Simple patterns precede the development of more and more complex activities. Many muscles acting in groups are required to carry out even a simple movement. Organization is the process of putting the components of a movement together.

The component movements of one activity differ from those of another, depending upon the degree to which the acts are similar or dissimilar. Singing and talking have many similar components and require little differentiation, whereas hanging on to something and running have few components in common. Growth is seen by Gesell (Gesell and Amatruda, 1945) as the progressive organization and differentiation of muscle components.

The processes of differentiation and organization are controlled and directed by the individual's inherited genes. Every species has a distinct set of behavior traits. Man's most fundamental behavior characteristics are those he shares in common with all other men—the species as a whole. While it is true that each person has individual variations of all those human traits, no human individual varies so much that he ceases to belong to his species (Gesell and Amatruda, 1945). The progressive differentiation and organization of growth, therefore, serves to produce humans who have great overlaps in their basic traits and behaviors. Each man is therefore more like other men than different from other men, although each man is different.

The nature of behavior. Not only does the individual grow, but also his behavior grows, and as behavior grows it takes on characteristic patterns. These two far-reaching propositions—behavioral growth and characteristic patterns—are fundamental to the developmental-maturational theory (Gesell and Amatruda, 1945). *Behavior* is a term used by Gesell to represent all of man's reactions, whether reflex, voluntary, spontaneous, or learned. The complex pattern of events necessary for an individual to coordinate eye and hand movements well enough to pick up a dime is behavior. An eye blink or a knee jerk is behavior. Reciting the Gettysburg Address is behavior. Since growth is the process of differentiating and organizing, and since behavior grows, man's behavior can be said to have characteristic patterns of differentiation and organization.

Gesell and Amatruda (1941) point out that there is nothing strange or mysterious about the concept of behavior growing, since behavior can readily be observed. For Gesell, the behavior that we observe is a defined response of the individual's neuro-motor system to a specific situation. Behavior patterns are the end result of the individual's total development. As the genes guide the development and maturation of the physical structure of the individual, the capacity for a given behavioral pattern also develops. Thus, behavior patterns take shape in the same way that the underlying structures take shape. As the nerves and muscles of the throat, larynx, tongue, and mouth grow into maturity the child, through interaction with others in his environment, may learn to speak. The physical maturation must precede the behavior. Thus, for Gesell, behavior and behavior patterns are seen as symptoms of neurological development. Growth and development lead to ever more complex and varied forms of behavior. The ever more complex patterns are indicators of an ever more mature nervous system. The fully mature individual has all the behavior patterns necessary for survival in his culture.

The concept of development. Development, for Gesell, is a continuous maturation process. It begins with conception and proceeds in an orderly series of stages, each stage representing a degree or level of maturity. Development takes time, of course. And we mark the amount of time consumed by our age.

It is difficult to measure mature behavior with measurements as precise as those we use to measure height or weight. We can, however, measure behavior against age. Gesell and his students measured hundreds of normal infants and young children. As a result they were able to determine the average age for infants and young children to perform hundreds of ever more complex physical acts. As the children grow older, Gesell and his co-workers uncovered uniform sequences in which patterns of behavior appear. By noting the age or ages at which these patterns typically appear in normal children, Gesell developed a set of norms against which we may measure the development of any given individual. If we give careful consideration to the range of ages (how early the behavior begins with the earliest child and how late the behavior is acquired by the latest child), we can determine with some accuracy the individual's progress toward maturity. If we assume, as Gesell does, that behavior is a symptom of neuro-muscular maturity, then an individual's age-graded development is a measure (although indirect) of his overall maturity.

We must take note of the fact that development, while continuous, does not proceed in a straight line. Gesell and Ilg (1949) point out that development seems to fluctuate to the right and left, up and down, and sometimes it even appears to move backward. The overall trend is forward, however, as the individual develops more and more complex behavior patterns. Gesell states that the growing individual seems to pass regularly through periods of relatively comfortable adjustment to the world, or periods of "equilibrium," when his attempts to develop new patterns of behavior seem to disrupt his total organization. According to Gesell, these periods of equilibrium and disequilibrium are characteristic of the psychological growth of man. The fluctuations are not lapses but are the efforts of the growing organism to reach further organizational stages. Individuals vary widely in the amount of equilibrium and disequilibrium they show in their adjustment. Some individuals seem relatively self-contained and unperturbed throughout their lives. Others seem to have very few periods of their lives which could really be called tranquil. Nonetheless, the broad trends seem to be characteristic of human growth, and periods of relative equilibrium seem to appear at 4, 16, 28, and 40 weeks; 12 and 18 months; and 2, 3, 4, 5, 10, and 16 years (Gesell, Ilg, and Ames, 1956).

The four fields of behavior growth. Gesell and Amatruda (1941) suggest that man's growth occurs in four fields at once. The four fields of behavior which represent differing aspects of growth are motor behavior, adaptive behavior, language behavior, and personal-social behavior. Motor behavior includes the growth of gross bodily control and the finer motor coordinations. Adaptive behavior is made up of coordination and the use of motor ability to solve practical problems, such as picking up an object. Adaptive behavior also leads to new adjustments, such as going from crawling to walking. Language behavior includes verbal and nonverbal messages. It also includes, for Gesell, mimicry and the ability to understand the messages of others. The fourth area of growing behavior, the personal-social field, includes the individual's personal reactions to the social culture in which he lives. It is the personality, the emotions, and the mind. The accompanying table shows the sequences of development in the motor, adaptive, language, and personal-social fields of behavior.

We can gain a greater understanding of Gesell's developmental-maturational theory by looking at the way he might explain the growth of the personal-social field of behavior. For Gesell, the nervous system grows in a patterned and patterning manner. It develops patterns in response to people as well as to time and space. Therefore, for Gesell, emotions, personality, and the mind are all subject to the same mechanisms and laws which govern growth. Personality is an organized and ever-organizing set of behavior patterns. "They are neither more nor less mysterious than his sensori-motor patterns of posture, locomotion, and manipulation" (Gesell and Ilg, 1949; p. 30). Growth of the mind, personality, and emotions are subject to the same patterns of up and down, forward and back that occur in the physical growth of the individual. Because of this the child is sometimes friendly and outgoing and at other times withdrawn and negative. Personality and emotions are seen by Gesell not as operatives behind the scenes, but as the individual's collection of patterns and behavior potentials operating in response to the social situation. Just as crawling foreshadows walking, so the patterns of personality proceed in an orderly sequence. The personality patterns of the infant precede the personality patterns of the child; the child the youth; and the youth the man. Increasing maturity leads to increasingly more complex personality patterns.

As seen by Gesell, man as an organism is the result of eons of organic development. As a result, man's behavior can be traced to the potentials and limitations inherent in his genes. Growth is characteristic of living organisms and growth is, therefore, characteristic of man. Man grows as a whole: his body grows, his mind grows, and his personality grows. Growth is from the inside out. Neuro-muscular growth precedes behavioral growth. Behavior is man's characteristic, genetically given patterns of responding to or organizing the environment. The maturity of an individual's responses can be measured by comparing his characteristic behaviors to others of his same age. Though each person will have an individual approach, he will have more behavior in common with other people for a given trait than he will have differences.

Development of Behavior in the Four Major Fields

Level of Maturity	Motor Behavior	Adaptive Behavior	Language Behavior	Personal-Social Behavior
5 years	Skips on alternate feet.	Counts 10 pennies.	Speaks without infantile articulation. Asks "why."	Asks meaning of words. Dresses without assistance.
4 years	Skips on one foot.	Builds gate of 5 cubes. Draws "man."	Uses conjunctions. Understands prepositions.	Can wash and dry face. Goes on errands. Plays cooperatively.
3 years	Stands on one foot. Builds tower of 10 cubes.	Builds bridge of 3 cubes. Imitates cross.	Talks in sentences. Answers simple questions.	Uses spoon well. Puts on shoes. Takes turns.
2 years	Runs. Builds tower of 6 cubes.	Imitates circular stroke.	Uses phrases. Understands simple directions.	Verbalizes toilet needs. Plays with dolls.
18 months	Walks without falling. Seats self. Tower of 3 cubes.	Dumps pellet from bottle. Imitates crayon strokes.	Jargons. Names. Pictures.	Uses spoon with moderate spilling. Toilet regulated.
12 months	Walks with help. Cruises. Prehends pellet with precision.	Releases cube in cup.	Says two or more words.	Cooperates in dressing. Gives toy. Finger feeds.
40 weeks	Sits alone. Creeps. Pulls to feet. Crude prehensory release.	Combines 2 cubes.	Says one word. Heeds his name.	Plays simple nursery game. Feeds self cracker.
28 weeks	Sits, leaning forward on hands. Grasps cube. Rakes at pellet.	Transfers cube from hand to hand.	Crows. Vocalizes eagerness. Listens to own vocalization.	Plays with feet and toys. Expectant in feeding situation.
16 weeks	Head sags. Hands fisted.	Competent eye following. Regards rattle in hand.	Coos. Laughs. Vocalizes socially.	Plays with hands and dress. Recognizes bottle. Poises mouth for food.
4 weeks		Stares at surroundings. Restricted eye following.	Small throaty sounds. Heeds bell.	Regards faces.

From *Developmental Diagnosis* by Gesell and Amatruda. Copyright 1941, Harper and Row. Used with permission of Harper and Row.

The Developmental-Maturational View of the Nature of Children

Children are intrinsically good, according to Gesell (1952). The child is a growing organism who must follow a long but lawful cycle of growth. Since the child inherits nothing in complete form, he must grow in all aspects of his life, including the psychological aspects of self. Fears and affections, judgments and moral sense, attitudes and ideas grow as part of the child's response to his genes and in relationship to his experience. Graded steps of growth can be constructed which represent the natural maturational stages. The child's genetic inheritance guides his growth, and since growth is a natural process the child cannot be seen as anything but good.

The concept of individuality. The genetic inheritance not only guides the child's patterned growth, but also leads to his individuality. Infants are individuals from birth, or even before birth. Many of the child's characteristics were decided at conception. The individuality of the child is so strong that he will never be exactly like any other child at any given age. An infant's individuality can be seen in his natural patterns of sleep, feeding, and activity.

Gesell and Ilg (1949) make the point, however, that individual variations are never so great as to not follow the basic plan of human growth. All children follow a relatively stable developmental pattern. Gesell and his students feel that the study of hundreds of normal infants and young children has permitted them to describe that set of characteristic growth patterns and to ascertain the characteristic behaviors associated with any given age of the child. "For any selected age it is possible to sketch a portrait which delineates the behavior characteristics typical of the age" (Gesell and Ilg, 1949, pp. 60-61).

Gesell and his associates (Gesell and Amatruda, 1945; Gesell and Ilg, 1949; Gesell, Ilg, and Ames, 1956) have built a series of norms which describe the characteristic behaviors of children from birth to age sixteen. By describing the mature behavior of large numbers of children, the maturity norms become a standard against which the development of a child can be measured. Naturally, any such scale must be used with the same care that one would use in applying the norms of height and weight. The norms should be used only for interpretation and orientation of the child's behavior, and not as standards to which he must conform. Care should be used to look at the range of behaviors and the range of ages given for each step along the scale.

Behavior trends. Gesell and Ilg (1949) point out that in the end each child is his own best gauge of development. Parents should focus on the individual patterns of growth of the individual child. From birthday to birthday they should compare him to his former self. In this way his parents can begin to understand his way of growing. Under normal circumstances the child is never likely to fall below his previous levels of attainment. The long-range tendency of growth is toward optimum development rather than toward decline, as can be seen in this brief description of the trends of behavior development given by Gesell and Amatruda (1941):

> In the *first quarter* of the first year the infant gains control of the twelve oculomotor muscles.
>
> In the *second quarter* (16-18 weeks) he comes into command of the muscles which support his head and move his arms. He reaches out for things.
>
> In the *third quarter* (28-40 weeks) he extends command to his legs and feet and to his forefingers and thumb. He pokes and plucks.
>
> In the *second year* he walks and runs; articulates words and phrases; acquires bowel and bladder control; and attains a rudimentary sense of personal identity and of personal possession.
>
> In the *third year* he speaks in sentences, using words as tools of

thought, and he shows a positive propensity to understand his environment and to comply with cultural demands. He is no longer a mere infant.

In the *fourth year* he asks innumerable questions, perceives analogies, displays an active tendency to conceptualize and generalize. He is nearly self-dependent in the routines of home life.

At *five* he is well matured in motor control. He hops and skips. He talks without infantile articulation. He can narrate a long tale. He prefers associative play and feels socialized pride in clothes and accomplishment. He is a self-assured, conforming citizen in his small world (Gesell and Amatruda, 1941, p. 10).

Developmental principles. A number of important developmental principles can be seen in the description of development given above. Gesell and Amatruda (1945) suggest seven principles which describe the structural development of the individual. They are the principles of individuating fore-reference, developmental direction, spiral reincorporation, reciprocal interweaving, functional asymmetry, self-regulatory fluctuation, and optimal tendency.

The principle of individuating fore-reference suggests that each pattern of behavior emerges, not as a result of experience with the environment, but as a result of the development of the neurological structure necessary for that behavior. Development results in the organism and the environment fitting together. An action system, such as the ability to pick up a block, comes to have a unitary whole, a completeness at a certain stage of development. There are individual differences in the growth pattern which lead to individual differences in the action system. Individual differences are thus the result of the child's genetic structure and not the result of the environment. Individuating fore-reference is Gesell's term for the genetic basis of individual differences and the biological basis for behavior. The genes are telling the child what to do, when to do it, and how to do it.

The second principle is the principle of developmental direction, which is clearly illustrated in the description of behavior trends given above. The principle states that maturation proceeds from head to body to legs to feet (referred to as cephalo-caudal direction). Organization also goes from the center out (proximal-distal pattern). That is, the child gains control of his trunk before he can control the shoulders, shoulder control precedes arm control, and arm control precedes hand control.

The principle of spiral reincorporation notes the fact that directionality seems to pass through the head-to-foot pattern several different times. For example, trunk control goes through three complete cycles: lying down control, seating control, and standing control. In this way the child's development returns time and again to being a component of muscular organization. The child at first grasps in an awkward palming fashion, later with the fingers, and still later with the thumb and fingers nicely opposed.

The principle of reciprocal interweaving is suggested by Gesell's observation of the dualities of development. The child first develops the flexor muscles and then the extensor muscles. The child seems to develop control over the right and left extremities unevenly, sometimes pushing ahead on one side and then pushing ahead on the other. There are periods when we cannot tell if the child will be right- or left-handed. One of the important tasks of development, according to Gesell (1952), is to bring the opposing systems of the neuro-muscular system into effective control. The growth pattern of reciprocal interweaving is said to counterbalance one extreme of behavior by setting it against its opposite.

Closely related is the principle of functional asymmetry. Gesell and Amatruda (1945) observe that handedness is paralleled by unidexterity of eye and foot. They suggest that this may be important for the child in focalizing psychomotor orientations, thus helping him to gain control of his physical body.

The principle of self-regulatory fluctuation describes the basis for the child's periods of equilibrium and disequilibrium. As the child begins to develop an action system, such as standing, he is "in a state of formative instability" (Gesell and Amatruda, 1945). Growth is a progressive movement toward stability. Thus stability and variability coexist, with now one more noticeable, then the other. "Growth gains represent consolidations of stability" (p. 165). The child's forward thrusts are struggles to reach new levels of maturity.

Gesell and Amatruda (1945) use the child's sleeping and waking patterns as an example of self-regulatory fluctuations. Sleep and waking are differentiated aspects of brain functions. At first there appears to be little difference between the period of sleep and the period of wakefulness. As the child matures, however, sleep becomes deeper, more regular, more clearly defined from wakefulness. In the same period of time his wakefulness is more "vigilant," more active, in a sense more purposeful. Wakefulness is regulated by internal mechanisms. "The capacity to stay awake is based on ages of phyletic evolution. The infant reacquires this capacity progressively through the growth of the higher levels of his nervous system" (Gesell and Amatruda, 1945, p. 149). The fluctuation between sleeping and wakefulness is "self-regulated" by the child's internal biological structure.

The seventh and last principle is optimal tendency. Behavior growth is always toward maximum realization of the individual's genetic potential.* Growth potentials are, to some extent, guaranteed by reserve mechanisms which may be called into action if the primary mechanisms are damaged or blocked.† If, for example, some of the muscles in the shoulder are missing, others can take over and compensate. If a kidney is weak or damaged, the other may enlarge slightly to handle the additional load. Thus the biological structure provides for continual movement toward maturity despite obstacles. Individual differences result from the fact that each person needs to overcome different weaknesses and each does so in somewhat unique ways.

Individual differences are most clearly the result of principles one and seven—individuating fore-reference and optimal tendency. Gesell's reliance on genetic influences to describe the growth and development of behavior can most clearly be seen in these two principles.

The development of personality. As we have stated before, development is a continuous process. Beginning with conception, the child grows stage by stage in orderly sequences, with each stage representing a level of maturity. Following birth the child's personality begins to be influenced by other personalities. The child begins to build up expectations and associations related to the people around him. He begins to assimilate or take in the world and to make it a part of his personality. At the same time, those that are closest to him make accommodations for him. He takes on the culture and at the same time, to some small degree, he changes the culture. This process of acculturation is important for the child, according to Gesell, for it is through this interchange of back-and-forth interaction that the child comes to be aware of others and of himself as an individual. "A personality cannot take root and cannot flourish except through interpersonal relationships" (Gesell and Ilg, 1949, p. 34).

Thus the personality of the young child forms little by little, pattern by

---

*See Chapter Six for a similar approach proposed by the existential-phenomenological theorists.

†Adler held a similar view and applied the idea to psychological characteristics (Chapter Four).

pattern, as illustrated by a memo sent by Hymes (1945) to the nursery school staff at Oregon State University (*see* Appendix, page 127). Personality is made up of an infinite number of patterned responses to environmental situations. For Gesell, personality is a progressive finding of the self through interaction with other persons, especially the child's parents. Personality grows in the same way the child grows. The growth of the body and the growth of the child are not separate events.

The same can be said of the mind. The mind is indivisible from the growing organism. As such it is responsive to both the genes and the environment. As the nervous system changes because of growth, so too does mental behavior change. "At one age [the child] seizes with his fist; at a later age, he plucks with neat opposition of thumb and index—a concrete example of the way differentiation produces specialization of function and new behavior patterns" (Gesell and Amatruda, 1941; p. 3). Gesell sees each of these changes as evidence of the child's growing ability of "mind."

The personality, the mind, the child: all grow as a unit. All are the result of the organizing processes of growth. Growth then is the key concept for understanding the nature and needs of the child. If parents wish to understand children they need to understand the nature of growth.

The Relationship of the Individual to the Group

Each child is an individual, as shown by his natural patterns of sleep, feeding, and activity. Therefore, Gesell concludes, it is best for the family to give the child his head in eating, sleeping, and playing, and to follow the child's natural patterns; in other words to follow a *demand schedule* rather than place the child on a fixed schedule which fits the family's needs (Gesell, 1952). In fact, parents cannot postpone responding to the child's natural patterns. From birth each child has distinctive individual drives and needs which we either ignore, indulge, combat, or attempt to control (Gesell and Ilg, 1949). Parents are responding to the child's natural patterns by whatever action they take or do not take.

For Gesell the family is the pivotal point in which the interaction of growth and culture take place. The family is seen by Gesell as "a cultural workshop for transmitting the social inheritance: a democratic household fosters a way of life which respects the individuality of the growing child" (Gesell and Ilg, 1949, p. 4). The family and the child influence each other. However, for Gesell, the behavior of the child is primary. Each child must "do his own growing" with the help of the family. The parents can help him achieve his developmental potential, help him learn, by creating a helpful setting in which the child can interact with others, and in which the child has access to the right equipment for his age. But in the end the child's learning is always limited by his natural growth processes. The child and the group come into conflict when the parents' attempt to promote learnings which are not appropriate for the child's maturational level.

The mechanisms of growth and development are seen as so lawful and fundamental that children of the same or similar chronological ages are most similar with respect to their emotional development. "The intellectual prodigy capable of fifth-grade work at the age of six is at heart more like a child of six than a child of eleven" (Gesell and Ilg, 1949, pp. 36-37). This suggests that parents need to be aware of the emotional patterns which are appropriate for a child of a given age and that the parents should not expect the child to respond beyond the level he is capable of. Gesell feels that the make-up of personality comes from deep-seated genetic factors which cannot be transcended except at great cost to the individual child. Therefore, it is best if parents learn to observe the individual needs of the child and work with his characteristic patterns of growth, rather than trying to impose some pattern of their own.

Patterns of civilization cannot be imposed upon the child; they must be newly learned by each generation (Gesell and Ilg, 1949). Children acquire civilized behavior just as they acquire other behaviors, by gradual stages which are equated with the child's developmental maturity. The child is the best gauge of what he can do and what he cannot do, of what he should do and what he should not do. This is true because the child is responding to his innate genetic predisposition toward growth. The family should not attempt to impose behaviors upon the child which he is not developmentally ready to accept.

In viewing the development of man from birth to death, Gesell concludes that the first five years of life assume the greatest significance. The child receives from his family many of his views of the nature of the world. These early events form a deep and lasting impression. Acculturation (learning) begins in the home, and the influences of other cultural groups are limited by the basic patterns established at home.

Not until the child is five years of age is he ready to launch out from the family and take his place as a regular member of the community. The child has reached this level of readiness, just as he has reached all other levels of readiness, by successive progress through innumerable stages of development. Development and growth have prepared him to become a member of the community just as they have prepared him to walk or talk. The result of the child's growth has been a steady penetration into the life of the community. The child has moved from womb to bassinet to crib to high chair and to community in sequence, stage by stage. Just as with other patterns of behavior, Gesell sees this as evidence of genetic influence on behavior.

By age five we have a fairly clear picture of the child's physical and mental make-up, according to Gesell. And even though the child has not yet experienced adolescence he is, for the developmental-maturational theorist, very nearly a finished product. Later developments in personality and thinking are primarily variations on a well-established theme. By age five the child's personality already consists of an infinite number of reactions, which are released in his social world. These patterned reactions will guide and shape his further development.

Other Dimensions and Issues

In some of his early research Gesell and his co-workers demonstrated the importance of maturation in the learning process (Gesell and Thompson, 1929). This was done by comparing the learning experiences of twins. For example, one twin might be given the opportunity to climb stairs rather early while the second twin was kept from this experience until the first had mastered the skill. At a later developmental age the second twin was exposed to stair climbing. It took the second twin very little time to master stair climbing in comparison to the first. The greater speed in acquisition of stair climbing skill by the second twin was attributed to greater maturational readiness. Gesell appears to have taken this evidence of the importance of maturation as license to slight environmental influences (Zigler and Child, 1973). This is important because it colors Gesell's view of how children learn, and consequently what parents and teachers can and should do in their child-rearing practices.

The developmental-maturational theory states that all basic behavior traits are products of organic evolution (Gesell and Amatruda, 1945). Thus, the behavior we think of as learning has been developed over long periods of evolutionary development. The result is a human organism that is a significant mixture of stability and modifiability. The human organism appears sensitive to cultural influences from the moment of birth. However, growth creates progressive changes in structure and the changes in structure produce changes in functional behavior (Gesell and Amatruda, 1947).

According to Gesell, the infant does not teach himself, nor is he taught. The changes we observe in his behavior come about through the intrinsic growth forces that shape and reshape his nervous system. Naturally, he needs an environment in which to display and utilize his behaviors. Environmental factors do not generate developmental changes; they merely support, inflect, or modify the behavior (Gesell and Ilg, 1949).

Maturation and acculturation (Gesell often uses the term acculturation for learning) interact in the development of behavior, but maturation is seen as the most fundamental influence. Maturation is so fundamental that learning can never exceed maturation. Gesell's long-range studies of infants and children have convinced him that such behaviors as social responsiveness, readiness of smiling, self-dependence, and motor agility tend to show up early in the child's life and tend to persist under varying environmental situations. Thus, while the infant has great capacities for learning, there are lawful limits to his conditionability. "He has constitutional traits and tendencies, largely inborn, which determine *how, what,* and to some extent even *when* he will learn" (Gesell and Ilg, 1949, p. 40). Growth, therefore, is the limiting factor in the child's learning.

The laws of child development ". . . literally establish the basic patterns of behavior and of growth . . . " (Gesell and Ilg, 1949, p. 358). The maturational matrix is the basic determiner of the child's behavior, whether we are referring to language, personal-social behavior, or motor behavior. The culture, through the parents, requires the child to gain control over bladder and bowel; but attainment of that control depends almost totally upon neuro-motor development. The same is true of the child's skills in feeding himself, his sense of personal belongings, his development of independence, his ability to cooperate with others, and his responsiveness to such social conventions as dressing and table manners. While personal-social behavior is especially susceptible to individual variation, these variations have normal limits established by the genetic inheritance of the child. The child learns what his genetic structure allows him to learn.

Application of Developmental-Maturational Theory to Child Rearing

Gesell's theory has from the first attempted to relate directly to the problems of child rearing and socialization. Three of Gesell's texts are especially given to this task: *Infant and Child in the Culture of Today* (1943); *The Child from Five to Ten* (1946); and *Youth: The Years from Ten to Sixteen* (1956). The assumptions and theories which we have already discussed form the underlying theme for each of these works. The fundamental concept used by Gesell and his co-workers is growth or development. As stated earlier, growth is seen as a continuous process of integration and differentiation of nerve tissue, muscle structure, and behavior. All sequences of integration and differentiation are dictated by genetic factors. They are invariant sequences for all humans. The sequences form repeated cycles of "equilibrium" and "disequilibrium" as the individual moves from relatively integrated stages to newer, more complex forms of differentiated behavior. Knowledge and understanding of these broad cycles are seen by Gesell as helping parents be aware of and respond to the needs of the ever-growing child.

Gesell believes that parents should become perceptive of and sensitive to the needs of the child. The child is an individual from birth and therefore parents should plan to respond to the child's needs, to help him reach his fullest potential. Parents should work to create the most favorable conditions for the child's self-regulating functions so that he can come to a state of self-adjustment. To accomplish this, parents direct, intervene, assist, postpone, and encourage or discourage many times. But assuming a developmental approach, the parent's guidance is always in accord with the child's maturational level. The child will come to a gradual acceptance of the cultural demands if parents take notice of the fundamental self-demand cues from the child himself.

The developmental orientation. The child's first year of life is the easiest period for the parents to acquire a developmental orientation to the child's individuality (Gesell and Ilg, 1943). During the first year parents should refrain from using harsh emotional methods of discipline. Rather, they should attempt to come to understand the way the child's immaturity must be met and helped. Parents should expect the child to crawl before he walks. They would not, therefore, punish the child for crawling. Neither do they need to push the child into walking. The same is true for the child's emotional growth and development. Parents should expect the child to act "childish" before expecting him to act with wisdom.

It is important for the parents to learn the child's mechanisms of self-regulation in the first year while the patterns are relatively simple. The hunger of the four-week-old child results in crying that can only be stilled with food. At 16 to 28 weeks the child can wait a little while for feeding, since the hunger pangs are less intense. The child's inner growth is now more and more directed toward discovery of self and others in his environment. At 18 months the child has begun to learn to respond to environmental cues.* Thus he may cry at lunchtime when he sees the table where he usually eats. Mothers wisely accommodate to this stage of development by having lunch ready before they bring the child to the table. When the child is 2½ years old his mother helps him learn to wait by saying, "In a minute." By the age of three the child can accept, "When it's time." At four he can help prepare the meal. Thus the child is led to more and more mature responses, but always in relationship to his innate readiness. Parents' ability to respond to the child's self-regulative patterns throughout his early years will be considerably easier if they make an effort to understand his particular style in the first year.

Because the cycles of infancy are repeated again and again, the first year of life is important for the parents, for they may discover more than the child's individual patterns. They may observe the larger rhythmic pattern of development characteristic of all children (Gesell, Ilg, and Ames, 1956). Thus the infant of 28 weeks is seen as having overcome the period of disequilibrium characteristic of the newborn. Gesell, Ilg, and Ames (1956) describe this as "a phase of relative equilibrium; [the child] tends to be self-contained, outgoing, and amiably adjusted . . ." (p. 18). This is followed by a period at 32 weeks in which the child, now more aware of his environment, fears strangers. More emotionally withdrawn, he undergoes a period of disequilibrium only to be followed at age 40 weeks by "better equilibrium." At this time the child has established routines; he is able to amuse himself for up to an hour, and, more outgoing, he likes having others around.

The period from two to five years of age is described by Gesell and others (1956) as another turn of the same cycle. "Years Two and Five, in some sense, are similar. Not that abilities at the two ages are alike; the difference in skills is vast. But in mode of adjustment to the world around him, Five shows a poise and equanimity reminiscent of Two" (p. 18). The authors go on to suggest that after two years and five years of age "Behavior 'loosens up,' perhaps even 'goes to pieces' . . ." (p. 18). The cycles continue to alternate, "Three and Six-and-a-

---

*The importance of cues to potential reinforcing events such as food is discussed at length in Chapter Seven.

half bring increasing amenability," while "Three-and-a-half and Seven bring in-wardizing thrusts. . . . Four and Eight reverse these thrusts. . . . Four-and-a-half and Nine try to bring inner and outer thrusts into unity, . . . achieve greater self-sufficiency." "With ages five and ten a resolution is temporarily achieved as growth forces are integrated (Gesell et al., 1956, p. 18). "Eleven, like Five-and-a-half to Six, is 'loosening up,' 'snapping old bonds;' Twelve is more positive in mood. . . . Thirteen pulls inward; Fourteen thrusts out; Fifteen specifies and organizes; Sixteen again achieves a more golden mean" (p. 19).

The cyclic reformulation of behavior is a key concept for Gesell and his fellow students. It appears as the basis for much of what they seek and find in their research. Understanding this fundamental law of development is important for parents and others who want to understand children, since it serves to help parents get through the difficult periods of disequilibrium by knowing that with normal growth, periods of equilibrium are sure to follow. It also serves to signal when something is going wrong in the course of normal development.

Awareness of the child's usual orderly patterns of adjustment may alert the parents to problems should the child not follow the usual sequences. Failure to adjust in this orderly fashion may be due to two possible causes. First, he may be hanging on to the earlier patterns because he has not matured enough to be ready to make the adjustment. In this case parents are advised to wait and watch with the assurance that the time will come when the child's physical equipment will be ready and that the behavior will follow.

A second reason that children fail to make the necessary adjustment is often that the situation itself is too complex. In this case, parents may need to simplify the child's environment enough to help the child make the change. "Through such mutual accommodations between [parents] and child, human relationships are improved at all age levels" (Gesell and Ilg, 1949, p. 55). In this way parents teach the children while children also teach the parents. Parents can become more and more familiar with the laws of growth and development and the potential of each of their children.

Early in the life of the child, parents may begin to give the child oppor-tunities to develop purposes and responsibilities. Consideration of the child's individuality is probably the first step. The child's individual differences cannot be ignored by the parents without their paying a price. If parents begin with the assumption that the child is an individual with unique individual needs they will set as their task the understanding of that individuality, and try to give him the best chance to grow. They may then assign responsibilities to the child which are within his ability to do successfully.

The developmental philosophy. One should not assume from the above that the developmental approach put forth by Gesell and his colleagues equals indul-gence. The developmental point of view makes a healthy deference to the limita-tions of immaturity while emphasizing the need for parents to give direction, set reasonable limits, and structure the environment in such a way that the child can test out his growing behavior patterns.

The developmental philosophy does not imply overindulgence or excessive individualism because the parents as the representatives of culture are continu-ally making demands on the individual for responsible behavior. The goal of self-regulatory guidance should be to increase the tensions and the fullness of growth. In the infant, the self-demand schedule builds up the child's physical strength while developing a psychological sense of security. Because the infant's most vital needs have to do with his cravings for food and sleep, we should meet those needs as promptly and generously as possible. By meeting these needs with certainty we help the child to experience satisfaction of expectations. This in turn develops in the growing infant a sense of security and confidence in the lawfulness of the universe (Gesell and Ilg, 1949).

The developmental approach may be contrasted with what Gesell (1952) and others (Osborn, 1957) term the authoritarian approach (including behaviorism) and the laissez-faire points-of-view. The authoritarian method insists on the priority of the groups' needs; that is, the child should be taught to fit into the needs of the culture. The laissez-faire approach, on the other hand, imposes no limits on the child or his parents. In the laissez-faire model the child is said to know what is best and will find it for himself if allowed the freedom to seek his own solution. Gesell (1952) states that the developmental method would fall between the two. The developmental approach avoids authoritarian absolutes but does not accept license. The developmental model is sensitive to the subtle changes demanded by the child's growth and adjusts the guidance to the child's needs.

For Gesell and Ilg (1949), "child guidance is growth guidance" (p. 5). Therefore, a genetic approach takes precedence over rules of thumb and clever discipline techniques. The developmental outlook is designed to help us see the overall flow of development. In this way parents may look forward to the continual growth and development of their children instead of becoming bogged down on some specific difficulty or problem. By understanding the genetic basis of behavior they may take a more tolerant view of the difficulties encountered in immaturity.

The demand schedule. The child's self-demands and the parents' cultural demands must be brought into balance. This will come about by the parents becoming appreciative of the essential wisdom of the child's body and behavior manifestations. Parents need to learn to respect the child's behavioral changes and be able to understand their meaning. The changes are the way the child is growing and learning. If parents respond to these changes, then they can develop a flexible schedule of care geared to the infant's needs. This is a *demand schedule* as distinguished from an imposed schedule. Parents are likely to find that difficulties increase when they impose a hard-and-fast schedule without responding to the maturational level of the child.

The self-demand schedule takes its cues from the child's organic clock rather than from the clock on the wall. The infant is fed when he is hungry, changed when he is wet, allowed to sleep when he is sleepy, and allowed to play when he desires to play. The parents' adoption of a self-demand schedule sets up a favorable situation for the parents to observe and really learn the basic characteristics of their child. They will escape the problems which come from forcing the child to eat food he does not want and from the child's long crying spells while waiting for feeding time. Parents should record the various behaviors of the child, such as feedings, waking time, and play times on a chart so that the pattern of the child's behavioral day may become more apparent.* In this way the parents may satisfy their instinctive interest in the child's growth. The parents make the child a working partner in his up-bringing. The child helps the parents to work out a flexible schedule suited to his changing needs.

Self-adjustment, or the child's self-regulation, is a fundamental law of child development, which has important cultural implications (Gesell and Ilg, 1949). It applies to sleeping, eating, and infant play, as well as to higher forms of learning and mental organization. The child during his entire period of development is in a state of "formative instability" combined with progressive movement toward stability. This opposition between stability and variability produces

---

*Behaviorists (Chapter Seven) also recommend record keeping but of specific behaviors parents wish to increase or decrease rather than routine schedules. Both may prove helpful.

continual changes. Parents must learn to look upon these changes as positive thrusts or movements toward greater maturity. They may be viewed as self-demands, which if adequately satisfied by the parents result in optimal growth of the child's personality organization.

The child's personality is a product of slow and gradual growth. All of him grows; his nervous system grows, setting the stage for growth in mental activities and in personal-social patterns of behavior. This growth follows natural stages and sequences. The child "sits before he stands; he babbles before he talks; he fabricates before he tells the truth; he draws a circle before he draws a square; he is selfish before he is altruistic; he is dependent on others before he achieves dependence on self" (Gesell and Ilg, 1949, p. 11). The parents' task is not to force the child into a predetermined pattern but to guide his growth. Parents must be aware of the growth needs and the growth demands of the child. Yet "the child must do his own growing" (p. 5). The extent of his growth and fulfillment of his potentialities is dependent upon the insight and wisdom of his parents in meeting his individual needs.

Criticisms of the Developmental-Maturational Approach

One of Gesell's major assumptions is that all human behavior may be traced to growth and development. This assumption seems to hold very well as long as one confines his attention to physical growth and maturation. However, when Gesell and his coauthors turn to the vast array of adaptive behavior acquired through interaction with the environment the focus upon genetic influences to the almost total exclusion of the control exerted by environmental factors seems unjustified. While of course the physiological structure must be capable of sustaining the behavior, the same physiological structures may be used to perform so many acts and actions that to insist that each is dependent upon further maturational development requires some evidence. As Stolz (1958) points out, Gesell and his associates have not yet produced convincing data to substantiate their claims.

Even the principles of reciprocal interweaving and spiral reincorporation, which are invoked to support the development of more and more complex behavior, serve only to describe the process, and do not lead to any clear explanation of how it takes place. Gesell suggests that all the nerve cells are in place at birth. Therefore, increased differentiation is not the result of adding more complex nerve patterns. Nor is further organization the result of adding new muscle groups. Differentiation and organization can only come about through learning to use the existing organism in new and different ways. However, Gesell insists that the processes of organization and differentiation are the result of growth. He does not give evidence for such development. Nor does he give directions that would be of help in promoting such skills as flying an airplane, sewing a knit suit, or working out the solution to a complex business problem. He does not, of course, believe that the behavior necessary for these and countless other complex skills lies buried in the gene structure. There must be interaction between the individual and his environment for such complex behaviors to be developed. Gesell does not develop the nature of this interaction; in fact, he treats it so cavalierly that one almost comes to think that he *does* believe that it is all in the genes. It is difficult to argue with his thesis that mental maturity is only one aspect of the organism itself. But it is difficult to accept his suggestion that it is the organization of the organism which determines ultimate behavior.

Stolz (1958) has criticized Gesell's work on the basis of the sample he and his associates used to arrive at their descriptions of behavior for infants and children. Their sample is largely a sample of opportunity, taken from those children and parents who presented themselves at the Yale Clinic of Child Development and later at the Gesell Institute. These children represent an upper-middle-class group, with few of the difficulties encountered by lower and middle-class children and families. Gesell and his assistants argue that the developmental sequences are normative and that all children must pass through the stages regardless of class or status. (All developmental theories make similar claims; *see* for instance Freud's descriptions of the psychosexual stages in Chapter Two, and Piaget's descriptions of the cognitive stages in Chapter Five.) However, as Stolz (1958) points out, many of the behavior patterns described by Gesell for older children, especially adolescents, have been shown to be highly variable both within and between social classes. Sexual behavior of adolescents varies between classes (Hollingshead, 1949) and between cultural groups such as Danish, midwestern U.S., and Intermountain U.S. (Christensen and Carpenter, 1962). It becomes difficult to hold to the thesis that the disposition toward certain behaviors is genetically inherent and not learned. (For the argument from the other extreme *see* Chapter Seven).

A final criticism of Gesell's work is aimed at the use of the "ages and stages" approach so long associated with this theoretical point-of-view. Despite a throwaway warning in most of their writings, the authors still act as if the ages and stages were viable units; for example, in Ilg and Ames (1955): "Do not take the 'timetable' which follows too seriously. Do not try to match your own child exactly to it. We are here describing more or less *average* behavior for each age level" (p. 8); yet when they repeat over and over again that "Five is more self-contained than he was at four" (Gesell and Ilg, 1946, p. 79), "Seven is becoming more responsive" (p. 155), "Ten is not what you would call a worker" (Gesell, Ilg, and Ames, 1956, p. 50), and "Fifteen has a more defined ethical sense than he has ever had before" (p. 246), parents are likely to come to the conclusion that being a particular age has some magical quality which makes the child more self-contained, responsive, or ethical. There is, of course, nothing magical about these behaviors, and parents want to know how to help a child be self-contained, responsive, and ethical. Little that is found in Gesell's work will teach them how to provide that help. They are admonished to "give the best teaching possible and set the best example possible" (Ilg and Ames, 1953, p. 277). But they are not told how to proceed in those actions. And at the same time they are told more or less not to worry about it: "We should always remember that the child's ability to accept and profit by teaching about right and wrong develops slowly." In the end, parents are left with the impression that they can give some help but that their job is mostly to sit back and watch the children grow.

The prejudicial and stereotyped descriptions of children at various ages and stages is bad enough at 8, 10, or 14 weeks—but it becomes increasingly more difficult to swallow at 3, 5, 10, and 16 years of age. If parents expect their children to match the descriptions given by Gesell and associates they are very likely going to be disappointed. Still, all their descriptions of the early physical development of children can be very useful, *if* parents are careful to recognize that children do develop at very different rates and that they are very much influenced by learning.

The Socio-teleological Approach

4

The socio-teleological theory was first formulated by Alfred Adler following his split with Sigmund Freud. Adler, a physician, saw a parallel between psychological development and physical development (Way, 1962). For example, when an organ, such as a kidney, is defective, the other kidney and other organs often compensate for the physical disability by enlarging to meet the needs of the body. Similarly, Adler saw the individual as compensating psychologically when a weakness in a personality trait occurs. The individual was conceived by Adler as always moving from a felt psychological minus to a hoped-for plus (Ansbacher and Ansbacher, 1956). This striving to go from a feeling of weakness or inferiority to a feeling of strength or superiority takes on the characteristic of goal seeking in the individual's total pattern of interacting with others. Thus, the term *socio-teleological* refers to social striving or social goal-seeking.

Adler was always very interested in the family and did much work with parents. His student Rudolph Dreikurs did a great deal to elaborate Adler's theory with young children, and spent almost fifty years of his life helping parents to better understand and help their children. We shall rely heavily upon the writings of Dreikurs (1968; Dreikurs and Solz, 1958) for much of the discussion in this chapter.

The Socio-teleological View of the Nature of Man

From the socio-teleological point of view, man is a biological organism which reacts as a psychological whole to his environment. Physically weaker than many other biological organisms and capable of realizing this inferiority, man also develops feelings of psychological inferiority or weakness. The small child, unable to control many events in his environment, stands in awe of the magical, powerful adults who so easily open doors or get drinks from taps far above the child's head. Observing his powerlessness and the powerful capability of others to control the world, the child seeks to find ways to compensate. He tries out various ways of behaving that might help him overcome his feeling of weakness. He may try to act weak and helpless, or he may act brave and blusterous or angry and aggressive. After a few years he settles upon a characteristic pattern, or as Adler put it, "style of life," which will unconsciously guide his behavior. By five years of age the child has usually assumed a very individualistic set of goals which will be with him throughout his lifetime.

The teleology or goal-striving described by Adler and his students (Ansbacher and Ansbacher, 1956; Allred, 1968; Dreikurs, 1968) is a "soft" teleology often referred to as a "fictional finalization." By this Adler means that the goal or goals the individual strives for are entirely a product of his own conscious and unconscious needs. These ideal states are, therefore, really unattainable by the individual. Because they are a fictitious creation they are forever out of reach. Nonetheless, they are the primary source of motivation. The goal is "the final cause, the ultimate independent variable" (Ansbacher and Ansbacher, 1956).

Biological and historical factors are all used by the individual in terms of his personal goal. Biological factors and learning provide mere possibilities, or at most probabilities. The individual uses the objective facts in accordance with his lifestyle.

The goal the individual assumes is a product of self and environment. It is formed in early childhood in response to the child's image of himself and his response to the environment. Other people, especially his parents, form an important part of the environment. However, it is the child's view of himself and his environment and not the objective facts which determines his lifestyle. In this way the socio-teleological approach is very similar to the existential-phenomenological approach discussed in Chapter Six.

Genetic endowment plays a part in the individual's early goal development. The child's physical characteristics help to determine the self-image the child develops. If he perceives himself to be strong and coordinated he will form a picture of himself quite different than if he perceived himself to be weak and clumsy. Parents play a role here too. If a child is born with a defect, such as a club foot, the child's view of the problem will be shaped in part by the parents' reactions. If parents behave as if the child can overcome the difficulty and will be a capable person despite the handicap, the child often accepts this point-of-view also.

If the child forms a concept of himself as capable and worthwhile, he will develop into an adult with a sense of "social feeling" or "social interest." Adler (1964; Ansbacher and Ansbacher, 1956) assumed that social interest is a unique human trait, genetically bestowed on all men. Events in the child's life tend to enhance his sense of social interest or "belonging" or to decrease it. Evidence for these feelings is taken from the amount of cooperation and the useful contributions the individual makes to others. Fear of failure leads the individual to seek *personal superiority* rather than to seek solutions to problems which will benefit others as well as himself (Ansbacher and Ansbacher, 1956).

A through-and-through evolutionist, Adler felt that the goal of all human life is the perfection of that life (1964). The goal for perfection is inherent in social interest. Since individual men cannot become perfect, they can only reach the goal of perfection through cooperation with others. The goal of personal superiority is a perversion of the goal of social interest, for it limits or subverts the development of others and thus prevents the individual who practices it from cooperating for the perfection of all.

Ultimately, for Adler, each individual must find solutions to three basic human problems: first, how he will relate to society; second, how he will meet his needs (i.e., work); and third, how he will meet his emotional needs, his need for love. These challenges remain with us throughout our lives and are a fundamental part of our evolutionary history.

Adler argues that since human perfection can only occur in a perfect community, we must all strive in whatever way possible to bring about a more perfect society. Whatever we do that improves the common good is in accord with the inherent nature of social feelings. The tendency to act for the common good is rather weak at the present stage of evolutionary development, but eventually it should become as automatic as breathing or walking in an upright position (Adler, 1964). The solution to society's problems will bring about the solution of our own problems. Thus every man is involved in the solution of society's problems to the extent that his social interest has been aroused or learned.

Solving the problem of meeting one's basic physical needs requires cooperation and the division of labor. Social feeling leaves its mark here in the need to work together for the benefit of all. The individual's solution to the problem of apportioning his time between his personal needs and the needs of the group has meaning for all men. His choice of work is strongly influenced by his lifestyle and the extent to which he has developed his feelings of social interest. The person who performs useful work lives in a self-developing community and contributes his share to that community. Thus in work he is again tied socially to others.

In no other area of human behavior is social interest so clearly seen as in the way the individual works out his solutions to his emotional needs. Love is essentially a task for two persons. Cooperation is required, whether one is sharing in a friendship or in a sexual union with one's spouse with a view to having offspring. Although one person can merely use another in such an exchange, it is not the same act. Love and friendship require a certain commitment to the other person. Child rearing, which is the only certain way of continuing one's self throughout eternity, cannot be fully successful if left to one parent or the other. "The refusal to enter into a lasting union shows doubt and mistrust between the two partners in a common task" (Adler, 1964, p. 61). Such doubts and mistrust are not conducive to developing children's social interest. This "is bound to have unending results in the children and in the welfare of humanity" (Adler, 1964, p. 61).

Life, Adler concludes, is continually testing us in the problems it presents. Our solutions are correct inasmuch as they enhance our social interest and the social feelings of others. Inasmuch as we fail we are sowing the seeds of our own and our society's destruction.

Man is, therefore, a social being. Striving for perfection and to fulfill his own personal ideals or fictional goals, each individual acts out his solutions to life's basic problems. In so doing he adds to or takes away from the slow progression of the human species as it marches slowly forward in its evolutionary history.

The Socio-teleological View of the Nature of Children

According to the socio-teleological theorists, the child is born with a sense of social interest. That is, he has the capacity to become an adult with well-developed social feelings. Given the proper guidance he will be cooperative with others and will seek to make a useful contribution to the needs of other members of his society. He will treat others as his social equals, respecting them as individuals just as he would wish to be respected.

Social feelings are influenced by the child's heredity, his environment, and his perception of all these things. This relationship has already been noted above. It is important to note here how Adler (1964) and his students view the interaction of these variables in the development of the personality of the child.

As we have already seen, the child's genetic inheritance can influence the child's picture of himself and thus his developing lifestyle. Still another way in which the child's genetic inheritance influences his growing lifestyle is through the child's tendency to be more or less active in his interaction with the environment. Dreikurs (1968) pointed out that the child's activity level influences the way the child solves the problems he encounters in life. This is as true for the child who is working on the side of perfection or, as Dreikurs terms it, the "constructive" side of life, as it is for the child who has become discouraged and is working on the "useless" or destructive side.

Adler (1964; Ansbacher and Ansbacher, 1956) repeatedly points out that heredity and environment provide probabilities for the child's behavior; but they do not determine that behavior. Environment, however, seems to provide more probabilities than does heredity in his model.

Dreikurs (1968) and Allred (1968) follow Adler's lead in pointing up the influence of parents and siblings on the developing lifestyle of the child. The *family atmosphere* created by the style of interacting established by the husband and wife determines many of the similarities between family members. If the parents establish patterns of cooperation and mutual assistance, then the children are far more likely to establish cooperative patterns in their lifestyles. On the other hand, if the parents compete constantly for power and position within the relationship, the children will tend to adopt a competitive style of interacting.

Differences between the children within a family (such as one child being a good reader while another does poorly, or one child being a good student while his brother is a good athlete) may be fostered by the relationships between the siblings. The *family constellation* refers to the order of birth and the influence the relationships of birth order have on the child's developing lifestyle. Having been born first, second, or third presents the child with a different set of life experiences, depending upon where one is in the family constellation.

The first child experiences one or two years of his parents' undivided attention. However, as a rule, this special position as Mom's and Dad's one-and-only comes to a sudden end when the second child is brought home from the hospital. According to Adler, if the first child has been prepared for this event and has even been taught to help in the care of the younger sibling, the shock of this "dethronement" is generally quickly over. If, as is too often the case, the child has not been prepared, the pain of losing his favored position may be very great.

Adler suggests (Ansbacher and Ansbacher, 1956; Way, 1962) that firstborns often assume the roles of father or mother. They tend to accept or be given responsibility for the younger children. Research seems to bear this out. Harris and Howard (1968) found firstborns and first of sex children *expecting* to give more responsibility to their firstborn children. This is taken as evidence that they have internalized the ideal of responsibility more than their siblings.

One explanation of the firstborn's taking on the roles of his or her parents may be that he has no one else upon whom he may model (Sampson, 1965). He may well be taught, therefore, to attend more closely to approval cues from his parents and to match his behavior more closely to their expectations. Second-born children, as Adler (1964) points out, always have the older sibling as a model. The secondborn must distribute his attention between his parents and his sibling for important cues about forthcoming behavior and expectations. As a result, Adler feels the secondborn child is in a far better position to learn to be cooperative than is the firstborn.

Adler (1964; Ansbacher and Ansbacher, 1956) suggests that the pressure from the second child may accelerate the competition between the two. In response to this pressure the first may strive harder to achieve and stay out in front of his younger rival. There is some evidence to support such a theory. Schachter (1963) gives evidence that firstborns do receive better grades in high school, a factor which may lead to the fact that firstborn children are over-represented in college and greatly over-represented in graduate and professional training. Although the data is fairly consistent that firstborns do achieve relatively more than later born children, the *whys* are far more uncertain. Schooler suggests one reason for these findings: recent reviews of the birth order data by Schooler (1972; 1973) suggest that the differences found may be due to socio-economic and population factors. When social class trends in numbers of new families and family size are controlled, most of the findings related to birth order tend to disappear.

There seems to be some evidence that parents do give more attention to firstborns, especially in verbal areas (Sampson, 1965), although Schooler (1972) raises doubts about differences in parental practices. Sampson also found in his review of the literature on ordinal position that parents tend to be more restrictive, less permissive, less warm and approving, and less protective of firstborns as compared to later born children. Sampson concludes that the dethronement of the firstborn may lead the first child to spend much of the rest of his life trying to regain his favored position as the center of the family group. Thus the first child's trying to catch up to himself may lead to his high achievement motivation.

The data presented above seem to run somewhat counter to Adler's theoretical statements concerning the second child. Adler (Ansbacher and Ansbacher, 1956) felt that because the second child had the first as a pacesetter, the second-born child was more likely to be successful. Adler pictured the second child as always hurrying to catch up. This may be so in terms of his attitude, but does not seem to be borne out in the overall achievement of second children. It should be noted, however, that the data presented may not be a completely fair test, since much of the data compares firstborn children with *all* later born children and therefore may not be truly representative of the facts between the firstborn and secondborn children.

Adler (1964; Ansbacher and Ansbacher, 1956) also addressed himself to problems encountered by the youngest child. Youngest children remain forever the baby of the family. They can never be dethroned, so they remain in some ways forever special. The youngest child runs a very high risk of being pampered and spoiled, as there are all the other siblings before him to care for him. He tends, therefore, to expect others to care for him and to solve all his problems. In the end, Adler suggests, because the youngest has so many models and so many opportunities for competition, he often excells over all the others.

Problem children, according to Adler (Ansbacher and Ansbacher, 1956), are most likely to be first and last children. Adler suggests that firstborn children suffering from dethronement often fight for their mother's attention. In so doing they tend to become critical and demanding of the rights and the prerogatives of being first. They tend to be rule keepers and somewhat more conservative in that they want to maintain power and authority over others. Jensen (1971) found that older sisters in two-sister relationships had more influence over their younger sisters' behavior and attitudes in terms of choices the younger sisters made in response to immediate situations. They may be anxious and fearful as a result of their experiences with attempting to maintain their positions in the family, fearing that they will lose their rightful place if they let up even for a minute.

While some data tend to uphold Adler's theory about firstborns, it is by no means consistent. Firstborns do tend to have more difficulties maintaining friendships (Schachter, 1963; Sampson, 1965) although Koch (1954) found oldest girls were *more* friendly. The data concerning greater anxiety on the part of firstborns are also inconsistent. Sampson (1965) reports on two studies which suggest that there is no difference in authoritarianism between firstborn and later born children. And, finally, Sampson found evidence to support the conclusion that firstborns tend to have lower self-esteem than their siblings—this despite their greater achievement in life. One might assume that firstborns, having more clear cut adult models, may be forever reaching for goals that are impossible to achieve; thus their greater motivation to achieve, but at the same time their lower level of self-esteem. A cause-effect relationship between the variables cannot be drawn based upon our present data, however. Do the firstborns' lowered friendship levels come about because their high achievement drive keeps them close to their books and thus precludes their making friends? Or is their higher achievement the result of the fact that they are unable to make friends and are left with little else to do but study as Schachter (1963) suggests? Either answer seems equally likely, and further research is indicated.

Youngest children, according to Adler (1964; Ansbacher and Ansbacher, 1956), tend to be more spoiled. Spoiled children can never be independent, and youngest children often have so many others to care for them that they are likely to be spoiled in this way. The research data presented by Sampson (1965) does not uphold this theory, however. There appears to be little difference between the dependency needs of firstborn and later born children.

Adler's interest and attention to the interaction of the individual child with his parents and his siblings leaves little doubt of the important role he placed on the social environment. We have yet to discuss, however, the role of the child's view of his position in the family and what Adler (1964) frequently termed the child's creative ability or activity.

Every child is born with an individual set of potentials. And many children who have similar environments remain very different individuals. It is the child's creative power or ability which determines what he does with the genetic factors which he inherits and the problems created for him by his environment. The child surveys his phenomenal world* and by means of his creative power establishes the meaning of himself and his world. Out of his natural drive toward human superiority he fashions his own personal direction or *law of movement* which will serve to organize and give a self-consistent unity to events throughout his lifetime.

All of the child's inherited possibilities, all of the influences of his body, and all the environmental influences are taken into account, evaluated, and responded to by a living and striving individual, attempting to be successful according to his own personal goal. For Adler (Ansbacher and Ansbacher, 1956), this finalistic, teleological point of view is absolutely necessary for understanding the individual. The child shapes his life from his subjective, personal conception of life.

Because the child selects his personal goal and then works to make the world fit his perception, Adler refutes the idea that heredity and environment play an absolute causal role. Heredity and environment can only provide problems and influence in terms of probabilities. The child, and later the adult, makes his choices and acts upon the events; he does not merely react. The child's creative power is the ultimate deciding power. The child strives to overcome life's obstacles as he sees them. The possibilities for response are endless. Through trial and error the child establishes a goal and then follows it throughout his lifetime.

The element of trial and error leaves open the possibility of error. The child will make mistakes. No one can know the absolute best way to solve any problem. Within the thousands of possibilities available he may choose a poor solution. But from his mistakes the child will learn that it is not a good solution. Parents may help by pointing out, not what the child did wrong, but rather that he now knows one way that will not work. The wise parent will encourage the child to try again a different way.

The Relationship of the Individual to the Group

The only way one can fully understand the individual, according to the socio-teleological theorists (Adler, 1964; Ansbacher and Ansbacher, 1956; Dreikurs, 1968) is to understand his position in the social group. Man's social groups include not only the face-to-face groups with which he interacts daily, but also the whole of mankind. Ansbacher and Ansbacher (1956) suggest that "the individual must be seen and must see himself as embedded in a larger

---

*For a detailed description of the concept of *phenomenal world, see* Chapter Six.

whole, the social situation" (p. 127). Failure to come to grips with this "iron logic of communal life" is sure to be disastrous to the individual. Such a failure occurs when the person's social groups fail to awaken his sense of social interest.

The weakness and helplessness of the child at birth require that others take care of him. Thus from the very beginning there are interlocking ties of human relationships. However, it is not just the child who is dependent upon the mother; the mother is also dependent upon the child. The pressures of lactation in the mother's breast draw her to the child nearly as compellingly as hunger draws the child to the mother. Very quickly an emotional attachment develops between both mother and child. Thus the child and the mother develop the infant's first social ties.

Very quickly the child becomes aware of the fact that he must fit into the social group in some way to survive. This includes an awareness of the rules of the game of group living. The child acts as if his perception of those rules were the absolute truth. Merton (1957) recognizes this rule of human behavior when he states that what men believe to be true is the truth for that time. Adler (1964) illustrates this fact by suggesting that one's behavior is the same whether a poisonous snake is crawling toward one's foot or whether one merely believes that the snake crawling toward one's foot is poisonous. Since the child believes that his perception of the rules is the absolute truth he behaves that way.

If the child believes the people in his world will only accept him if he manages to keep their attention he behaves in such a way as to maintain their attention. It does not matter if others would actually accept him more readily if he would join with them in a more cooperative way. As long as he perceives the rules to be that he must have "center stage," he will continue to act to get attention.*

The "best-adjusted" individuals will be those whose view of the truth is most like the views held by others in his society. The rules of the game originate in the needs of the community (Ansbacher and Ansbacher, 1956). They are determined by the necessity for order to enable men to live together. Thus the rules and regularities arise spontaneously.

Group life is an evolutionary necessity, according to Adler, because the group allows man, through the division of labor, to solve problems that would be impossible to solve alone. Thus the group evolves rules through education, superstition, taboos, and laws by which it judges the value of the individual's actions. So far as the actions of the individual are likely to be rewarding to other members of the social group he would be said by Adler to be acting out of social interest.

The more one's private decisions have general validity, the more one is likely to act out of what Adler termed "common sense" rather than "private sense." Men need to have a feeling of certainty to guide their conduct; but because no one can have the absolute answers to life's problems, the most useful fiction, according to the Ansbachers (1956), is to consider the rules of one's society as if they were the absolute truth. "A man is called good when he relates himself to other humans in a generally useful way, bad when he acts contrary to social interest" (Ansbacher and Ansbacher, 1956, p. 139). The more a person's behavior supports the general needs of the society, the less likely that his behavior will be labeled bad, evil, sick, or crazy.†

---

*An equally plausible explanation is that the child is reinforced by the attention of others; see Chapter Seven.

†It is interesting to note the correspondence between Adler's thinking concerning the group and Skinner's considerations of the role of culture in shaping human behavior.

As seen by Adler (Ansbacher and Ansbacher, 1956), social interest is the measure of the child's normality. The degree of social interest a person exhibits is evidence of his mental health. As long as the child or adult is not lacking in social feelings (i.e., is relatively free from inferiority feelings) he will attempt to contribute to others in a worthwhile manner on the "useful side of life." Such an individual, while pursuing his own personal goal, is interested in others. This interest need not be of the hail-fellow-well-met variety: the back-slapping, hand-shaking "extrovert." Social interest expresses itself in some kind of contribution to the common good, but not necessarily in concrete participation. Ansbacher and Ansbacher (1956) also note that the contribution need not be to any specific here-and-now group, but may well be a contribution to some future, ideal society.

In the end, Adler (Ansbacher and Ansbacher, 1956) sees all the failures that befall mankind as failures in social interest. Neurosis, psychosis, alcoholism, delinquency, and suicide occur because the individuals involved are lacking in social interest. These individuals fail because they look for solutions to the problems of life in private meanings rather than in a common sense. "No one else is benefited by the achievement of their aims, and their interest stops short at their own persons. The goal of success is a goal of personal superiority, and their triumphs have meaning only to themselves" (Ansbacher and Ansbacher, 1956, p. 156). Adequate social feelings lead to "common sense" solutions so far as they make sense, not only to the individual, but also to members of his social group.

Adler felt that his position was the most consistent theory of the place of the individual in the social group. The important interplay between the group and the individual was continually stressed by Adler. His concept of social interest is that the individual cannot exist in any real sense without the group. The development of language as a tool for mankind is a good illustration: Adler states, "Language is quite unnecessary for a creature living by itself" (Ansbacher and Ansbacher, 1956, p. 130). However, the group has need of the individual as well. Language and even logical thinking are not private but common property, shared or lost.

Social interest is an innate potential of man, but it does not operate with the force of an instinct. Therefore, social interest must be encouraged and even taught. It is an important role of parents to instill social interest in the developing child. In this way it will act with certainty, shaping every thought and action and guiding the child toward the useful side of life.

Other Dimensions and Issues

Among the important concepts developed by Adler is his concept of lifestyle. The current popularity of this term suggests its usefulness. However, it is important that we understand how Adler used the term as part of his theory. We shall also take a detailed look at how Adler saw heredity and environment influencing the child's learning.

Lifestyle. It is important to note that the child forms his lifestyle, his personal goal for superiority, within the first five years of life. During this time he has neither the language nor the concepts to form this impression of life and his direction in it into words. As a result, the child's law of movement is preverbal and remains largely hidden to the individual throughout his lifetime. In normal times when the problems he encounters are not too great his personal goal may remain hidden to others as well. When the individual is under stress, however, the pattern he formed in the first five years of his life will be far more visible.

Once formed, the line of movement (the lifestyle or goal) tends to determine the direction the individual's choices will go in response to both heredity and environment (Ansbacher and Ansbacher, 1956). Adler believed that the adult's mental life, or *schemas*, differs markedly from that of the child. He also believed it is unusual for those differences to make a difference in the lifestyle. The adult ways of thinking and behaving only contribute to the variety of ways one may work toward achieving the already formed goal.

It is because the goal was formed in early childhood that the mistaken interpretations the child made of the world at that time continue to dominate his experience. Whenever the child or adult faces a new or difficult situation he in some way repeats his original misconceptions in his approach to a solution. It is in this way that the objective facts are, for Adler, rendered useless in predicting the behavior of the individual. If we do not understand the child's lifestyle we cannot predict how he will use the facts which confront him.

Early events strongly determine behavior in later years. The chief difference between Adler's view of this determination and the viewpoints of others is the role the child himself plays in the formation of his own personality. For the learning theorists it is the environment which molds the child; for Adler "the child creatively forms his subjective opinion of the world and himself, albeit utilizing his surrounding objective situation" (Ansbacher and Ansbacher, 1956, p. 191).

Socio-teleology and learning. Adler's conception of the individual as having the creative ability to form for himself a style of life from the raw material of his hereditary and environmental conditions strongly influences his conceptions of how the child learns. From Adler's point-of-view, the individual is self-determined by the meaning he gives to his experiences. We determine ourselves by the meanings we give to the situations in which we find ourselves.

Because experiences are ambiguous, the individual is free to draw whatever conclusions he wishes from his experience. The conclusion he draws is determined by his style of life, his line of movement. "It is not the child's experiences which dictate his actions; it is the conclusions which he draws from his experiences" (Ansbacher and Ansbacher, 1956, p. 209). The conclusion the individual reaches is to use the situation or the learning from the situation to help him reach a successful solution to his problems. As his ultimate problem is a fictional goal which he has created for himself, he cannot help but make some error in his solution. Thus he may behave in a way which appears to others to be quite irrational. For example, the child whose crying always results in a spanking but who continues to cry would, from the point-of-view of others, be solving his problem (possibly the need for attention) in a very irrational way. However, from the point-of-view of the child the goal was attention, and therefore crying serves his purpose very well.

The example above is a good illustration of Adler's (Ansbacher and Ansbacher, 1956) meaning when he states that the child does not learn from experience. If he learned from experience he would not cry if crying is always punished by spanking. "Of course we learn to avoid certain difficulties and we acquire a certain conduct toward them, but the line along which we move is not changed thereby" (Ansbacher and Ansbacher, 1956, p. 211). Any learning experience will be accepted only when the individual perceives that it will help him in his movement toward his private goal. Adler considered this concept to be a direct refutation of behaviorism.

The environment influences behavior only in the way the individual chooses to interpret it in relationship to his individual lifestyle. "Thus he also sees the environment which trains him with his own self-created perspective and accordingly changes its effect upon him for better or worse" (Ansbacher and Ansbacher, 1956, p. 212). It is for this reason that attempts to change the behavior of the child sometimes meet with failure. In one case, a delinquent high school student was treated for one year utilizing phenomenological techniques. The next year he was treated utilizing behavioral techniques. At the end of the second year when asked why he hadn't changed following all that therapeutic help he replied simply that he didn't want to. Evidently this individual did not see the attempts of the therapists to change his behavior as realistic from the point-of-view of his lifestyle. Thus he changed the meaning of their behavior and continued in his previous line.

Application of Socio-teleological Theory to Child Rearing

According to the socio-teleological theorists, the high degree of cooperation which men need in order to exist together requires spontaneous social effort. Therefore, the primary role of all socializing processes should be to evoke social interest. Because social interest is not inborn as a full-fledged instinct, but is rather an innate potential, it must be consciously developed. The responsibility for the encouragement of the child's developing social interest falls first upon the parents.

It is with the mother and the family that the child makes his first acquaintance with interpersonal relationships. It is within the circle of his family that the child makes his decision as to the nature of the world in which he finds himself. The decision depends upon the creative power of the child and is guided by the social environment and the experiences he has of his body (Ansbacher and Ansbacher, 1956). The decision as to whether the world is a safe place where he may take part as an equal among equals, or whether he must forever strive to be superior to others in order to survive, determines his lifestyle or goal. While the ultimate decision is the child's, the parents may play an important role through the atmosphere they provide and by their encouragement.

To bring about the development of the child's social interest, parents must understand the dynamics of personality development. The earlier sections of this chapter have been an attempt to point out Adler's theoretical conceptualization of the process of personality development.

Adler (1964; Ansbacher and Ansbacher, 1956) and his students (Dreikurs, 1968; Allred, 1968) see the child as acting and reacting to two sets of stimulation. The internal stimuli are his physiological and hereditary functions. The child also responds to his external environment. Both are acted upon by the child's creative potential, and after the first three to five years of life the child has settled upon a lifestyle that determines much of how he interprets the signals he receives from both his inner and outer environments. This goal is a fictional finalization: it is an attempt to reach a place in life from which the child will be safe from feelings of inferiority. However, because much of the child's experience is preverbal during this time, and because he has limited experience against which to evaluate his experiences, the child may draw faulty conclusions about the most effective approaches to social living. This may result in his taking ineffective or faulty approaches to the solution of life's problems.

Two reasons that a child may select a mistaken goal as an attempt to defend against feelings of inferiority are parental expectations and parental reactions to the child's mistakes.

Parents' expectations may lead them to give subtle and not-so-subtle cues to the child's behavior. The parent who says, "He's a little devil most of the time" or "She's always shy around strangers," may be signaling to the child that he or she is expected to behave in a certain way. The child may, without being consciously aware of it, respond as expected.

Expectations may be transmitted far more subtly, however. Rosenthal's (1966) work stands as a monument to unintentionally transmitted expectations. In one of a series of experiments to study the effects of experimenter bias in research, Rosenthal measured the achievement level of children in a grade school. The teachers were then informed that the children whose names appeared on a list were due to spurt ahead that year. The children whose names appeared on the list were selected randomly from the population of children tested for achievement. In the spring, the children were tested again and the children on the list were found to have achieved more than their peers. The experimenters conclude that the teachers' expectations for improvement were responsible for the differences in test scores. Evidently our expectations as teachers and parents can and do lead to differences in children's behavior.

Parental reactions to children's mistakes also lead the child to draw erroneous conclusions about himself and his worth in the social system. By always noticing the child's mistakes we tend to discourage him from trying again. We give him the feeling that he is not good enough the way he is, that he will only be acceptable to us if he changes (Dreikurs, 1968). By discouraging the child in this way, we keep him from experiencing his own ability to meet and solve his problems.

Dreikurs (1968) suggests that parents need to recognize that there are at least two ways to stimulate the child's development. We can stimulate him toward attitudes which will lead him to seek security by getting ahead of others—putting others down so that he feels "up." Of course, security cannot be found in achievement over others, since there is always the possibility of being put down. On the other hand, parents may stimulate their children to find success by contributing to the good of others. Rather than succeeding *over* others they can succeed *with* others. In this way mistakes are not failures but invitations to try another way.

There is yet another way that parents fall victim to the child's mistaken goals. Parents often react to the child's misbehavior in a way which strengthens it and maintains it. In part, Dreikurs feels, this is due to a tendency to treat children as inferiors. In a democracy all people come to feel equal to each other. Children can and should be treated as equals, too.

By equality the socio-teleological theorists (Adler, 1964; Ansbacher and Ansbacher, 1956; Dreikurs, 1968; Allred, 1968) mean social equality. The child is not equal in terms of experience and education; but he is still due equal respect as an individual capable of deciding and choosing for himself.

Dreikurs states that many of the mistakes made in child rearing are due to failures in maintaining self-respect—the adult's self-respect as well as the self-respect of the child. The parent who allows his child to rule over the household and constantly have his way allows the child to reach for personal superiority; but the child does not experience the necessity to share in the needs of the family and community. This spoiling or pampering diminishes the child's social interest.

Parents would do better to establish some rules of order within the family for the benefit of all family members. Within those limits children should be given choices and be allowed to make decisions for themselves. They should be allowed to be responsible for their own behavior and should learn by feeling the natural or logical consequences of that behavior. By recognizing the child's ability to care for himself and by showing their faith in him, parents would instill courage in the child, and his social interest will grow.

Unfortunately, many parents do not recognize the child's ability to solve even his most simple problems, let alone more difficult ones. As a result they often move in too quickly and solve the problem for the child. By doing this they increase his feelings of inferiority and his self-doubts.

However, even the discouraged child wishes to gain status and have a place in the group. Thus, the child who is misbehaving and denying the needs of others in the social situation "still believes that his actions will give him social status" (Dreikurs, 1968).

Typically, Dreikurs believes, the young child in this type of situation will seek to gain status in one of three ways. He will focus the attention of others on himself, strive to prove his power over others, or seek revenge for his real or assumed hurts. If he becomes even further discouraged he may attempt to avoid more hurt and failure by refusing to participate in the areas where he perceives the possibility of making a mistake. To avoid further humiliation, the child may assume disability and use his display of deficiency to escape from what he perceives as a dangerous situation in terms of his self-respect.*

The four goals of disturbing behavior, as Dreikurs has labeled them, are relatively easy to observe in children below the age of 10. After that they are more difficult to detect because we have learned to cover our motives with "rational" explanations. Dreikurs points out that it is difficult for parents to accept the fact that their children are seeking the parents' attention unduly or are seeking power over them, or that they are even seeking revenge upon them. The child is seeking status and at this young age the child receives his status from adults. Furthermore, when parents are unaware of the child's goals they often unwittingly reinforce the child's misbehavior by their reaction to it.

When the child seeks undue attention we often feel irritated and upset. Our response is to give them the attention they are demanding, when they demand it, and in the way they demand it. In this way the child continues to seek attention because he is convinced, according to this theory, that only in this way can he be an important part of the family group. It is as if he feels that if he behaved in any other way he would be left out, ignored, or unimportant. Attempts to correct the attention-seeking child usually result in his stopping whatever he is doing for a short period of time. Within a matter of minutes, however, he has returned to the irritating behavior or has found a new behavior which brings the same results.†

According to Dreikurs, attempts to control children may lead to a struggle between the parents and the child for power and superiority. The child acts as if he must prove that he can do as he pleases and refuses to do what the parents want him to do. Parents feel as if their rights and prerogatives to govern in their own homes are being attacked. They are often heard to make such comments as "He can't do that to me"—even while he is "doing that" to them. Emotionally, we react to the behavior of such children with anger. And the child meets our attempts at correction with refusals to cooperate and intensified anger and rebellion.

As parents intensify their efforts to influence the child through increased application of power, the child feels that his only recourse is to seek revenge and retaliate (Dreikurs, 1968). Having failed to win a place in the group through cooperation, attention, or even power, the child acts as if the only way he can gain recognition is through gaining a reputation as the most vicious. Individuals who are motivated by this goal are very sensitive to other peoples' weak spots and do not hesitate to attack them there. Our typical emotional response to the revenge-oriented child is a feeling of hurt. Any efforts that parents or others make to help these children are met with deep distrust as the children feel that they are unliked and unlikable.

---

*Adler (Ansbacher and Ansbacher, 1956) felt that the fear of humiliation, i.e., being proved inferior, was at the root of all human motivation. It is interesting to note that Sullivan (1953) similarly postulated avoidance of anxiety as the prime motivator.

†For a behavioral analysis of the same type of behavior see Chapter Seven.

Passive children and those who have been continuously and successfully discouraged may begin to feel there is no hope for them to be successful. Fearing to fail even one more time they may stop trying altogether. The deeply discouraged child may hide behind his real or imagined inferiorities as a defense against being asked or expected to perform. It is as if by avoiding taking part he can avoid further hurt and humiliation (Dreikurs, 1968). The discouraged child may only too easily convince us of his inability. His parents become discouraged and convinced that the child lacks the ability required to accomplish in the area he shows incompetence in. Instead of the parents influencing and teaching the child, he influences and teaches them not to expect anything from him. The parents' attempts to help only seem to push the child into deeper and deeper despair.

What can parents do about children who behave in these ways? First, of course, the parents must be aware of the nature of the child's goals and his typical patterns of interacting with others (Dreikurs, 1968). One might consider what the "typical" day is like with each child in the family. Does he or she get up ready to meet the challenges of the day? Or does this particular child need to be called several times before rising? Is getting out of bed a point of fighting and arguing between the parent and child? The cooperative child may be up and going; the attention seeker may need many reassurances that you care by demanding that you call several times; and the power-seeking child may make getting out of bed a declaration of war for the day.

Obviously, a single incident or a single episode is not evidence for a goal. We are looking for recurrent patterns, for variations on a theme, as it were, which recur over and over throughout the day and the week. The parents should continue their observations of the child's behavior through the "typical" day. How does the child get dressed, come to breakfast, depart for school? What is his behavior like at school, as reported by the teacher? How does he come home from school? What is his behavior like at suppertime, at bedtime? In all of these critical times when the child must respond to the needs and demands of others in the social group parents can see evidence of his goal.

We should notice in all these interaction periods who initiates the action; whether the child responds to requests, initiates his own, seeks attention, counters others' actions, or attempts to hurt or claim inability. After careful observation, we may come to some tentative decision about the direction of the child's goal. Our purpose is not to arrive at a label, however, but to gather information which will lead to action on our part as parents.

Once parents recognize the goal, they are in a position to change *their* behavior. Careful analysis suggests that if one member of a social group changes his behavior the others in the group will eventually need to change theirs (Watzlawick, Beavin, and Jackson, 1967). Unfortunately, most of us start off backwards in our attempts to solve our interpersonal problems. We say that we will change our behavior as soon as the other person changes his. As a result, no change ever occurs in the system. Parents who really wish to bring about a lasting change in their children's behavior and attitudes are advised to start by changing their own behavior.

In the case of the child who continually seeks undue attention and service, for example, parents may bring about a change by changing the way they respond to the child's demands. When the child seeks service or attention in an area where he obviously has the ability and the skill to act for himself, the parents should arrange to not hear his request and to be occupied with some important task of their own. They may acknowledge his request with a simple word or phrase of encouragement, such as "I know you can handle that." However, long lectures on the child's skills and abilities should be avoided.

Sometimes it is necessary that the parent leave the room or ask the child to go to another area of the house until the task is completed. In this way the parent is physically unable to respond to the child's demands for service.

In addition to changing how they respond to the child's requests for attention, parents need to change another pattern of their own behavior if they truly wish to help the child overcome his attention-seeking tendencies. Parents need to observe when the child is doing something right and replace the attention they have withdrawn. That is, they should give the child as much attention for doing the job by himself as they previously gave him by "helping" him get it done. This encouragement can be nonverbal, such as a smile, a wink, or a pat on the shoulder. If it is verbal it is a good idea to point out the child's role in the accomplishment of the task rather than praising the whole child. For example, on observing the child share a cookie with her sister one might comment, "I'll bet it makes you feel good to share with your sister," rather than, "You're a good girl." Such phrases highlight the child's actions and the related feelings. The long-range outcome is a child with increased social feelings.

When encountering a child whose primary goal is power, parents need to change another set of behaviors. The most typical reaction is often the least helpful. When someone attacks us our natural inclination is to fight back. Children and parents often teach each other to argue and fight in just this way. One crosses the other, the other responds, and on it goes. If parents desire to change this pattern, they should disengage from the battle. They must decide that *they* are no longer going to fight. Parents who choose this course should respect the child enough to allow him to choose to continue fighting for a while if the child wishes to do so. (Parents should note that this is really another way of saying that they will not fight with the child over whether he will fight or not!)

Disengaging from fights and arguments with children is often difficult. One method is to label the fight as such. Regardless of how it starts, as soon as the parent recognizes that they are engaged in combat he should simply state, "Oh, I see we're fighting again; I've decided to stop." This should be followed by action on the part of the parent. Strategic withdrawal is often a useful tactic.

Withdrawing from the area whenever the child engages us in a fight is often helpful. After all, it is no fun to shout and scream in an empty room. Many parents fear to withdraw in this way for several reasons. First, it is often very difficult to do because we have a tremendous personal investment in the fight. We feel that withdrawing will be a signal that we have lost either the fight or our influence over the child. As for losing the fight, we have only to remind ourselves that we have chosen not to fight and therefore we may congratulate ourselves for maintaining our resolve and winning our own personal battle. It helps, of course, if both parents are working together on this and can lend support and encouragement to each other when they do withdraw from the battle. And as for losing our influence over the child, we should note that changing our behavior from fighting to not fighting is influencing the child—just in a different way than in the past.

Having lost a sparring partner, the child is unable to solve his problems as he has in the past. At first his emotional response to the situation may get worse. Then, when we continue to remain uninvolved, he may begin to cast about for a new way to resolve the conflict. As he does so, the parents should encourage him and respond positively to his efforts to resolve the difficulty by a more useful means. When the child is in a more positive frame of mind, we might point up several possible solutions which tend to meet the needs of the child and of the other members of the family as well. In this way, strategic withdrawal from the fighting is merely setting the stage for better, more positive help on the part of the parents.

A second reason parents often give for not removing themselves from the fight with the child is the fear that the child will demolish the room or hurt himself. This rarely happens, unless the child has had a model of others doing the same thing in such a situation. If it should occur, the parents need to deal with that event as a separate problem. When the emotional reaction has passed, the parent and child should sit down and assess the damage. The child may learn a great deal about personal responsibility if he is expected to set things right. Picking up the mess and paying a reasonable share of the necessary repairs out of his own money or money he earns would seem a most logical consequence of his decision to "tear the house down." Often our fears act as effective blocks to taking action. If we fear the outcome of some act we often do nothing. Not everything that is faced can be resolved, of course, but we can only resolve those problems which are faced.* We must have the courage to change our behavior if we hope to help our child change his.

The child who perceives himself as having been hurt and, therefore, having the right to hurt others is often difficult for parents to cope with. They are given the feeling by the child that their attempts at helping are not wanted, and they tend to back away with hurt feelings. Here again, following one's first impulse is often the incorrect thing to do if one wishes to help the child. More than anything else these children need to learn that others may be trusted not to hurt them. It is often difficult for parents of vengeful children to notice even one thing the child does right during the course of the day or even the entire week. However, this should be the goal parents set for themselves with these children. The parents should concentrate upon finding the things the child does right. They should attempt to notice anything the child does that is acceptable to them, right now, as the child is at this moment. It is important that parents teach themselves not to respond to the child with statements which say or imply, "You'll be OK when you. . . ."

Often parents feel that they cannot compliment a child upon doing only part of a job right. The child only gets a positive response from these parents if they get the whole thing correct. Anything less than perfect is often punished. This is a mistaken tactic. As Dreikurs (1968) has noted, we cannot build upon the child's weaknesses, only upon his strengths. The child will be encouraged to keep on trying if we point out what he has done right.

Noticing the parts of the job which the child has accomplished often helps parents of vengeful children. Now they can begin to focus their energies on finding what the child is capable of doing rather than continually noticing his mistakes. It is difficult to maintain the constant effort to find out what the child is doing right, especially when so much of our effort is met with hurtful responses from the child. Nonetheless, it is only by our persistent efforts on his behalf that the child will learn to trust us again and to believe that he is accepted and acceptable, that he can win a place within the family by other than destructive means.

When attempting to change their own behavior, parents need each other's support and reinforcement. They especially need this cooperation when they are attempting to convince a vengeful child of his worth. Only by long and consistent effort are such children likely to abandon their mistaken goal and assume a more useful one.

The deeply discouraged child who assumes it is safer not to try is only further discouraged by having his mistakes and errors pointed out. Unfortunately, many parents do not know of any other way to help their children. As a result, while

---

*This statement has been attributed to James Baldwin, but the source is unknown to the author.

they are attempting to help the child to improve they often end up adding to the child's feelings of inferiority and humiliation. The child responds by further demonstrations of inability which only reinforce the parents' feelings of doubt in the child.

To change this behavior, parents must not allow the child to teach them to be discouraged. Instead, parents need to learn how to encourage their children. According to Dinkmeyer and Dreikurs (1963), the key ingredient of courage is confidence in oneself and one's ability to cope with whatever situation may arise. The courageous child is seen as the one who can work toward finding a solution to his problems. He will not feel diminished in his feelings of self if he does not find a solution to every problem, every time. He values himself as a person of worth, not for his successes, but for his ability to work toward success. He is all right with himself just the way he is, not as he might be at some distant, unknowable time.

The child becomes this type of person by being treated as this type of person. Thus the role of parents is to teach the child to view himself as a courageous person.

Dinkmeyer and Dreikurs (1963) suggest several ways parents may teach their children to be courageous. First, they suggest that parents practice placing value on the child just as he is. Parents should pick out the child's assets and abilities and focus their attention on them. They should not expect the child to do better than his best. Real accomplishment should be recognized. But, just as with the vengeful child, parents needn't wait to have the child do the whole problem before they notice the steps he has done correctly.

A second step in encouraging children is through the family group. Often by careful observation parents can determine how various members of the family are influencing one another. At times father may have more influence with one child; at other times a sibling may be more capable of helping a particular child. By rearranging seating at the dinner table, for instance, one might move a discouraged child away from a more talkative brother or sister. Such a move may allow the discouraged child more opportunity to talk about his accomplishments and gain recognition from the family for his attempts at solving his life problems. A shift in bedroom partners away from a sibling who is proving discouraging to a child into a room with a more supportive member of the family may prove beneficial.

Parents may work to establish family rules which assume that all members of the family win attention and praise. By following through with such a change, parents can help the discouraged child in the family, as well as all other members of the group. A weekly family council meeting established to act as a forum for family planning and mutual help serves as an excellent opportunity for such discussions.

Awareness of children's normal developmental stages* and of the individual child's progress is also important in working with discouraged children. By carefully pacing the child's work in keeping with normal developmental schedules we can avoid expecting unrealistic accomplishments. By breaking down new learning tasks into small, easily accomplished tasks we can be more assured that the child will find a solution to the problem. In this way the child will develop a concept of himself as a capable problem solver and gain the courage to try increasingly more difficult problems.

As can be seen, parents can play an important role in the developing child's choice of goals. While the socio-teleological theorists stress the creative and

---

*See chapters Three and Five for a discussion of developmental approaches.

decisive role in forming a lifestyle played by the individual child, there is ample room to be influential as parents within the confines of this theory.

By recognizing the nature of children and how they form their lifestyles, parents can foster social interest. Parents teach social feelings by helping their children find solutions to problems which take into account the needs of others. From the point-of-view of Adler and his students, those individuals with the greatest capacity for including others in their solutions in the fields of work, love, and society will be the most mentally healthy. It is through a fully developed sense of social interest that the individual reaches toward evolutionary perfection in his time. By developing social interest in their children, Adler felt the individual parents gained their best hope for immortality, as only by cooperation can the best accomplishments of mankind be passed on into the eternities.

Criticisms of the Socio-teleological Approach

One of the principle criticisms of the socio-teleological approach is its general failure to generate empirical research. The approach has been used and "tested" clinically, but such research does not impress the empirical-minded. Science tends to pass over theories which fail to demonstrate their usefulness in predicting specific outcomes which can be demonstrated in nature. Such theories may be useful in everyday practice by both the clinician and parents, but without careful testing it is difficult if not impossible to tell what aspects of the procedure being employed are bringing about the changes. As a result, we may expect to see less and less reference to socio-teleological theory in serious scientific circles. We can only hope that many of the workable concepts developed by this approach are incorporated by other approaches and tested. The elements of this theory which seem to work best appear to be closely related to many of the procedures utilized by the behavioral approaches, one of which is described in Chapter Seven.

Part Two

Part Two contains three theories that are generating considerable interest in psychology at this time. The three approaches start with very different assumptions about the nature of man and the best way to study human behavior.

Piaget, the biologist, approaches the study of man from the point-of-view of human cognitive development. Piaget is especially interested in the development of man's intelligence. Intelligence allows man to cope with his environment in a very special and unique way. Piaget believes that some aspects of the development of intelligence are a function of maturation. To the extent that this is true it should have an impact on our child-rearing practices. Chapter Five reviews the cognitive-developmental approach as it applies to child rearing and guidance.

Chapter Six presents the existential-phenomenological model. The existential-phenomenological view is that man is so unique that a special approach is needed if we are to truly understand human nature. Under the leadership of men like Carl Rogers and A. H. Maslow the existential-phenomenological approach has attempted to understand man from the point-of-view of the individual as he *experiences* life. It is each individual's unique set of experiences, and how the individual organizes his experiences to cope with the environment, that must be understood if we wish to understand man.

In marked contrast to the other two approaches is the behavioral approach developed by B. F. Skinner and presented in Chapter Seven. This approach assumes the biological aspects of man are "given," and attempts to understand not so much man as the *behavior* of man. Assuming that all behavior is caused by natural and physical causes, Skinner attempts to determine what the causes of behavior are and what lawful relationships might exist. If behavior is a function of environmental events then those events may be changed, and when that occurs behavior will change. As parents are charged with the responsibility of guiding and controlling their children's behavior, it would appear important that they understand the nature of conditioning and its functions in human behavior.

The Cognitive-Developmental Approach 5

Among the cognitive-developmental theorists the name of Jean Piaget is currently heard most frequently. This has not always been so. For years the work of this man has been relatively ignored by the larger scientific community. Recently, however, much of the research on cognitive development and problem solving in children has used Piaget's theory.

Piaget was trained as a research biologist and has maintained a lifelong interest in philosophy and logic. With this background it was only natural that Piaget would see the study of the child as an extension of embryology, or the growth and development of the individual. Piaget sees the mental growth of the child as synonomous with the organic growth of the individual, a viewpoint shared with other developmental theorists, such as Gesell (Chapter Three).

However, Piaget carefully integrates the environmental influences with the genetic development of the individual. As a biologist, Piaget stresses the relationship between the organism and the environment. Piaget states that the relationship is such that the organism must take action upon the environment in order to survive. The assumption that taking action upon the environment is inherent is fundamental to all of Piaget's work. He believes that the sum total of the actions we can take in response to the environment constitutes our ability to act intelligently for survival. Therefore, intelligence is the sum of all the things we can do in relationship to the environment.

Piaget assumes that the capacity to organize is inherent. The action schemes which are available to the individual as he adapts to the environment are a function of the individual's capacity for organizing information about the world. The more ways one can organize the available information, the greater the probability of acting intelligently. The ability to organize is seen to vary through species and during the lifetime of individual organisms. The changes in man's organization over his lifetime constitute the central subject matter of Piaget's research and theorizing.

Assimilation and Accommodation
Piaget and his students assume that man is inherently capable of organizing information about his environment and adapting to it. These two functions, organization and adaptation, are seen as "functional invariants" because they are characteristic of all biological systems. The ability to organize incoming events and to change in response to varying environmental conditions is fundamental to all life. The two invariant functions are not independent of each other. They are part of the process of living.

To adapt is to make use of the organization which exists either to *assimilate* (take in) some aspect of the environment and use it according to some already established scheme of action or to *accommodate* to the environment by changing an existing action scheme to meet the new situation. According to Piaget (1970) "biological adaptation is thus a state of balance between an assimilation

66

of the environment to the organism and an accommodation of the organism to the environment" (p. 153). Adaptation takes place best when the two processes are in a state of equilibrium.

As the child struggles to assimilate incoming data from the environment and at the same time accommodate to the demands placed upon him by that environment, he constantly reshapes the action schemes by which he has organized his understanding of "how the world is." The mental structures or collections of schemes form the basis of the child's thinking. The sum of all the child's schemes equals the sum of all he knows (Duckworth, 1973a). For the infant, prior to learning language and symbols, his schemes are the actions he can perform; he is what he knows how to do. According to Duckworth (1973a), "Schemes are similar to rules of grammar. Once the child understands the rule of grammar he uses it in all manner of sentences in which he has never heard it used before" (pp. 137-38). Once the child has learned a scheme it is available to him to apply in any new situation.

Assimilation. Assimilation is the process of bringing something from the environment into the organism and converting it to the use of the organism. Any event or stimulus is assimilated according to the existing organization of the organism. Thus the infant drinks milk and assimilates it. In the process, the milk is changed and so is the growing child. As the child grows, changes which are due to both maturation and interaction with the environment occur within the organization of the digestive system. Teeth begin to appear and the stomach and intestine become capable of assimilating more and more solid food. In a like manner the child assimilates information about the world outside his body. At first he reacts to the world through built-in reflexes, such as the sucking reflex. By exercising a reflex some aspects of it are developed, and other parts atrophy through disuse. This exercising slowly changes the reflex pattern. Sucking for food can lead to sucking on one's thumb, other objects, or on nothing; thus the sucking reflex gets generalized.At the same time, since sucking on the nipple and sucking on a toy give different results, the child develops "recognitive assimilation" (discrimination). The child learns the difference between the nipple and other objects. Piaget (Piaget and Inhelder, 1969) believes that the ability to discriminate is the result of qualitative changes in the internal mental structure, besides the response to the environment. Just as the digestive system changes to allow the child to accept solid food, so too does the mental organization change to allow the child to discriminate between objects and to organize space and time.*

Accommodation. Internal change comes with a new object or different aspect of external reality that cannot be adequately assimilated by the existing reflex patterns or schemes. Changing one's behavior to fit the environment is the process of *accommodation.* Intellectual adjustment is the process of balancing one's assimilation of experiences into his existing structural organization of "how the world is" and at the same time accommodating that structure to the new data from experience (Piaget, 1970). This is the great struggle throughout the child's developing years, and indeed throughout his life. We are constantly trying to make sense out of incoming information, to assimilate it to our present concepts and schemes of what is true and correct. When we are unable to fit the information into our present schemes we accommodate to the data by reorganizing our understanding in some way.

---

*The discussion of generalization and discrimination is very similar to that presented by Skinner (Chapter Seven) except that Skinner would not agree to a change in the mental organization. He would simply say that the processes described leave a changed organism.

The basic underlying idea is that the functions of organizing and adapting never change. In Piaget's terms, they are invariant. All organisms have the capacity to organize and adapt to the environment. And as a person organizes and adapts to his environment throughout his lifetime, the mental "structures" he uses to organize and adapt with also change. The change in an individual's mental structures is due to physical maturation *and* accommodation to the environment.

It is fundamental to the developmental position that changes follow a sequential pattern determined by the genetic structure of the individual. Piaget and his colleague, Barbel Inhelder, state that while the child is of interest and worth studying for his own sake, the child explains the man at least as well as the adult explains the child, and often better (Piaget and Inhelder, 1969). Many of the other theories we discussed appear to look at man and then ask about children almost in retrospect.

The Cognitive-Developmental View of the Nature of Man

To Piaget, man is a psychobiological organism adapting to his environment like any other organism. However, for Piaget (1970) intelligence is the highest form of adaptation. The human baby has all the adaptive mechanisms of higher animals, such as the ability to move about in space, the ability to discriminate between pleasant and unpleasant activities and to seek out those which are pleasurable, the ability to develop object permanence, and knowledge of physical objects and their organization in space. In addition, humans have a more complex central nervous system and thus greater biological potential for organization of information (Kamii, 1973a). Furthermore, man has evolved a complex society which helps to structure the activities of the developing organism. These serve to set human beings off from other biological organisms.

Man is a social animal. The child is social almost from the very beginning. By the second month, the child smiles at others and brings others into contact with himself in numerous ways. Through constant interchange the child adapts to his particular culture by assimilating the language, moral patterns, and all the mannerisms which are a part of that culture. In this way the patterns of human society are handed down from generation to generation.

Man's intelligence does not lead him to behave in a totally trial-and-error way; nor does it structure his behavior through a closed instinctive system of responses to the environment. Intelligence in man implies forms of both reaction and action (Piaget, 1970). Furthermore, the individual himself elaborates upon these forms of adjustment to adapt to the demands of the environment.

Although abstract thinking is seen by the cognitive theorists as "the great advance in the evolution of living species" (Schwebel and Raph, 1973), it is never divorced from the emotional or affective aspects of man. In fact, Schwebel and Raph (1973) make a point of contrasting the cognitive-developmental approach with that of the existential-phenomenological theorists (*see* chapter six). Schwebel and Raph indicate that the existential-phenomenological approach tends to deemphasize the cognitive development of man as if the development of cognitive behavior were at the expense of the affective. They insist that man is not partly cognitive and partly emotional, but is both of these completely and indivisibly at one and the same time. The way the individual structures his thinking about others as objects outside of himself and about himself as an object is obviously colored by the emotional experiences related to others and self.

The law of activity and the law of interest. While affective and cognitive behavior are completely interdependent, cognitive-developmental theorists do not see them as the prime sources of motivation in human behavior. Activity and interest are the determiners of cognitive and affective behavior. This is said to be true for both children and adults.

The functioning of the mind is seen as the same for all age levels. While particular mental structures are changed over time by growth and interaction with the environment, the functions of the mind are always oriented toward adaptation through assimilation and accommodation. The "Law of Activity" suggests that it is the nature of man to operate upon the environment, and that it is this activity and the individual's reactions to it that bring about changes in the ways he can assimilate new information.* According to Kamii (1973a) "the greater the amount of activity on the part of the [individual] the greater the probability of accommodation" (p. 199).

From the point-of-view of the cognitive-developmental theorists, intelligent behavior requires that the individual actively manipulate any new information in order to assimilate it to the organism. The data may be manipulated physically, as in the sensorimotor period; concretely, as in the concrete operations stage; or abstractly, as in the period of formal logic. From the position of the cognitive theorists, man is never a passive reactor to external stimuli, but is always actively assessing and evaluating those stimuli in relationship to his present structures of thinking.

Man is an active being whose actions are controlled by the "Law of Interest or Need" (Piaget, 1970). Interest or need is seen to be created in the individual, whether child or adult, when a discrepancy exists between the nature of the incoming information and the existing structures for handling that data. According to Kagen and Klein (1973), "The mind, like the nucleus of a cell, has a plan for growth and can transduce a new flower, an odd pain, or a stranger's unexpected smile into a form that is comprehensible. This process is accomplished through wedding cognitive structures to selective attention, activation of hypotheses, assimilation, and accommodation. The purpose of these processes is to convert an alerting unfamiliar event, incompletely understood, to a recognized variation on an existing familiar structure" (Kagen and Klein, 1973, p. 960). Treated this way, intelligence may be seen as an active process in which adaptation entails assimilation of things into the mind, just as does accommodation. Therefore, according to Piaget (1970), all work on the part of the intelligence depends upon interest.

True interest is said to appear when the individual identifies himself with objects or ideas. According to Birns and Golden (1973) the individual is more likely to accommodate his behavior to solve a new problem when the new behavior which is required is only slightly different from the behaviors already in his repertoire. Awareness of these slight differences cannot be imposed from without by parents or teachers, in the case of the child, or by others, in the case of the adult. Awareness of differences must be discovered by the individual himself, since only he is aware of his present state of organization as related to the new information becoming available to him. Insight or awareness occurs when the individual discovers the inconsistencies and is ready to respond with some new intellectual structures (Schwebel and Raph, 1973).

Man is, therefore, an active adapting organism. Guided by the law of interest, he seeks to bring into equilibrium the discrepencies between what he is forced to accommodate to from the environment and his ability to assimilate new information to his existing schemes of action or thinking. All thinking is action. It

---

*This definition is very similar to the definition given in Chapter Seven for operant conditioning. There too, behavior which causes an effect feeds back to the individual and changes the probability of similar responses in the future.

entails manipulation of the data either physically or symbolically. And while the way the individual can manipulate the data depends on growth and development, it always serves the same function: to help the individual adapt to his environment of the moment. Discrepencies between accommodation and assimilation force the individual to develop or learn new schemes.

The Cognitive-Developmental View of the Nature of Children

For cognitive-developmental theorists, childhood is far more than a necessary evil. Childhood is that most useful period of time when the biologically immature child makes progressive changes in the way he adapts to his physical and social environment. The child's physical growth leads him constantly to reach out and explore the nature of the world around him. Time and again in the course of that exploration he organizes cognitively "what goes with what." The child's mental growth is completely inseparable from his physical growth (Piaget, 1970; Voyat, 1973). It is typical of the theorists who take the child as the focus of their studies that they see the parts contributing to the whole. Thus, for Piaget, perception and intellect merely serve the organism as it adapts to its environment. How they serve is the basis for our understanding of the nature of children.

Kagen and Klein (1973) state, "From Locke to Skinner we have viewed the perfectibility of man as vulnerable to the vicissitudes of the objects and people who block, praise, or push him, and have resisted giving the child any compass of his own" (p. 960). For the cognitive theorists, at least, the child is deemed to have memory, a readiness to passively obey and imitate adults, and the receptive capacity to take in and make use of data from the environment. All of this is combined with the natural tendency to be spontaneously active (Piaget, 1970). These qualities lead him to act upon his environment as well as reacting to it.

For Piaget, interaction with the environment is critical for the development of the cognitive structures the child uses to order his environment. The structures the child uses are not the same as those of the adult. Therefore, when Piaget states that children differ from adults he does not mean that they are careless or that they prefer to be different, but that they cannot help but be different because their fundamental knowledge is structured differently (Sinclair, 1973a).

Because an individual can only understand reality in terms of the cognitive structures he has built through assimilation and accommodation, the very nature of the environment differs for the four-year-old and the adult. Even when the child and the adult share the same environment physically, they do not perceive it in the same way (Kamii, 1973b). For example, upon seeing a car in the distance the young child may remark that it is a toy car, whereas the adult perceives it as a normal car far away.

As the child explores his surroundings he attempts to match what he discovers to similar objects and events. If he cannot assimilate this new experience to an old structure he accommodates by building a new structure. The tendency to do this is a basic property of the mind and, therefore, the child has no other alternative but to respond to the environment in a mentally organizing way (Kagen and Klein, 1973). The structures that develop are similar to those of others of about the same age, of course, and eventually the child structures mental schemas similar to those of adults.

The sensorimotor period. Piaget has established in his almost fifty years of study that before the child can speak, and therefore before he can think in any abstract way, he develops a practical form of intelligence that allows him to conquer space and object permanence, causality and time. Through his sensorimotor apparatus the child learns to organize the world in a coherent manner at the level of his actions and the actions of things around him. By the time he reaches school age, the child has begun to construct from his experience a set of concrete concepts that help him establish the reasons behind things; but even this new power to reason has as its basis a solid practical intelligence based on actions.

The child is continually striving to reach some kind of match between his practical understanding of how the world is and his growing ability to reach beyond here-and-now events. Piaget (1970) feels that this striving for coherence is a fundamental given, a law of development. But it becomes clear that children of three or four and children of ten or eleven are satisfied with a different type of organization from that which satisfies an adult. Thus the child of four, if asked if he has a brother, may reply, "Yes." When asked if his brother has a brother he may answer, "No." He can reason in one direction only. The fact that he has a brother cannot be reversed in his thinking so that he *is* a brother to his brother. By the time he reaches seven to eleven years of age he will be fully capable of seeing that the relationship works both ways; in fact, he will be able to take the other's point-of-view in relationship to himself. This process of *decentering* is an important one, which the child must work through numerous times on his way to a mature adult outlook on the nature of the world.

According to cognitive theorists the central struggle in life is to find a balance between the practical world view and the conceptual understanding of what goes with what. The child must try continually to accommodate his sensorimotor organs to the external realities. He must continually adjust to the peculiarities of everything, for he knows nothing of the nature of the world. In order for the child to fully understand the nature of his world, he must assimilate it and make it a part of himself.

One major difference between the world of the child and the world of the adult is the development of systems. The child does not construct systems. Because he does not think about his own thought processes, the child does not see that he approaches problems in a characteristic way. We may see him behave in a more or less systematic manner to attack one problem after another, but he does not attempt to logically try one alternative after another. The four-year-old who begins by lining up the triangular blocks may, upon picking up two blue ones, switch to gathering all blue blocks. If asked why, he simply responds, "Because," and continues. He is not capable of reflecting upon the process and dealing critically with his own thoughts. In time he will be able to respond by ordering all the blue blocks and even all the blue round blocks. But in the beginning such systems are beyond him. In time, when the structural aspects of the nervous system have developed enough and the child has had the opportunity to interact with the environment, such formal thinking will evolve. The two processes, structural development and application to the environment, are inseparable for Piaget. Action leads to understanding and understanding leads to action.

Formal thinking has its roots in the child's earliest sensorimotor development, which occurs between birth and approximately two years of age. During this period, language is largely absent and the child is generally unable to symbolically replace a person or an object by some form of mental representation. Therefore, objects which are out of sight lack permanence. It is as if they did not exist. If, for instance, you move a set of keys in front of a very young child and gain his attention, but then drop the keys out of sight, he will not follow or seek the keys. As he becomes older, he will follow with his eyes and head but if you hide the keys he will look back to the source but fail to hunt for them. By eighteen to twenty-four months, however, he will begin to move the paper or pillow under which you have hidden the keys. He begins to actively seek for the missing object. This is taken as evidence by Piaget that the child can now symbolize the keys in some manner, that objects are known by the child to have permanence.

Thus is born "representative" intelligence. The child now has two ways to deal with reality. He can manipulate the object itself, and he can evoke the object mentally and manipulate it "in his head." Representative intelligence has its beginnings in the child's own actions and manipulations of the objects around him.

From birth, infants act in intelligent ways (Duckworth, 1973a). They seem to come equipped with three tools for acting upon the environment. First is a set of reflexes which are basic to immediate survival: sucking, rooting, and feeding (Sameroff, 1972). Second, the infant seems armed with a motivational rule of action which states, "If I can do it, I will." And third, he appears to have an intellectual rule of action and repetition which could be stated as, "All else being equal, things will turn out the same" (Duckworth, 1973a). Given this type of structure in his genetic inheritance, the child simply cannot help acting upon his environment.

The infant begins by simply repeating his reflexes in all kinds of situations. As he does so he meets with resistance here and a new sight there. He accidently stretches, or he stretches because of a tickle, and something moves. He stretches again and whatever moved before moves again. The more he acts the more he is rewarded by finding new sights, feelings, tastes. He continues to act. He discovers that in order to pick something up he has to open his hand, move it over the object and, even if the object goes out of sight, clasp his hand. Any other order will not do (Duckworth, 1973a). All these new discoveries are prerepresentational; that is, he does not have language with which to describe them. He merely knows that he acts and that this brings about an effect. In behavioral terms, the effect is rewarding and the behavior is repeated until satiation sets in.* But in the cognitive view, the important thing is that the child is developing schemes of action with which he can order, classify, and see the relationship between previous, present, and potential future states of things and events.

Schwebel and Raph (1973) point out that it is not the activity alone which develops intellectual behavior on the part of the child. The key factor lies in the nature of the interaction. The twelve- to eighteen-month-old infant playing with a pan lid is learning the nature of lids by touching it, seeing it, hearing it as he bangs it, tasting it, and interacting with it in terms of muscular actions such as lifting it, pushing it, and pulling it. And, most importantly, at the same time he is learning coordinated actions such as looking, reaching, and space and distance cues so that he becomes more and more successful at reaching the right distance and looking accurately at the source of a sound or flash of light. These coordinated actions can be applied in other situations and to other objects when the child needs to solve a problem.

The child's experience with the world of things also leads to representational thought. At first he seems to gain the ability to represent the thing itself in memory. Thus at nine to twelve months the child will search for the object which has just disappeared. Presumably he can retain a mental picture of the object on the basis of recent cues. At eighteen to twenty-four months the child begins to represent the out-of-sight object with a signal or signifier such as a word, a picture, or another object. Piaget gives the example of his daughter using a piece of wood to represent the kitty. She makes the wood walk on the wall

---

*See Chapter Seven for a detailed discussion of the behavioral approach.

just as she saw the kitty do some time before. She also makes meowing sounds which are imitative of the cat, adding strength to the hypothesis that the block of wood represents the cat at this time.

Piaget and Inhelder (1969) suggest that there are five important behavior patterns which may be taken as evidence that the child has acquired the ability to use signifiers to represent objects which are not present. The first is deferred imitation. Deferred imitation is imitation which takes place after the model has disappeared. If the cat has gone over the wall, for instance, and the child picks up a block and runs it over the wall we may infer that the block represents the now-missing cat. The second pattern that gives evidence of the use of signifiers is the child's symbolic play or pretending. In play the child may assimilate behavior patterns without the need to accommodate to the demands of reality. Pretending in play has been suggested as almost a pure form of assimilation for the child (Piaget and Inhelder, 1969; Phillips, 1969). While pretending, the child imitates behaviors he may never have performed before. He is aware that his action stands for the behavior not present. In imitating the behavior of the other, the child develops the schemes of action necessary to understand the object or other person.*

A third set of behaviors Piaget would have us consider as part of the child's ability to represent objects with something other than the object itself is drawing. Drawing rarely occurs before two or two and a half years of age (Piaget and Inhelder, 1969). Inasmuch as the child says his scribbles are a dog, a house, or a tree, they are an attempt to represent one object with another.

Mental image is given as the fourth piece of evidence for the development of representative thought. The ability to think of a missing object certainly requires some form of mental imagery.

And the fifth and possibly most important evidence for the use of signifiers is the development of language. Both verbal and nonverbal methods of calling up events which are not currently happening allow the child to transcend the here-and-now events of life. Saying "beep, beep" after the bus has faded from sight adds verbal representation to imitation and mental imagery.

We can conclude with Piaget and Inhelder (1969) that there is evidence for intelligent action on the part of the child even before language develops. We can see that the child has learned something of the relationship between himself, his acts, and the world around him. He has discovered that objects have permanence. He has also found out some very rudimentary things about space: he can reach the right distance for things, and he can generally avoid falling down stairs. He has learned something about time: for example, if a toy train moves through a tunnel he can judge the time it will take to come out the other side. And he has discovered something about cause and effect; for example, if he hits the mobile it will swing, or if he drops things they will fall.

The child's sensorimotor intelligence is basically practical. That is, it is aimed at getting results rather than stating truths. However, a basic truth has begun to emerge. The child has begun to discover that the world is not entirely centered in his own body and in his own actions. While at first the child is totally egocentric and unaware of himself as separate from his experience, he has slowly become aware that objects and persons are not part of him.* This important process of recognizing the difference between self and others, *decentering*, may be the most important thing the child learns.

The sensorimotor period has been a time of cognitive development without language. Only at the very end of this period have we seen the rise of representa-

---

*The process appears to be similar to modeling (Bandura and Walters, 1963) and role rehearsal (Burr, 1972).

tional thought as described above. The child's adaptation to reality has been primarily on the basis of his observation and perception of the environment and the action he can take upon it in a direct physical sense.

The preoperational subperiod. From about three or four years of age to about seven or eight the child's thinking takes on a new pattern. Building upon the action-oriented intelligence of the sensorimotor period, the child begins to internalize his actions by means of verbal symbols. Even more important during this stage of development is the ability to reverse his thinking, to mentally cancel out one action and perform another (Schwebel and Raph, 1973). An example of reversibility may be seen in the child's ability to put the big blocks and the long toy trucks together on the shelf, and then see that grouping blocks of all sizes could be another way of putting things together. The ability to reverse his thinking comes to the child only after overcoming a number of important obstacles.

Throughout most of the preoperational subperiod the child's thinking remains tied to his overt actions. The child's thinking has been compared to a slow-motion film, or, perhaps more appropriately, a filmstrip. He seems to think only one frame at a time. He seems incapable of taking an overall view of action or events.

During this period, too, we see a marked tendency for the child to behave in a particularly egocentric way. According to Piaget and Inhelder (1969), the child at the preoperatory level seems to assimilate events to his own actions, whereas later in the operational stages he will assimilate to the general coordinations of action. That is, at the preoperational stage he will tend to focus on one striking feature of an object to the neglect of other important features. For example, if you show the child three pennies spaced out six inches apart and five pennies with their edges almost touching and you ask him to take the most pennies he most likely will take the three pennies. He attends to the greater apparent length rather than to the number of pennies. This may occur for the four- or five-year-old even if you take his finger and help him count out each row of pennies.

Still another example of the preoperational child's rigid and inflexible thinking is his tendency to pay attention to the result of an action rather than the process which brought the end about. If you pour the water from a tall thin jar into a low flat one and ask the child which has the most water he will undoubtedly say the low flat one "because it is bigger" or the first one "because it is taller." It never occurs to him that it is the same water even though he has seen it poured right before his eyes.

The preoperational child's egocentrism is manifest in his social life as well as in his understanding of the physical world. Although he has become decentered enough to know that the world is people with responses similar to his own, he still lacks the ability to differentiate between his and the other person's points-of-view. The child in the preoperational subperiod tends to be the "prisoner of his own point-of-view, which he naturally looks upon as absolute" (Piaget, 1970). Gradually, through the give and take of interaction with his peers and following appropriate maturation the child of seven or eight can begin to take part in truly cooperative activities. He can accept the fact that in playing store he may wish to put all the frozen food in one area while his friend may want to put all the big boxes together and next all the little boxes. While there may be a great deal of discussion about the merits of either one, the seven- and eight-year-olds can agree to take turns or to compromise: for example, putting all the big frozen food containers together, and then the little frozen food boxes.

---

*The relationship of this concept to Freud's description (Chapter Two) of the discovery of "object reality" should be obvious.

Looking back over the child's life span we can see that the child has been decentering in cognitive, social, and moral planes all at once. As an infant, the child was subjectively centered in all areas. He felt that he, and he alone, controlled all the world. Slowly he came to differentiate himself from the world of objects. With time he has learned to separate his point-of-view from the point-of-view held by another person. In adolescence he comes to differentiate his point-of-view as an individual from the point-of-view of the group, which he at first hopes to assimilate to his point-of-view. When he does achieve a decentered position in relationship to his total world picture he can reach a somewhat stable level of equilibrium between assimilation and accommodation. Part of this later decentering takes place in the concrete operations period of development.

The period of concrete operations. By about age six or seven the child has constructed his first stable concepts. These concepts Piaget calls "operations." According to Furth (1970), these operations eventually permit the child to mentally consider the possibilities of a problem solution. He can then take the perspective that a given physical reality is only one concrete instance from among the many theoretically possible outcomes.

An example of operations is the union of two classes of objects—it is because the child's thinking is still primarily tied to "objects" that this is known as the period of *concrete* operations. At this point in his cognitive development the child can agree that fathers united with mothers constitute parents. Another example of an operation is the addition of two numbers. The ability to handle these *actions* gives the child great power because the actions may be widely generalizable to new situations and problems. The operations of uniting, arranging things in order, adding to, and taking away from enter into the processes of coordinating many particular actions. For instance, adding children to the union of mothers and fathers gives us all people. That the operations are reversible is easily seen; taking away the children from the mothers and fathers leaves only parents. And finally, as Piaget and Inhelder (1969) explain, the operations are not idiosyncratic, belonging only to the individual, but are shared with all people on the same mental level.

Once again Piaget emphasizes that these operations apply to the child's cognitive, emotional, social, and moral development. Once the concrete operations are formulated, the child can apply them in all spheres of his life. The development of the operations allows the child to be freed from single-frame-at-a-time thinking and to begin to grasp the whole in a single action. This sets the stage for the final decentering. The child is now ready for formal thought.

Formal thought. Formal thought differs from concrete thought in that the adolescent can think of what might be—the future, the whole world of possibilities. He is no longer tied to concrete objects. He can and does evolve theories and great ideals. He can form hypotheses and reason away from the concrete or present set of observations. Whereas the child in the concrete operations stage is centered on reality, the individual at the formal operations level grasps the "possible" and can assimilate reality in terms of imagined or deduced events. This change of perspective holds for the affective domain as well as for the cognitive world of the adolescent; for shortly after the child became capable of separating himself from the world of objects, including other people, he became capable of putting an affective value upon the objects in his world, including himself. With the development of formal reasoning, the adolescent becomes capable of freeing his values from concrete and perceptible reality and thus can encompass many new interpersonal and social possibilities. The period of formal operations takes place sometime between the ages of eleven and fifteen.

The period of adolescence. Adolescence is, for Piaget and Inhelder (1958, 1969), the age of introduction into adult society. The primary change from adolescent to adult is the change from idealistic reformer to active achiever. Unlike the child, the adolescent can and does study his own thought processes and construct theories about their meaning. The ability to construct theories makes the adolescent equal to other adults in his society. To be fully adult, however, the adolescent must come to think of himself as fully equal to other adults. *Equal* in this sense means that the individual judges other adults with complete reciprocity and on the same plane as himself. A second adult quality taken on by the adolescent is the capacity to be future oriented and to attempt to find for himself a place in society. And, third, the adolescent has an idea about how to change society. The adolescent does not fully become an adult until he takes on a real job. Then he shifts from idealistic reformer to realistic achiever. Once again he is forced to decenter from his subjective thinking to accommodate to the demands of reality.

The idealism of the adolescent is sharply contrasted with the lack of such feelings in the child (Inhelder and Piaget, 1958). Children are sensitive to their families and their homes, even to their native language, but at the same time they remain relatively free from strong feelings of nationalism in terms of belonging to a collective whole. This should not be surprising, since the child from seven to eleven years of age applies his logic only to concrete or manipulable objects.

The adolescent's ability to formulate theories and ideals leads to two basic changes that socialize him into adulthood. First, he adds feelings for mankind as a whole instead of only having feelings for individuals he interacts with on a face-to-face basis. Second, the adolescent acquires social roles and values that result from his considering his place in society. He is no longer limited in his thinking about himself and the world to only the contacts he has made with his physical environment and the persons with whom he has had direct contact. Having developed such a world view, the adolescent is prepared to meet other adults as equals and to take his position in adult society. Inhelder and Piaget (1958) suggest that these ideals and values are the final building blocks of the personality.

The Relationship of the Individual to the Group

From the point-of-view of the developmental theorists, the individual and the group are clearly not independent. Just as the individual organism is in constant interaction with the environment, so the human organism is in constant interaction with that most important environment, other members of the human group. Inhelder and Piaget (1958) point up the circular nature of the relationship between the individual and other members of the group. At first the child is unable to distinguish the group from himself. His initial egocentrism leads him to believe that all the world is just an extension of himself. He attempts to assimilate others into his own needs and frame of reference. Only slowly does he come to recognize that others are separate and distinct objects outside himself, and that they view the world through the same processes he uses but from a different perspective. Eventually he learns how to accommodate to the needs of others and even to take their role in fact or thought. He also develops the capacity to anticipate the consequences of his acts for himself and others and to develop alternatives. According to Piaget and his students, this leads, developmentally, to two important intellectual and affective processes: *cooperation* and *moral reasoning*.

The development of cooperation. Cooperation develops from social interaction. According to Kamii (1973a), the proposition is: The greater the amount of social interaction among children, the greater the cooperation. The suggestion is not that a great deal of interaction all at once is important, but rather that a great deal of interaction over time leads to cooperation. Thus, true cooperation does not occur until about age eight.

The child's initial egocentricism precludes cooperative play in the true sense of cooperation, which means taking into account the other person's needs as well as one's own and acting accordingly. Young children, if allowed to play freely, appear to like to be together. They often split into small groups of two and three children to carry on some shared activity. However, they are acting singly in company with others, rather than actually coordinating their activities. Each child is acting on his own, with or without mutual assimilation. This continues to occur as late as five or six years of age, where even in a shared activity, such as a game of marbles, each child is applying his own set of personal rules and each child wins at the same time, just by participating (Piaget, 1970).

With the development of object reality the child grows to see himself as separate from others. He comes to value himself as an individual and, according to Piaget and Inhelder (1969), this leads him to oppose others. He becomes at odds with the social group. Having discovered that he can make an impact upon the world, he acts upon that impulse and finds himself at odds with others. Thus, autonomy precedes cooperation.

However, the need to value himself also leads to the child's seeking to win other people's affection and esteem (Piaget and Inhelder, 1969). While the child wishes, on the one hand, to be free of others, he at the same time wants their esteem. This conflictful situation comes to be resolved, at around age eight, by submitting himself to rules he sets for himself or works out freely in interaction with his peers. He finds that he wins freedom and esteem by true cooperation. At this point the child can coordinate his way of seeing things with the other person's point-of-view, and so he can now cooperate in both action and communication.

Children's ability to develop their own rules of cooperation, and the freedom to do so, are seen as extremely important by Piaget (1970). It is precisely this capability which leads the child away from an excessive individualism. Too much restriction and imposition of rules from parents and teachers is likely to prevent the child from developing the ability to take the role of the other person. The child may come to depend upon the direction of others instead of reasoning through the needs and demands of the situation on his own. The ability to reason through the consequences of a course of action is one important aspect of moral reasoning.

The development of moral reasoning. Moral reasoning or moral judgments are the child's use and interpretation of rules in conflict situations. They are his reasons for moral acts (Kohlberg, 1964). According to Piaget (1970; Piaget and Inhelder, 1969), the developing child passes through three major stages of moral reasoning. First is the stage of *moral realism*, followed by the stage of *objective responsibility*, and eventually the stage of self-directed morality or *autonomy*.

The first step in moral reasoning can be seen in the early preoperational period, ages four to six. During this stage the child's moral response is based on imitation of his parents and others in his immediate environment. The child's behavior is seen as primarily *heteronomous*; that is, guided from others outside himself. Two things must be present in order for this type of morality to work. First, others must give orders or directions which have rather indefinite time spans, such as: "Always be on time for dinner" or "Never tease your sister." And second, the child must be willing to respond to such orders.

Children seem likely to respond to persons who have prestige in their eyes and who have the power to dispense rewards and punishments. Piaget and Inhelder (1969) feel that respect for parents is a combination of fear and affection. Fear alone results only in self-interested submission, and affection alone is not able to instill a sense of obligation in the child. The respect the child thus develops is that of an inferior toward his superiors, in this case his parents. This type of respect is labeled "unilateral respect" (Piaget and Inhelder, 1969).

The problem with a morality based simply upon imitation and unilateral respect is that the adult is the source of all morality and all truth. All statements from the adult are taken as unquestionable, and the authority of others, therefore, does away with the need for the child to reflect on the outcome for himself. Since the child already has a strong tendency toward egocentrism, such an attitude may get translated into a belief that whatever he believes is true is the only truth, and that others cannot legitimately differ from that point-of-view. As a result, the child sees himself as an authority and does not enter into the reflective thinking and critical discussions that constitute reason. Moral reasoning, according to Piaget (1970), can only be developed by cooperation and genuine intellectual exchanges on the part of children. This is why the adolescent peer group plays such an important part in the decentering of teenagers. In his discussions with friends the adolescent often finds that his great theories are really very fragile and do not hold up in the light of other persons' realities.

Fortunately, most children have ample opportunity for interaction with their peers to develop a sense of objective responsibility. In interaction with his peers he learns that there are rules of conduct he must adhere to if he is to get along well in his society. At first his adherence to the rules follows the same pattern as his responses to authority; that is, the rules are seen as absolutes and good and bad behavior are judged only by how much the behavior conforms or does not conform to the rules. For example, if a child is asked not to help a lazy pupil in the classroom but later teaches the child the correct way to solve a problem, he would still be "bad," as judged by most six-year-olds, even though the situation is different. Regardless of the intent of the child who helped, he would be seen as in violation of the rule by six-year-olds. Further, six-year-olds would assume that everyone would agree. By the time children are nine, they can see that there is more than one way to look at the situation. Rules have begun to lose their absolute quality and seem open to flexibility of interpretation.

Advances in intellectual development through social cooperation and the development of operations in the child's thinking lead to a new basis for moral behavior. Mutual respect for self and others leads the child to a certain *autonomy* in moral judgments. Rules lose their sacred, unchangeable character. Rules now are regarded as agreements between contemporaries. Rules can, therefore, be changed by mutual consent between agreeing parties.

At about this same time (eight to nine years of age) children begin to recognize the operational concept of justice. Parents at this time are often called to task with what seems to be the watchword of the day: "But that's not fair." Justice at this point may become far more important to the child than obedience. Other abstractions follow in the child's growing awareness of reciprocal relations among people. Equality and a true understanding of the golden rule appear at about this same time.

It can be seen from our discussion of the development of cooperation and moral reasoning that the child stands *opposed* to the group at times and *with* the group at other times. Thus in periods of egocentrism the child tends to place himself above others, at first exclusively and then in terms of first his concrete thinking, for example about rules, and later in his more formal thinking about man in general. However, if given opportunity to try his thinking out in the world of his peers we see this egocentric thought giving way to more realistic thinking which increasingly places the child in a position to take the other person's point-of-view and to stand for a morality which meets the needs of the majority—to be oriented toward mankind rather than toward the individual.

Other Dimensions and Issues

Because Piaget's theory is a theory of intellectual development, it is only natural that this theory gives us some insight into how and what children learn. Among the important intellectual achievements the child must develop is the ability to mentally structure events in his world through grouping, classification, seriation, conservation, and number. The capacity to achieve these mental structures is inherent, according to the cognitive-developmental theorists, but must develop in response to the child's personal experience with the environment.

One of the most critical issues for any developmental theory is the establishment of genetically controlled responses to the environment which are in some way independent from the individual's experiences with the environment. The arguments given by the cognitive-developmental theorists for internal control over the organizing concepts such as grouping, classification, and conservation will be given following the discussion of how and what children learn.

How children learn. Piaget feels that children come equipped to learn so far as they have a natural tendency to be social and also to imitate others. Even so, the child has everything to learn. The infant is purely egocentric. During his first few months of life he has almost no capacity to exchange with others. However, through the use of his built-in preparation to learn, the child eventually masters what Piaget (1970) deems as the two essential skills for getting along in society: the capacity to share mutual understandings with others through speech and a sense of social discipline based upon standards of reciprocity; that is, the ability to see a social situation from the point-of-view of the other person.

Piaget's conceptualization is similar to the definition of socialization given in chapter one. "To educate," says Piaget (1970), "means to adapt the individual to the surrounding social environment." In so doing we help the child to develop his intellectual and moral reasoning power. And since that power cannot be invoked from the outside the challenge is to find ways to arrange the environment to help the child develop these powers from his experience. Parents and teachers must seek methods of establishing an environment suitable for the child to develop intellectual coherence, objectivity, and moral reciprocity.

According to Piaget, change in children's behavior can only come about through time. There are no procedures that increase intellectual functioning without involving a slow and sometimes uncomfortable groping for a correct solution. However, it is not time itself which brings about the change. Here the cognitive therapists can be seen to contrast markedly with the developmental-maturational school. It is not heredity alone which leads to development, but the activities of the child in interaction with his environment that lead to new structuring of the mental organization.

In structuring the child's learning, understanding the role of heredity and environment means that we need to recognize and understand the processes of mental development. It is important to take into consideration the child's needs at each of the various stages. It also suggests that the environment can play a very meaningful part in the development of the child's intellect. The thought content of each of the stages is not immutably fixed, as can be seen from the differences in children from differing cultures and subcultures (Sinclair, 1973). Careful attention to the environmental influences available to the child may increase his learning efficiency even though it may not be possible to accelerate his intellectual development.

In looking at how the child learns, the parents' goal should be to gain a more complete understanding of how infants gain knowledge of their world (Birns and Golden, 1973). Such an understanding will bring the parents to see that what the child needs is the opportunity to have what Duckworth (1973b) terms "wonderful ideas."

The child's wonderful ideas are his discoveries of what the world is like, what goes with what, and what causes things to happen. These ideas may not be new and wonderful to the adult (although they once were), but they are wonderful and new to each child as he discovers them for himself. Our goal should be to help the child have wonderful ideas and to feel rewarded for having them. The more we are able to do this the more likely that he will come upon a wonderful idea that has *not* been thought of before.

We can help children have wonderful ideas by providing materials and questions which lead to their manipulating the materials in all kinds of ways that are new for them. If the child says he believes the lead soldier will float we can encourage him to try it and see. If he believes that the balloon will cause the balance beam on a scales to go down and the silver dollar on the other side to go up, he should be encouraged to test it out for himself.

Kamii (1973b) notes that the child is not normally discouraged if the physical world does not confirm his hypotheses. Such natural consequences are merely taken as a part of nature. Wise parents can, therefore, refrain from giving the child answers and allow him to discover the results for himself. In this way the child builds up his repertoire of thoughts, actions, and connections. He develops the ability to predict things in nature and develops the capacity to integrate such actions and his feelings about himself and the world around him. Merely to be told the answer often does not lead to making the necessary connections between the relevant aspects of a problem. For example, in the case of comparing the balloon and the coin on the balance beam of a scale it is highly doubtful that telling the child he must compare size (volume) *and* weight (mass) to determine whether the beam goes up or down will help him make the connection between these two important variables. His best teacher will be his experiences with things large and small, heavy and light in various combinations of the two variables. In the end the child must do the work for himself to make the connections. The important connections the child makes are the important things that the child learns.*

What the child learns. One of the two key skills for getting along in society is language. Through play, imitation, and language the child may represent to others what he knows of the world. Language develops as a way of representing the events and objects in the world. Words may accompany an event or point it out or even express the feelings which accompanied it, but they are not the event itself. Because of this the child who is just beginning to learn language can not be sure that a given word and its referent are correctly connected. He is likely to believe that the word refers to what *he* has in mind at the time. At bedtime I often held my three-year-old daughter up at her second-story bedroom window and said goodnight to the houses, fences, and trees. We were surprised, therefore, when Chris frequently talked of "walking on the trees" as we played outside on the grass. It later occurred to us that the trees and grass were all below us when saying goodnight and that Chris had assumed that our downward glance was focusing on the grass, as hers was. It takes time and a great deal of experience to connect words and their referents correctly.

This tendency to focus on what is the most salient aspect of a situation is part of the child's egocentric thought. What is at the front of the child's thoughts is what he believes others are attending to also. Furthermore, according to the

---

*Recent reviews of the literature (Baer and Wright, 1974; Gollin and Moody, 1973; Lipsitt and Eimes, 1972) all point out that children can be assisted in learning these concepts by various teaching approaches, and that children who have acquired understanding of conservation "naturally" and those who have been trained to conserve do not differ in resistance to extinction by countersuggestion (Gollin and Moody, 1973).

cognitive-developmental theorists, children tend to deform verbal messages systematically. They do this in accordance with the basic patterns of thinking which are characteristic of their stage of cognitive development. For example, Sinclair (1973) found that four- and five-year-olds rather consistently reverse roles when asked to repeat statements such as "The car is pushed by the truck." The child is likely to focus on the concrete statement and say, "The car pushes the truck." This is taken as evidence that information which comes from outside the child is assimilated to the basic cognitive schemes which the child possesses at that time.

Piaget and his followers believe that while the child must discover his own links between events he does so in constant interaction with the environment. The developing nervous system, in conjunction with environmental stimulation, serves to produce characteristic patterns of thinking within all children. The culture or subculture may speed up or retard a given pattern, but little can be done to change the direction of the child's thinking. Outside influences can strongly influence what a child thinks, but how he goes about it is less susceptible to influence, for some changes in thinking are the result of changes in internal structures. Piaget and his colleagues have carefully mapped the development of the child's capacity to organize and order events in his environment. In addition to learning that objects have permanance and that they can be located in space and time, the child learns that things may be ordered into groups for convenience in his attempts to assimilate them into his experience. From grouping objects the child moves to classification, seriation, conservation, number, and further understanding of space.

According to Schwebel and Raph (1973) and others (Phillips, 1969), *grouping* consists of the child's ability to do three things. First, the child learns that objects have identity or equivalence. Adding one bear and another bear does not change the fact that the objects are bears. Second, the child learns a logical system of classes which may have two or more classes included within it. For example, the class *people* may be said to be made up of the subclasses *men, women,* and *children*. Classes may overlap or exclude other classes. And third, the child learns that there are relationships between parts and wholes of concrete objects or collections of objects or persons. The child also learns to reverse the process. If we show a young child three toy cows and six toy horses and ask, "Are there more animals or more horses?" he is likely to answer, "More horses." He is not yet able to relate the parts to the whole. Later he will be able to give the correct answer and reverse the processes. "There are more animals than horses and there are more horses than cows," or "There are fewer cows than horses."

The child of four or five tends to arrange objects according to their proximity or closeness to each other; he begins to use *classification*. He may begin by putting all the green blocks together, when he happens upon two round blocks, whereupon he gathers all round blocks regardless of color. It is not until about eight years of age that the child has developed the ability to coordinate his classifications on the basis of both similarity and relationships. Schwebel and Raph (1973) suggest, "The true basis of classification depends not upon recognition of perceptual likenesses, but upon the child's control of logical quantifiers, such as *one, some* and *all*" (p. 27). By age eight the child has also learned to classify on more than one criterion at once, such as "all the tall, red-haired dolls." Taken all together, Piaget sees this as marking the achievement of genuine operatory classification (Piaget and Inhelder, 1969).

Seriation consists of arranging objects according to increasing or decreasing size, graded heights, graded hues, or some other criterion. With time and experience the child can compare two or three and later ten to twelve sizes. He learns to look ahead and plan his seriation: "First we'll put the different shades of yellow straws in order from darkest to lightest." He can also reverse the process and go from lightest to darkest.

At about the same time that the child is discovering how to deal with groupings, classification, and seriation, he also discovers *conservation*. Conservation is a way to internally compensate for external changes in objects such as a lump of clay or the shape assumed by water poured from one container into another. As in the case of groupings, one of the key events in the child's intellectual growth is his ability to reverse the processes he encounters. Now he can recognize not only that the water is the same whether in the tall container or the flat one, but also that it will resume its former shape when poured back into the original glass. Piaget and Inhelder (1969) note that the concepts of conservation are not won all at once. The child recognizes the conservation of substances at seven or eight, the conservation of weight at nine or ten, and the conservation of volume at eleven or twelve.

Schwebel and Raph (1973) suggest that the understanding of *numbers* is a synthesis of class inclusion and seriation. The child must be able to ignore differences in items and recognize random or one-to-one correspondences. At first the child can identify a qualified correspondence based on the resemblance of elements, such as a nose for a nose or an ear for an ear. Only later does the child see that one dime, one chair, and one toy dog are the same so far as the number of items is concerned. Seriation enters in when he does not count the same object twice in a series.

Piaget and Inhelder (1969) point out that we should not assume that the child understands numbers simply because he can count verbally. In the preoperational child's mind, number is judged by the quantity of space occupied (Sinclair, 1973). Piaget and Inhelder conclude that there can be no question of numerical ability, in an operational sense, before the child develops the ability to see numerical grouping independently from spatial arrangement.

The child has developed a comprehension of *space* almost from the start. Reaching to touch and to grasp have helped him to coordinate eye and hand movements in space. Location of objects both in sight and out of sight has helped him to form a sense of object permanence. This has led to the recognition that some objects are fixed in their relationship to each other and that others are not. In this way he comes to know where his house is in relationship to school, the store, and other places of importance to him in his community. He has also come to grasp the fact that objects remain the same although they may appear different on his visual retina. That is, two boys the same height remain the same height although one is a block away and appears shorter than the boy two feet away.

The cognitive theorists assert that these cognitive functions—grouping, classification, seriation, conservation, number, and space—are learned naturally by all children in response to hereditary and environmental factors. As the child actively attempts to adapt to his environment, he is able to assimilate many new experiences to his existing patterns or schemes of intellectual action. When he encounters an event that does not fit with his present schemes, he is forced to accommodate to the new situation. The new accommodation may be, for this child, an entirely new way of organizing information about how the world is. Typically, the ways of organizing include a nonverbal sensorimotor knowledge of the world, followed by a concrete understanding capable of symbolizing cause and effect and the nature of events in verbal terms. The concrete stage is at first nonoperational; that is, it is a period when the child's thinking is "one-way." Events follow one another concretely, as if fixed in that particular order. They cannot be reversed and retraced. The child cannot mentally envision the water in one glass being returned to its previous container and looking the same as it once did.

Finally, the child's growth and his experiences lead him to be able to organize the world in terms of formal logic. He can see events as sequenced and reversible. Further, through symbolic manipulation he can envision sequences and processes which are and have not been seen. He can think abstractly, formulate plans, and act in accord with ideals. He can see himself in relation to others, both as individuals and as mankind in general, and act for the common good. Piaget and other cognitive theorists believe that it is the nature of all children to develop these capacities.

Arguments for cognitive-developmental stages. It appears quite natural that in a developmental theory early experiences will influence later experiences as each stage forms a basis for the next. However, such a position is not unique to the developmental theories. For example, B. F. Skinner's discussion of the development of complex behavior repertoires (see Chapter Seven) suggests the necessity for simple patterns to precede certain more complex patterns simply because the simple patterns form a part of the overall behavior. The problem for the developmental theorists is to demonstrate that certain behaviors or behavior patterns are universal and appear in an unvarying sequence.

Piaget and his students claim that they are describing just such a universal and unvarying sequence of developmental events. Kagen and Klein (1973), for example, state that separate maturational factors set the time of emergence of man's natural intellectual functions. Experience, in the form of an enriched or an impoverished environment and can speed up or slow down that development by months or even years; but they cannot prevent the emergence once the proper environmental stimulation occurs. Kagen and Klein are careful to distinguish between intellectual competencies which are universal, such as the capacity for perceptual analysis, imitation, language and symbolism, inference, deduction, and memory and culturally specific competencies such as reading, arithmetic, spearing fish, and building snow houses.

Two points seem important in relationship to the development of universal and cultural intellectual competencies. First, the universal functions will be learned, given time and the opportunity for the child to interact freely with objects and events in his world. And second, the culture-specific learnings require specific teaching if the child is to become a fully functioning member of that particular culture.

Piaget and his students are quite emphatic on the point that the child needs time to discover for himself the nature of conservation, reciprocal justice, and so forth; they insist that the child cannot be "talked" into comprehension of these responses. Kamii (1973) says, for instance, that for the preoperational child the more of the learning that is verbal the less the child will be able to assimilate and accommodate. "Memorization of meaningless material," according to Schwebel and Raph (1973), "is on a par with learning nonsense syllables as far as development and learning are concerned" (p. 16).

The assertion that experiences must precede verbal learning is taken from Piaget's works, which suggest that the sources of thought are found in the preverbal sensorimotor actions of the young child. Play, imitation, and physical representation of events that are no longer present are all taken as evidence of nonverbal representation occurring before verbal representation. Schwebel and Raph (1973) cite the work of Furth to further support this position. Furth reportedly showed that deaf children have the same ability to handle logical symbols as do hearing children. Blind children, however, solved the same types of tasks four years later than did the sighted and deaf children. It is suggested that the blind children's lag in this skill comes from the lack of opportunity for imitation and learning about relationships through active manipulation of objects. The child's early nonverbal experiences are critical in the development of his intellectual skills.

Culture-specific learnings. Kagen and Klein (1973) have pointed out that there are culture-specific learnings, such as arithmetic and reading, that must be deliberately taught in order for the child to survive in our particular culture. In other cultures it might be far more important that the child learn to build ice houses and stalk game with a harpoon in a kayak.

Schwebel and Raph (1973) insist that the best basis for verbal learning is varied and active encounters with real objects in the environment. For example, they suggest four things that a child needs to do to facilitate his learning to read. First, the child needs to have the opportunity to develop his skills at imitation. By learning to represent objects and events in the environment through his movements, the child is better able to respond to the objects in other symbolic ways, such as the use of words. Second, the child needs to develop the ability to use one object to symbolize another. Using a rock to represent "food" and a stick to represent the family car all prepare the child to accept other symbols in the same way. The third thing a child needs to do on his way to reading is to put several objects together to form a new whole. Thus, linking several chairs together to make an airplane is a step beyond using a single chair or block. And fourth, having had plenty of experiences with real things, the child can begin to identify pictures of objects. Schwebel and Raph feel that pictures serve to bridge the distance between the object and more abstract representations such as the sign or word.

It appears that impoverished environments retard the child's development of the culturally specific intellectual skills. However, it remains unclear as to why this should be true. Does the impoverished environment preclude the child's manipulating objects so much that he is unable to develop the underlying intellectual capabilities to handle culture-specific tasks? Or does the impoverished environment prevent the child from receiving the direct teaching that is necessary for the child to learn the required cultural skills?

Kagen and Klein (1973) point up the fact that American parents must be interested in the development of the culturally significant skills regardless of whether the source is experience or teaching. Once behind in these learned skills the child catches up with great difficulty, if at all. Once behind in reading, arithmetic, and similar school behaviors the child may begin to see himself as incapable, which will influence his motivation in other culturally relevant pursuits. The child whose development in the universal cognitive behaviors has been retarded merely catches up when the environment stimulates the necessary accommodations. This is all that is necessary if the culture does not stress learned skills.

There is little comfort in this knowledge to the average middle-class American parent. The parent is probably well advised to give his child ample opportunity for interaction with the widest number of objects and events his community offers, including the opportunity for formal training when the child shows his readiness and ability to handle it. It seems reasonable that the younger the child the more these experiences should be physical, nonverbal events. So far as Piaget is correct, these nonlanguage experiences will serve to stimulate later intellectual growth and development.

The Role of the Parent with the Child

One of the major problems in applying Piaget's theory to child rearing is the fact that his work is primarily concerned with how intelligence develops in the child (Schwebel and Raph, 1973). However, parents are more specifically interested in the child's learning specific skills and information. And while it is necessary for the child to develop his intelligence in order for him to develop skills, the processes required for the development of the two are fundamentally different (Furth and Wachs, 1975). Piaget and his followers would emphasize that concentration on the development of skills and information to the exclusion of the development of knowledge may be folly.

Nonetheless, it is still necessary to teach children the conventional spellings and that two and two make four. As Duckworth (1973a) points out, we standardize spelling and grammar so we can give our attention to what is said rather than having to struggle over how it is said. But this leads parents into a trap. If the correct way is important but it is also important for them to let the child make his own mistakes and learn from them, how can they teach? Should parents just sit back and do nothing?

Not at all. Two or three principles from Piaget and his students seem to be helpful in this dilemma. Parents can learn to ask the right questions and they can learn how to accept mistakes as one of several alternative responses in a given situation.

The "right" questions lead the child to explore the outcomes, to evaluate the solution *for himself* rather than for adults. Also, questions that lead to new actions on the part of the child promote the development of his intelligence. Wickens (1973) suggests that parents avoid evaluating the child's efforts and encourage the child to appraise his own work in terms of future efforts. For example, if the child says, "Is this a good picture?" The parent might respond, "Do you like it?" "Does it make you feel good?" "What other ways could you draw the tree?" "How would it look from a worm's eye view?" "From a bird's eye view?" By asking questions that lead the child to look in a new way at the event, we encourage him to develop his intelligence. We increase the ways the child can operate upon his environment.

Helping the child to ask his own good questions is another way of achieving these same ends. This is especially useful because we cannot always know exactly where a child is in his own thinking, but we can develop the kind of atmosphere which makes asking questions all right. Duckworth (1973b) feels that children cease to be creative because they become discouraged by adults who make them feel that their questions are unimportant, unacceptable, or socially embarrassing. This may lead the child to believe that he has no important ideas of his own that are worth sharing.

Parents should not be surprised when they do not get the answers from children which seem to "fit" the adult's questions. Sinclair (1973) suggests that disappointing answers to such questions as "What did I just ask you?" or "What did I just tell you?" are not always due to lack of attention or faulty memory. This is not a case of infantile senility. It occurs because the child does not copy literally what he has just heard. He must assimilate each incoming message to his basic knowledge of how the world is. Therefore, the response is likely to be in *his logic* rather than ours.

In addition to learning to ask good questions and allowing children the right to ask all kinds of questions, parents can also learn to accept mistakes as alternative ways of solving problems. But shouldn't we be concerned if he makes mistakes like spelling cat *k-a-t?* Duckworth (1973a) suggests that we need not be afraid to explore alternative ways to solve the problems of spelling. We might even encourage it. After all, our conventional methods do not seem to prevent children from making errors. They see words correctly spelled hundreds of times, but still misspell them. Why not help them to see the alternative ways but then point out that the conventional way is to help us all communicate with each other more easily. Children accept this logic and have learned how the word looks right and wrong. After all, an *A* is still the letter *A* even if it is lying down. We stand it up just as a matter of convenience for us all.

We might conclude, with Duckworth (1973b), that it is just as necessary for parents as for children to gain confidence in their own ideas. If parents feel good about themselves and their ideas, then they can feel good about their children's ideas. If parents feel that their value as parents depends on the child's doing things by the book, they will find it difficult to allow their children to be free and creative, to have their own "wild and wonderful ideas." According to Duckworth, books designed to help teachers and parents should give only enough information to get parents started while making it possible for parents to feel free to follow their own directions when they have new and interesting ideas.

Some Specific Helps for Parents

In addition to the general principles to guide parental behavior given above, some specific helps may be given about each of the major developmental periods. Cognitive-developmental theorists have worked to apply Piaget's theory to the education of young children, and many of their findings may be put to use by parents. In a survey chapter there is room for only a few examples from each period. Interested parents may create activities of their own or turn to the additional sources cited in the text.

The sensorimotor period. The sensorimotor period lasts from birth to approximately two years. It is in this period that the child learns what he can do to and with the environment. He learns what he can do with his body. He learns to reach, roll over, grasp, stand, sit, and walk, and he begins to talk. All the physical actions he can do he tries and puts together in countless patterns, each elaborating on the others. All this sensorimotor development is a normal prerequisite to orderly symbolic functioning, according to the Piagetians (Phillips, 1969). During this time the child builds a kind of internal map or body image based on his discrimination of left from right (Phillips, 1969).* The child's understanding begins with his own body and gradually extends to the world around him. His understanding of differences between the left and right parts of himself is soon transferred from simple lateral control to control in terms of direction. To grasp an attractive toy, he not only must move the arm and hand on the proper side but also must move in the proper direction. And since space is three dimensional, he must locate objects within a given area at the right altitude as well as in the correct direction. The child slowly maps the space around him, and each of these maps is a "program" or "action scheme" for the control of behavior.

To help the child develop his understanding of what and how he can do things in this period, parents should give him many opportunities to learn about visual relationships, form, and space. They can do this by giving the child opportunity to interact with a variety of objects, many of which are freely available in the child's normal environment. Opportunity to climb on, over, and around a footstool, couch, or chair, or some large building blocks, forms one part of this developmental stage. Walking on a low brick or cement wall or a well-braced two-by-four presents an opportunity to learn balance and laterality. By walking and losing his balance and then regaining it, the child learns how to locate himself in space. He also learns how to correct for an error in judgment when he gets off balance. By numerous opportunities of this sort, the child develops his sensorimotor intelligence. He learns who he is and what he can do. Each of his experiences of walking on, crawling over, jumping from, and climbing on all

---

*There appears to be a relationship here with Gesell's concept of reciprocal interweaving, Chapter Three.

manner of things leads the child to further assimilation and accommodations. As long as the tasks are challenging but not too difficult, the child remains motivated to learn. He continues to pursue the activities he is engaged in for long periods of time.*

During the sensorimotor period, it appears that the cognitive-developmental theorists' statement that it is not necessary to "teach" children (Piaget, 1970) is most nearly correct. All that appears necessary is that we put children into an environment where they may interact with a variety of objects and let them learn in response to the environment. If the child falls off a block he learns to correct for his overbalancing by trying again and not letting his weight shift quite so far next time. (Perhaps this lays the groundwork for understanding later the concepts of center of gravity and other scientific laws of motion. Piaget's theory seems to imply that this is so.) It certainly does not appear wise or useful at this time to *teach* a child how to jump, or run, or walk up an incline. He appears to learn these things well enough on his own. The extent to which this procedure will work at later stages is open to some questions; however, before we turn to those criticisms we need to see what Piaget and his followers might recommend that parents do to help the child's development in the concrete operations period.

Concrete operations period. The concrete operations period extends from approximately two years of age until about the eleventh year. It is during this period of time that the child learns about his physical world, about the nature of things in his natural environment (Phillips, 1969). There is evidence to suggest that children from many cultures achieve the capacity to use the thinking processes Piaget has labeled "concrete operations" during these years (Kagen and Klein, 1973). The concrete operations consist of the ability to deal with space, time, dimension, order, and causality. Our discussion will focus on only one part of the child's development during this time period: the development of an understanding of what Piaget labeled *conservation*.

To help the child develop an understanding of conservation parents may do several things. They may bring the child into contact with a wide variety of experiences in which things change or have a variety of relationships to each other. If during these experiences parents point out the changes and label various attributes of the objects and experiences, children may learn to abstract the various properties of space, time, dimension, order, and causality. As has been pointed out earlier in this chapter, the cognitive-developmental theorists feel that the child understands these principles best if he discovers them for himself.

As a specific example of what parents may do to help children discover these principles, they might frequently and with a wide variety of objects proceed as follows:

Holding up an orange the parent asks, "What is this?" "What color is it?" "What can we do with it?" "What is its shape?" What is being accomplished is that the child is directed to focus on, in this case, the various aspects of the orange. If he does not have a label or a name for the aspect, we teach it to him, thus giving him a verbal method of describing the properties of things. By frequent practice with many objects the child begins to build up an understanding of objects, which may later be used by him to form classifications.

Once various attributes of objects are known by the child, he may then be led by the parents' questions to compare and contrast the various attributes of two objects; later he could compare several. The child begins to form concepts of

---

*For other activities involving sensorimotor development, parents may wish to refer to Chapters Six and Seven of Furth and Wachs (1975).

class, such as inclusion and exclusion. Classification is at first based on a single attribute, such as the shape or color of a group of objects. In comparing apples, oranges, and grapes, the child may say they are all round. Later he may be asked to classify them on two or more attributes; in the case of the fruit described above the child may respond, "They are all round, and we can eat them."

Finally, after the child has the above skills well in hand, he may be led to an understanding of reversibility. Phillips (1969) describes using a stack of pennies to teach reversibility. The pennies may be divided in various ways among several children. Regardless of how they are divided, the original stack may be reconstituted by gathering together all of the pennies. By dividing things up and bringing them back together, the child develops the ability to see the relationship between whole and part, and some measure of causality.

As in the sensorimotor period, discrepancy between the child's current set of operations and his environment is brought to the fore (Phillips, 1969). This time, instead of being off balance physically, the child is brought into disequilibrium by the parent's questions. The parent raises questions that make the child look at environmental events in new, unfamiliar ways.* The result, according to the Piagetians, is the development of a new set of mental operations which the child may use to operate upon his environment: the concrete operations. Following this period the child comes to be able to formulate answers to problems on the basis of logic, without the benefit of direct experience with the actions and objects he is thinking about.

Preparing children for formal operations. The ability to reason formally develops over the years from ages eleven to fifteen. During this time the child develops skills in dealing with the "real" versus the "possible" and develops skill in using "rules about rules" and rules about how to solve problems.

During the latter part of the concrete operations stage, parents may begin to introduce activities to help the child form hypotheses and make guesses about things that are not immediately present or of which the child is not currently aware. The goal here is to present material to the child in such a way that he looks for his own answers about causes of and connections between events. As mentioned earlier, this is what Duckworth (1973b) called "having wonderful ideas."

Furth and Wachs (1975) caution that the games the child plays to develop formal thinking are played not to find the "right" answer, but to learn how to think about things. While on a trip the parents may therefore ask, "I wonder how many pickup trucks we will see in the next twenty minutes." The idea is to help the child think about the probability of a given event, and then verify the probability by checking against the facts in the objective world. Furth and Wachs present a number of games and other activities to increase the child's ability to logically relate events and classifications. Furth and Wachs especially recommend games that use symbolic logic as preparation for formal thinking. As an example (pp. 227-29), they suggest development of logical expressions which include a class, an arrow which is used to indicate the truth or falsehood of the statement, and a drawing which represents a class of objects; for example,

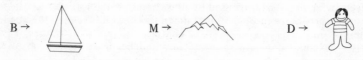

---

*Additional games related to the concrete operations stages may be found in Furth and Wachs (1975), Chapters Eight, Nine, Ten, and Eleven.

The parents could comment, "B goes with this, M goes with this and D goes with this." This can be expanded by showing that

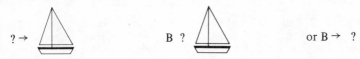

In addition, B →

Next, parents can give children problems to solve, such as:

? →   B ?   or B → ?

The game can be further complicated by introducing a symbol ↛
for negation:

B ↛

Following this, parents may wish to introduce multiple classifications by having the child indicate which symbols go with the classes included in the circle, thus:

↚D

← B

Furth and Wachs (1975) suggest that activities such as these help the child to realize that there is more than one way to think about an objective situation. As can be seen, there is more than one way to classify a group of objects. Different solutions to a problem are probably more common than a single solution, and games of this type help children understand this.

From the point of view of the cognitive-developmental theorist, parents can best help their children by giving them opportunities to interact with their environment in such a way that they must continue to work out a balance between assimilation and accommodation. This means giving them chances to imitate the actions and behaviors of things and people, for imitation is nearly pure accommodation (Piaget, 1954). Play, on the other hand, is seen as almost pure assimilation.

Criticisms of the Cognitive-Developmental Approach

Piaget's approach is an attempt to use both inner structures of development and environmental influences in explaining the behavior of organisms. As such, he contends that the action one can take upon his environment is limited by the internal structures available at that time for adapting. The internal structures are changed over time as the result of physical development *and* interaction with the environment. The principal criticism is not over whether such changes occur, but rather over what brings about these changes (Skinner, 1974; Zigler and Child, 1973).

One aspect of the criticism applies to developmental theory in general. It is the question of whether "stages" exist in fact or whether they are merely arbitrary divisions. Zigler and Child (1973) present arguments for both sides, but conclude that there "stands a very considerable body of evidence that qualitative changes occur in thought processes and in the very nature of learning at various times during childhood" (p. 14). However, their evidence does not prove very convincing when one asks *why* these changes occur.

If developmental changes are due to underlying physiological changes, then these changes should be evident as changes in the brain or other neurological structures. It may be, as Skinner (1953, 1974) argues, that such changes occur, but if so they should be discovered by the methods used by the physiologist. On the other hand, if changes occur in behavior patterns which are the result of environmental influences, then we should not allow our attention to be diverted from the environment to internal forces. Unfortunately, the theory and research presented by Piaget and his followers do not seem to help us understand the many differences between individuals at various developmental points in time (Zigler and Child, 1973, pp. 18-19). It appears that the answer to these questions awaits further research into both physiological and environmental changes and their influence.

The Existential-Phenomenological Approach

6

Although a number of theorists have contributed to the existential-phenomenological approach, the work of Carl Rogers has had perhaps the greatest impact on contemporary thinking in existential-phenomenological psychology. Rogers's theory was applied to clinical efforts with children as early as 1947, when Virginia Axline published her work on play therapy. More recently, Rogers's colleagues have applied his theory and techniques directly to families and the problems of child rearing (Raskin and van der Veen, 1970; Gordon, 1970a, b).

In order to understand the use of the terms *phenomenological* and *existential* in the title of this chapter, we need to examine the central idea of Rogers's approach: the self-concept (Raskin and van der Veen, 1970; Rogers, 1951). The existential-phenomenological approach begins with the assumption that man's *self-concept* is an organized and organizing set of concepts or ideas about himself which stand at the center of his own ever-changing phenomenal world. Man experiences his phenomenal world primarily in his moment-to-moment existence.

According to Rogers, the individual's self-concept is based upon how the individual sees, feels, and responds to the events or *phenomena* around him, the way those events fit, and the way the individual typically thinks of himself. The phenomena which occur in the individual's environment can only have meaning as they are received and responded to by that particular individual. The same events may have entirely different meanings to different people. A loud sound heard on the street by two people may be "experienced" as a car backfiring to one and as shots from a gun to another. The individual only knows about the world of phenomena from his personal experience. The self stands at the center of his private world. Therefore, the most appropriate method for studying man is *phenomenology*, which begins with the world of personal experience (Hitt, 1969).

Rogers (1951) believes that everyone lives in a world that consists of continually changing experiences. The individual is at the center of his own phenomenal world. Rogers has called this private world the individual's "phenomenal field," or "experiential field." It includes everything that is experienced by the individual, whether he can consciously express the experience or not. Consciousness, for Rogers, is the ability to symbolize, or put into words, our experiences. For most of us only a small part of our experience is ever put into words. Since only the individual really knows his own experiences, the best way to understand the individual is from the point-of-view of the individual himself.

The *existential* approach centers on the ability to make full use of all one's physical and mental apparatus to feel and experience life as it is right now. This intensive focus on the moment-to-moment experiencing of the individual has led to a here-and-now approach to counseling and child rearing (Gordon, 1970a; Raskin and van der Veen, 1970). The important information is the internal and external events available to and perceived by the individual at this moment.

The Existential-Phenomenological View of the Nature of Man

The phenomenologists see man as uniquely individual. Maslow (1962b) would agree that each person has some characteristics that all other persons have; however, the E-P theorists state that man also has characteristics which are idiosyncratic, unique to the person himself; and in this way the individual differs markedly from others in style and behavior (Allport, 1955). Because of this uniqueness the E-P theorist believes that man is largely unpredictable and thus can only be described in relative terms (Hitt, 1969). The biological aspects of man define the stage for man's uniqueness.

Biological underpinnings. Maslow (1962b) suggests that man has an inherited inner nature that leads to similarities and differences between men. This inner nature consists of "raw material" influenced by significant others and by the environment. This raw material becomes differentiated from others and from the environment as the *self*, which can in turn influence the "raw material" (Maslow, 1962b). We must understand what the raw material consists of, if we wish to understand the nature of man.

Man's inner nature consists of his ability for what Rogers calls *self-maintenance* (Rogers, 1951). This includes the ability to take in food and to defend against physical attack. It also includes the ability to adapt to the environment, to be creative, to overcome obstacles in the way of growth toward maturity. All of this makes for biological survival and assures further development in human evolution (Rogers, 1962).

Self-maintenance also includes, according to the E-P theorists, the tendency to work to enhance the self. This has been variously termed *self-fulfillment, emotional maturity, individuation, productiveness,* and *self-actualization* (Maslow, 1962b). Combs (1962) has referred to it as developing adequacy. The tendency to develop a self-concept in response to the environment is seen as inherent in the nature of man.

One of the more specific characteristics of the nature of man described by the E-P theorists is the ability to act assertively (Allport, 1955; Maslow, 1962b; Rogers, 1951; 1962). Not only is assertiveness seen by these theorists as biologically given, but also man has the capacity to be unabashedly self-seeking, to strive toward what Allport called *ego-enhancement* (1955). However, as Rogers (1951) and Maslow (1962b) hasten to point out, the tendency for this to become unwarrantedly hostile is removed if the individual is sufficiently in touch with both his inner instinctive feelings and the environment itself. Man's capacity for aggressive and angry behavior may be directed away from destructive hostility and toward what Maslow calls healthy self-affirmation, forcefulness, and righteous indignation.

Man is, according to Maslow (1962b), neither good nor evil. Rather, man is "prior to good and evil." By this he means that what man becomes is a reaction to what happens to him in his environment. Given the proper conditions of empathic understanding, warmth, and honest feedback, man will become fully actualized; that is, he will fulfill his biologically given potential to become fully constructive and trustworthy (Rogers, 1962). In contrast to Freud's view of man as a victim of his own hostile and aggressive drives, the E-P theorists take the optimistic position that man's potential is positive.

The biological aspects of man appear to be a set of inherent potentials: the potential to strive for survival through self-maintenance, to develop a self-concept to serve self-maintenance, to be assertive in defense of self when necessary, and through the self-concept to work toward the actualization of the individual's full capacities.

The cognitive aspects of man. Rogers (1962) sees man as "exquisitely rational." Having evolved the self-concept from the biological structure of the organism, the individual may use this collection of constructs about self to guide the organism toward the goals he is striving to achieve, including the biological goal of maturity.

The self-concept serves its guiding function through the processes of *consciousness*. Hitt (1969) draws upon Jaspers's arguments for consciousness, stating that consciousness has four main parts or characteristics: first, "an awareness or feeling of being active or having the capacity to act," second, "an awareness of unity or wholeness," third, "awareness of identity," and fourth, "awareness of self as distinct from others and the world (me, not me)" (Hitt, 1969, p. 754). Consciousness gives the individual an awareness of self, with the capacity to direct his own actions.

According to Rogers (1951), a large portion of the individual's phenomenal world may become conscious if awareness serves a purpose in fulfilling a need. Allport, too, recognizes the ability of the individual to treat himself and his feelings as objects, and to weigh and evaluate his needs in the situation in relationship to the events which surround him (Allport, 1955).* Rogers notes that in all this weighing and balancing the organism will always give the best possible answer with the data available, but that at times some data will be missing. The healthy self accepts this and makes corrections as new information becomes available. Maintenance of a reasonably coherent and acceptable self-concept is the goal of all this conscious cognitive activity. "Life is a continual series of choices for the individual in which a main determinant of choice is the person as he already is (including his goals for himself, his courage or fear, his feeling of responsibility, his ego-strength or 'will power,' etc.)" (Maslow, 1962b, p. 36). The degree of rationality varies in the individual's decision-making processes. However, as Allport (1955) points out, the focus of all action is the person. For the E-P theorist, behavior is the result of the interaction between the individual as he interprets himself (through the self-concept) and the environment.

The affective aspects of man. Man's goal-seeking behavior is always accompanied by emotional responses (Rogers, 1951). The intensity of the emotion is related to the importance of the behavior as seen by the individual himself. The more important the behavior for enhancement of the self or for self-actualization, the greater the intensity of the related emotion. The feeling process or affective behavior serves as a feedback mechanism to the individual to guide continued behavior (Rogers, 1962).

The E-P theorists believe that healthier people are capable of making their emotional responses conscious through symbolization. Less healthy people are seen as fearing their emotions and thus avoiding this important source of data relative to their phenomenal field (Maslow, 1962). Rogers (1951) suggests that people who deny these emotional experiences must continually defend themselves against the symbolization of their emotions. The result is often a generalization of the defensive behavior to all experiences (Rogers, 1951). Words and behaviors of other people that can possibly be construed as related to the denied emotions are seen as threats, even when they are not so intended. Therefore, not only do the less mature individuals lose information from their own emotional processes, but also they begin to distort information from their environment.

The E-P theorists believe that the affective experiences of man can play a crucial part in man's behavior. Maslow feels that the most mature individuals are those who can integrate the rational and the irrational aspects of themselves. In

---

*For an interesting discussion of how the individual may come to know himself and his actions, *see* Skinner's explanation as described in Chapter Seven.

this way the mature individual can permit and enjoy his emotional experiences. The mature person is more able to enjoy and value his experiences of love, silliness, humor, and even fear and anger. In a sense this is a childlike quality of experiencing fully the emotion as it is happening.

Having achieved this childlike quality, the mature individual can respond more creatively to the situations he finds himself in (Rogers, 1951; Maslow, 1962b). By daring to accept his feelings, instead of using a great deal of energy to control the emotion, he has more energy to meet the needs of the situation. Accepting and symbolizing his feelings also gives the individual just that much more information about the problem. As a result, the more mature individual is more likely to develop a creative solution.

The goal of actualization. Rogers (1951) places the tendency toward self-actualization within the genetic structure of the species. Actualization is evidenced for Rogers in the differentiation of organs and of organ functions. Expansion of the organism through growth is part of the tendency toward enhancement, as are reproduction and the use of tools.

The striving for greater independence and responsibility is also seen by Rogers as part of the movement toward self-actualization. Self-actualization leads the individual closer to other people, and is the one basic tendency toward which the organism is continually striving. It is directed by the cognitive, knowing aspects of the self, and is most likely to occur when the individual is aware of and responsive to the affective reactions he is having to the situation.

To this the E-P theorists add that the nature of man is such that he reacts at all times as a total organized system; that is, a change in any part of the system will lead to changes in the other aspects of the system. Thus the individual reacts biologically, emotionally, and cognitively to a situation he perceives as physically threatening. Rogers would say that the individual reacts as an organized whole to an event in his phenomenal field. Therefore, we do man an injustice if we only examine his cognitive, emotional, or physical responses to an event. We must consider the total reaction.

The more actualized individual is capable of responding in this wholistic manner, using his entire being in response to the many choices presented by his environment. There is widespread agreement among E-P theorists (Combs, 1962; Kelly, 1962; Maslow, 1962b; Rogers, 1951, 1962) that the more a person becomes actualized the more he is likely to have a positive view of himself, the more he is likely to identify with others, and the more likely he is to be open to new experience—to change in himself and others.

Maslow (1962b) points out that the actualized person is not above all human problems. He still must face anxiety, frustration, and conflict; he still will feel hurt, anger, sadness, and guilt. But he will be free from false or neurotic problems. He will be able to distinguish the important from the unimportant tasks in front of him and deal with them without unnecessary worry or concern. The actualized person is a person of conscience and will therefore be troubled by real guilt over hurt to others—but not by neurotic guilt over things he does not control.

For the existential-phenomenological theorists, actualization is a state of being or becoming. The person is not static or stationary, but is always shifting to and from a state of more or less actualization. To be more fully actualized is the universal goal.

The Existential-Phenomenological View of the Nature of Children

Allport (1955) suggests that the key problem for existential-phenomenological theorists is to account for the processes by which the unsocialized infant becomes the socialized adult. Because the young infant is without any of the personality structures that require learning, such as conscience, imagination, and an organized and organizing self-concept, it is important that we understand how these structures develop.

The infant is considered to be an immature human being and all immature growth is considered as steps toward self-actualization (Maslow, 1962b). As an immature person, the child has needs, as do older children and adults (Gordon, 1970a).* The child is seen as needing love, security, and acceptance as he struggles toward maturity. The needs are viewed as inherent, and comprise one of the first characteristics of children.

A second characteristic of children is their dependence upon parents or other adults for the satisfaction of their needs. While the infant is completely socially dependent he is by no means socialized. The infant's dependency needs are tied up completely with his immediate demands. He is unable to form and maintain long-range plans. He has few means for meeting his own needs other than to engage in even more dependent behavior. And his inability to communicate his needs through verbal symbols further complicates the problem (Allport, 1955; Gordon, 1970a). Yet despite the problems of immaturity the child is seen as having *within himself* the potential for overcoming these difficulties and becoming a capable adult.

The child's ability to change in the direction of becoming a normal, healthy person is fundamental to the thinking of the E-P theorists. Raskin and van der Veen (1970) note that no other system of therapy has stated so unequivocally that the child may be helped to change because he has within him the potential for healthy growth. Maslow says, "In the normal development of the normal child, it is now known that *most* of the time, if he is given a really free choice, he will choose what is good for his growth. . . . This implies that *he* 'knows' better than anyone else what is good for him" (Maslow, 1962b, p. 39). A fundamental respect for the child and his ability to become self-actualized is necessary for our understanding of children (Kelly, 1962).

However, while the child has within him the potential to become self-actualized, there are conditions which will greatly increase the chances of his developing most fully. Children who have felt loved and accepted by their parents tend to be more loving and accepting individuals. For most children, one of their earliest experiences is that of being loved by their parents. Out of this experience the child begins to see himself as lovable and worthy of love from others (Rogers, 1955). He experiences these feelings with a great deal of satisfaction. In this way he begins to develop a sense of self in which he sees himself as a lovable person. The Christian dictum to "Love thy neighbor as thyself" certainly seems appropriate in this light. Having a sense of self as lovable and worthy of love is a first step toward loving others.

In addition to a sense of being loved, children develop best, according to Allport (1955), when they have a feeling of security. Children who have had a generous helping of security in their early life tend to be able to give up their habits of demanding gratification, and are better able to deal with frustrating situations later in life. Self-acceptance grows out of a sense of security, and therefore whatever develops feelings of security in the child will build his ability to be open to himself and thus to others (Combs, 1962).

According to Allport (1955), this means that the child's needs for love, acceptance, and security are the basis for his healthy becoming. The child's

---

*The concept of needs as an explanation of behavior has been criticized by Skinner (1953) and others (Gewirtz, 1969) on the basis that needs must always be inferred and therefore they cannot be used as a causal explanation.

dependency demands are designed to get his affiliative needs (love, acceptance, and security) met by the adults in his community. Aggressive behavior is a protest aroused within the child when his affiliative needs are blocked (Allport, 1955).

One key to the development of a healthy self-concept in the young child is social interaction. Through the process of adjusting to the actions of others, the child is forced to realize that he is not the other person, but a separate individual. The young child's actions are directed toward immediate satisfaction of his needs. But others have needs in the situation as well (Allport, 1955). At these times the child will learn to experience his parents' negative evaluations as well as their positive feelings.

Just as the child experiences feelings of satisfaction when his parents express loving and accepting behavior, so too does the child feel satisfaction about much of his own behavior. Passing a bowel movement when the fancy strikes him is experienced by the child as satisfying. So too might striking another child be perceived by the child himself as pleasant. Rogers (1951) states that when the child is presented simultaneously with his own feelings of satisfaction in his actions and a negative evaluation from his parents in the form of "No, No, that's a bad girl," the child is put into a psychological bind. While an accurate assessment of the situation might be "My parents do not approve of this behavior," the child distorts this message into "I feel this behavior is not satisfying." The bind is that although the child experiences the behavior as satisfying, he symbolically distorts his parents' message and acts as if he himself were not experiencing the behavior as satisfying.

Binds which place the child's inner feelings against his parents' wishes pose a threat to the child's self-concept. According to Rogers, the child's dilemma might be schematized in these terms: "If I admit to awareness of the satisfactions of these behaviors and the values I apprehend in these experiences, then this is inconsistent with my self as being loved or lovable" (Rogers, 1951, p. 500). The child places positive value on events which are perceived by him as helping him to grow; he also places negative value on events which prevent him from growing. Yet to maintain his concept of himself as a person who is loved and lovable in his parents' eyes the child must devalue his positive feelings and accept his parents' negative feelings. The problem is that the child often places the negative feelings upon himself rather than upon the act being censured by his parents. When this occurs frequently, the child may develop as part of his self-concept the idea that he is not an acceptable person, that he is unworthy of the love of others.

The solution is not to smother the child with love and acceptance, for while the child needs generous amounts of love and affection, especially in the first year or two, he does not want his parents to interfere with his freedom—his preferred ways of behaving. To accept love and security alone would lead to a slavish obedience. The result would be children who are always conventional and who behave like patterned robots (Allport, 1955). Therefore, running parallel to the child's need for dependence is his need for self-direction or, as Allport terms it, *autonomy*.*

Allport (1955) suggests that life is one continuous struggle to bring together the two basic needs, the need for dependence and the need for autonomy. The need for dependence may be seen as a need for the group and group acceptance,

---

*It is interesting to compare the two opposing needs, the need for dependence and the need for autonomy, with the opposition of id, ego, and super-ego found in Freud's conceptualizations as described in Chapter Two.

and the need for autonomy may be seen as a need to be independent from the group. "If the demand for autonomy were not a major force we could not explain the prominence of negativistic behavior in childhood. The crying, rejecting, and anger of a young infant as well as the negativistic behavior of the two-year-old are primitive indications of a being bent on asserting itself" (Allport, 1955, p. 35).

The struggle for self-identity is long and difficult. The child's dependency needs and autonomy needs both contribute to his growing sense of self. The child's self-concept seems to be very flexible and changing until about age four or five. From that time forward the individual's self-concept becomes the most clear evidence he has of his own existence (Allport, 1955).

The establishment of a positive self-concept is probably the most important task of early childhood (Rogers, 1951). The child must learn to balance the needs of self and sensitivity for the needs of others. Children are capable of justifiable anger and acts of self-protection as well as autonomous assertion; they must learn how to control these feelings and how and when to express them (Maslow, 1962b). To continue the infant's destructive ways—his insistence that every desire be instantly gratified, his selfish possessiveness, his violent and immediate expression of all his feelings—would be to develop adults with what Allport calls "infantile and potentially evil" personalities. The E-P theorists believe that given adequate amounts of love, acceptance, and security, the child will develop a positive self-concept leading away from the infantile, toward an adult with positive, creative feelings toward himself and others.

The Relationship of the Individual to the Group

For the existential-phenomenological theorists, the individual and the social group are closely related. Kelly (1962) suggests that the self is developed through the interaction of the organism with others. The ability to communicate, both vocally and nonvocally, does not develop without social relationships. Man, as we know him, does not exist outside of his relevant social groups. The infant has the potential for the development of a positive self-concept; however, it seems apparent that nothing like the self-structure can be built without interaction with other people.

Given a nonthreatening environment, the child will be free from defensiveness. In such an environment the child will be open to all his inner feelings, and he will also be open to the whole range of environmental and social demands. Rogers (1962) believes that under these conditions the child may be trusted to develop a positive self-image, to move forward in a constructive manner. One need not ask who will socialize the child, for he has within him the need for affiliation and communication with others. His need to be liked by others and his willingness to give affection are at least equal to his aggressive tendencies. Certainly he will learn to be aggressive in situations in which aggressive behavior is realistically called for; but aggression for aggression's sake is not likely to occur. By providing a relatively threat-free environment, parents can trust the child to form for himself a positive and healthy self-concept.

The child quickly learns to achieve, to a certain degree, the other person's point-of-view. This is so because many of the people in his perceptual world— parents, teachers, and playmates—have counterparts in his personal experience. As he gains experience with anger, fear, love, hate, jealousy, and satisfaction, he can begin to relate the other person's behavior in a given situation with his own. The more he has learned to accept his own feelings, the more he will be receptive to, and understanding of, the feelings of others.

Identification with others is an important aspect of the child's relationship to the family, the peer group, and other social groups. Combs (1962) hastens to point out that the E-P theorist is not referring to "togetherness" or some frantic need to be with people. The identification referred to here is a feeling of oneness with one's fellow beings. It is fully conceivable that the individual might not care for parties or large groups. He may prefer the company of only a few close friends. He might spend a great deal of his time in individual pursuits. The feeling of belonging is not a hail-fellow-well-met feeling, but rather is a feeling of unity, of sharing a common fate. In this way it is an extension of self to include one's fellows. Given such an identification, the boundaries between self and others fall away and the actions of the individual take into account the needs of others.

Identifying with others in this way, the individual is unlikely to act aggressively unless it is to right a wrong as he perceives it. When a person has the feeling that others' fates are tied up with his own he is far less likely to do others harm or injury. The individual who perceives himself and others to be one is unlikely to ignore or reject others. Responsible and moral behavior follow from fully understanding the needs of others and the needs of self in any situation.

Identification of this nature is obviously learned. The child needs guidance and security as he learns to place his own and others' needs into perspective. Recently the E-P theorists (Gordon, 1951; Kelly, 1962; Raskin and van der Veen, 1970) have recognized the importance of family and other social groups in the development of these attitudes in the child.

One important aspect of family life that fosters the development of identification within members of the family is participation in the making of important family decisions (Gordon, 1951). Children who have an opportunity to express their opinions in an atmosphere where their opinions will be accepted as important tend to show better social adjustment in their later school years. Opportunity for group members to participate in group decisions seems to be important for their growth. Lack of family consultation and involvement appears to be one cause of continuing conflict between parents and children (Kelly, 1962). When individuals feel they are part of the decisions made by a group, they often feel responsible for the successful outcome of those decisions.

Cooperation is another important part of family life which leads to positive identification with others. Cooperation is important because a cooperative atmosphere leads to involvement (Kelly, 1962). According to Kelly, "The growing self must feel that it is involved, that it is really part of what is going on, that in some degree it is helping shape its own destiny, together with the destiny of all" (pp. 16-17). Cooperation is seen not only as shaping unity and identification but also as contributing to autonomy through fostering a feeling of guiding one's own behavior.

Maslow (1962b) suggests that as the child learns to see and understand other people's points-of-view, he learns to place some checks upon his natural spontaneity. The child learns to be less free; he becomes more inhibited and less trusting of himself and others. The family has a dual role here. While the family must develop the child's ability to exercise control through caution, will, and self-criticism, they must at the same time recognize the inner nature of the child, which is given to free expression of needs and feelings.

According to the E-P theorist a society, culture, or a family may be growth-permitting or growth-inhibiting (Maslow, 1962b). The basis for growth and humanness are within the child himself. However, the more the family serves to gratify all the basic human needs of acceptance, love, and security, thus promoting self-actualization, the "better" the family. The family or society did not invent the potential for development into humanness, but they can help or hinder the growth process. This is true because a culture or social group is absolutely essential for actualization.

Other Dimensions and Issues

Development of the Self-Concept. Allport (1955), suggests that the infant and young child learn many habits and behaviors through the interaction of their impulses with the rewards and punishments supplied by the environment. Such learning would be guided by the principles of reinforcement described at length in Chapter Seven. However, by the time the child is three, Allport contends, life is already too complicated for this single method of learning. Life presents issues which must be sorted and assessed in terms of their relative importance. Events need to be ordered and plans evolved, and this can best be accomplished around a reference center. Thus the child develops a self-concept because he needs such an organized and organizing concept to help him interact with his complex human and physical environment.

Rogers (1951) postulates that the child structures his self-concept as a result of the interaction between himself and his environment. Events are experienced and valued positively if they are seen as adding to the child's growth, as *he* perceives that growth. Events which are not perceived as growth promoting are evaluated negatively by the child. Eventually a portion of the total phenomenal field is differentiated as the self. A portion of the child's private little world becomes *me, I, myself*. The self-structure is an organized set of concepts about one's self which can be allowed into awareness. The self-concept includes the typical ways one relates to others and the environment, the values we place on experiences and objects, and our positive and negative personal goals and ideals.

Children learn who they are and what they are, not only from their own personal experience, but also from the evaluative responses of others around them, especially parents (Combs, 1962; Rogers, 1951). Children develop feelings of being liked, accepted, wanted, and capable from experiencing being liked, accepted, wanted, or successful, particularly when their parents express those feelings about them. The parents' role in these specific learnings is most critical because of the child's extreme dependence upon them in the early years when the initial self-concept is forming.

Once formed, the self-structure plays a role in all new learnings. As the child strives to meet his needs in the environment, the form of his struggle is determined in part by the self-concept (Kelly, 1962; Rogers, 1951).* The form of the striving must now conform to the expectations established by the child's internalized concepts of self. The child who sees himself as thoughtful and kind cannot seek recognition through unkind or hurtful means. The child utilizes the concept of self to further develop or enhance the self. The individual tends to select those methods for further enhancement which are most consistent with his concept of self.

It is interesting to note that the self in the self-concept is not necessarily limited to the physical body of the individual. Rogers (1951) suggests that an object or experience perceived as within the control of the individual is included in the self-concept. Ask any college student where he is parked; he will most likely reply that he is parked in lot 3A just beyond the student union building. Clearly the car is a part of his self-concept, since he himself is not parked on the other side of the student union. The car, as an extension of himself, is treated as part of his "self."

In a similar way our behavior may be treated as if it is not a part of our self. When some event occurs in which we perceive our action as not within our control, such as an act of courage in a sudden emergency, we often dissociate the

---

*The student will recall the similar use of goals to guide behavior in the socio-teleological approach in Chapter Four.

act from our self by such statements as "I just wasn't myself." Thus it is the extent of perceived control over the object or action which seems to determine whether or not it is claimed as part of the self.

Rogers (1951) points out that experiences which are not consistent with the self-concept are usually excluded because they are contradictory to the self-concept—not because they are derogatory. Derogatory information which is consistent with the self-concept held by an individual is accepted. Often it is as hard for the individual to accept data that would alter his self-concept in a positive direction as it is for him to accept a negative comment. The child who perceives himself as the meanest kid on the block rejects any information to the contrary, just as the friendliest member of the class of '67 would find it hard to accept data that suggested that much of his friendly behavior is an attempt to cover up his fear of failure.

This should not be construed to mean that the child—or anyone else, for that matter—cannot change his self-concept. Under conditions where there is little or no perceived threat to the self-structure, the individual may examine the corrective feedback and begin to revise his view of self in the direction of this new evidence. Rogers gives the following example: "The child who feels that he is weak and powerless to do a certain task, to build a tower or repair a bicycle, may find, as he works rather hopelessly at the task, that he is successful. This experience is inconsistent with the concept he holds of himself, and may not be integrated at once; but if the child is left to himself he gradually assimilates, upon his own initiative, a revision of his concept of self" (Rogers, 1951, p. 519). Merely telling the child he is capable is of little value and may even lead the child to reject parental statements. Forceful attempts to convince the child may lead the child to act in such a way as to prove to his parents his lack of ability. This in turn frustrates the parents even more.

Under conditions of threat, little positive learning is likely to occur. Learning that influences the child's self-concept is most likely to take place when the parents provide opportunities for experiences under conditions of acceptance. The child who has a good basis of love, acceptance, and security is able to learn a great deal from nicely graded frustrations (Maslow, 1962b). Overcoming difficult situations teaches the child he can meet and deal with frustrating events. He adds to his self-concept the picture of himself as a person who can solve problems and meet difficulties. The child may learn that even failure is acceptable as a challenge to try again in a new or different way.

It is important to recognize that most parents have been taught to believe that if you accept a child, he will have no reason to change and therefore will not change. As a result, most parents concentrate on telling the child what is unacceptable to them. But learning is blocked when parents spend a great deal of time with their children judging, evaluating, and criticizing the child's behavior (Gordon, 1970a). Parents are better teachers when they learn to trust the child's inner push toward growth. They can then express approval of the child as he is right now and allow him to find his own creative solutions to the problems life will inevitably bring him (Gordon, 1970a).

Early versus later experience. The existential-phenomenological approach is focused primarily on the here-and-now. For Rogers (1951) and his colleagues, the present contains all of the effective elements for the individual to base his actions on. A person's behavior is not determined by events of the past, as suggested by the psychoanalysts (*see* Chapter Two), but by the response of the individual to the needs of the present. The past is represented in the present by the current structure of the self-concept, which has been shaped by past events. Events which strengthen or alter the self-concept through interaction in the present determine to some extent the future. The individual is continually becoming what he will be tomorrow.

The self-structure is unique to each individual, having been built out of his total life experiences (Kelly, 1962). It is this unique self which the individual brings to the present as he responds to the events in his phenomenal world. Rogers states that all the effective elements exist in the present and that there is no behavior except to meet the needs of the present.

The fully functioning individual has access to his total feelings in response to the situation. He is aware of the social demands of the moment. He is open to his own complex and even conflicting needs. He brings to bear his memories of similar situations and his impressions of the uniqueness of this situation. Taking all this data in as part of the immediate perceptual field, he then comes to a conclusion close to meeting all his needs (Rogers, 1962).

Rogers (1962) suggests that many fail in this process because they include data which does not belong to the events of the moment, or fail to perceive information which does pertain. People include memories and other learnings as if they were this event rather than associated events. Threatening perceptions that are withheld from consideration or are distorted to "fit" the situation also lead to erroneous conclusions. Obviously, the more areas of our experience we are unable to use properly in meeting a problem, the less likely we are to arrive at a satisfactory solution.

Existential-phenomenological theorists suggest that neither parent nor child has anything to fear from past experiences. The ability to become a fully functioning individual lies within each of us. Given freedom from threat, we can all make progress toward self-actualization. The crucial problem, according to Kelly (1962) is not so much what you are as what you think you are. And since we are all in the process of becoming, we have within our grasp the potential for changing our self-perceptions. The past is no more dangerous than we perceive it to be.

Application of Existential-Phenomenological Theory to Child Rearing

If the family can influence the child's developing self-concept, what should be the role of the adult with the child? Rogers (1951) and others (Gordon, 1970a; Raskin and van der Veen, 1970) suggest that there is a great deal that parents can do. Basically, parents can work to change themselves and to change the patterns of their relationships with their children.

Changing ourselves as parents. Gordon (1970a) states that often when people become parents they assume the role of "parent" and forget to be human. They try to match a role they have seen their parents play, or else to do the opposite of what they saw their parents doing. They may try to meet some standard that they feel others will accept or that they have read in a book or heard preached from the pulpit. They expect themselves to be perfect in their new role, without human failings or weaknesses. Parents often fall prey to the belief that they should always be consistent, that they should always think and act alike toward their children, and that they should love each of the children in just the same way.

According to the E-P theorists, acceptance of self and of others is an important key to being a good parent. The more accepting one is of oneself, the more one can accept others. Therefore parents need to learn to listen to and accept more of their own feelings. This includes occasional feelings of not accepting their own children or their children's behavior. Just as we do not respond the same to all the adults we meet, we should not expect ourselves to respond the same to all the children we encounter, including our own (Gordon, 1970a).

Parents' feelings of acceptance toward a child will vary according to the nature of the child (we are attracted to some children more than others); according to their feelings at the moment (worries, illness, or preoccupation, interfere with our accepting feelings); and according to the situation (we are more accepting of loud playing in the backyard at home than in the foyer of the church, for example; Gordon, 1970a, 1970b).

As there are so many variables influencing acceptance of a child and his behavior, it can be seen that parents need not feel they must be the same with their children all the time. One need not be consistent to be an effective parent (Gordon, 1970a, 1970b). Parents can accept themselves as persons who sometimes feel positive and sometimes feel negative toward their children. Neither is it necessary to feel the same degree of lovingness toward all the children. Feelings vary according to the child, the adult, and the situation. Therefore both parents need not feel the same about each of the children. According to Gordon, parents do not need to put up a united front; in fact, it would be best if they did not put up *any* front, but felt good about being themselves, as they are right at that moment.

Parents who need to maintain a front, such as the front of being "good parents," are often not in contact with their own feelings (Rogers, 1951). Such parents maintain the concept of themselves as good and loving. Their self-concepts are based in part on accurate perceptions and in part on inaccurate, distorted perceptions of their feelings and responses. This often results in acceptance and assimilation of internal feelings of love which they may have toward the child. But feelings of hate, anger, or distaste which they may also have are distorted and denied symbolization.

When hostile feelings are denied symbolization there exists within the parent the need for aggressive acts to fulfill the negative attitudes and tensions which exist (Rogers, 1951).* The parents' organisms strive for the fulfillment of these needs, but they may only do so through methods consistent with their concepts of themselves as good parents. Good parents can only be aggressive with their children if the children "deserve" punishment. One possible outcome of this is that the parents may come to see much of their children's behavior as being bad and therefore deserving of punishment. The parents' hostile feelings may then be expressed without being counter to the picture they have of themselves as good and loving parents.

Parents can overcome the tensions which lead to constant punishment if they can learn to accept their own inner feelings of dislike for their children when those feelings occur (Rogers, 1951). Rejecting parents, who accept their own negative feelings, often find that their acceptance leads to a more relaxed attitude toward their children. They begin to be able to observe the children more as they are and less as they wish them to be.

From such a comfortable, realistic basis the parents begin to develop a deep and real relationship with their children. Obviously, such a relationship will not be without problems. However it will be far more real and comfortable than a relationship built upon false perceptions of the children. A good relationship will be based on the knowledge that the children are separate persons, very much individual in their responses to life.

Parents need not attempt to be unconditionally accepting of their children all of the time (Gordon, 1970a; 1970b). The adage so popular among some parents

---

*The action appears similar to repression as described by the psychoanalysts; *see* Chapter Two.

that you "can love the child but not condone his behavior" is impossible to put into practice. The child is his behavior.* Whenever the parent responds with nonaccepting behavior toward the child's acts, the child perceives this as not accepting him. There is a story of a boy who was about to receive a spanking for his misbehavior from his father: when the father said, "I'm just doing this because I love you," the boy replied, "I can't wait until I'm big enough to return your love, dad." The myth of unconditional acceptance seems to be just that—a myth.

Parents who pretend to be accepting of all the child's behavior often create a communications problem (Haley, 1963; Waltzlawick, Beavin, and Jackson, 1967: Raskin and van der Veen, 1970). When the parent is *feeling* unaccepting and *acts* accepting, the child receives both messages. Mother may say it is all right for him to yell and scream around the house, but her nonverbal messages say that she is upset by his yelling and screaming. The child is now in a bind. He wants to yell and scream but he also wants his mother's love and acceptance. Which message is the real one? How should he behave?

It would appear far better for the child to receive a clear and unequivocal message of nonacceptance if that is how the parent feels. If the parent's message is clear the child may evaluate his behavior, his needs, his feelings, and his parent's response. His decision to act would then be based on the realities of the situation rather than on a distorted and confused set of messages. The child may not come to a socially acceptable solution. His behavior may not conform to his parents' desires. However, according to Rogers (1951), "Its great advantage, as far as psychological health is concerned, is that it would be realistic, based upon an accurate symbolization of all the evidence given by the child's sensory and visceral equipment in this situation" (p. 502). The important difference lies in the parents' acceptance of the child's *feelings* in the situation. When the parents can accept the child's feelings, then the child can accept his feelings also. The child can continue to use his own experience as an accurate guide to his behavior.

Changing interaction patterns. Not only can parents work to change their own feelings, but they can also work to change the nature of the interaction between themselves and their children. Parents can learn to listen and to express their feelings of acceptance and nonacceptance in a nonthreatening way. Love which remains unexpressed can hardly be effective in changing another person's concept of himself. It may seem strange to suggest that parents must be trained in methods of expressing acceptance and listening to their children. This is so because our society trains us best in not listening and in expressing nonacceptance.

Active listening is the process of listening not only to what the child is saying but also to the feelings that the child is trying to convey in his message. Gordon (1970a) says that whenever a child attempts to communicate he does so because he is trying to express a need. The disequilibrium created inside the child by the need sets up the desire to communicate to others in order to return the child to a state of equilibrium. Parents should attempt to decipher the child's need message and to communicate that understanding back to the child. Successful communication of the parent's understanding of the child's needs and deep feelings is the best demonstration of acceptance. Such acceptance is almost always perceived as an act of love.

When parents are attempting to listen actively they should listen for the need message and send back a message of understanding of that need. At this point they are not sending their own message, which is most probably a message of

---

*A point certainly agreed to by the behaviorists, Chapter Seven.

nonacceptance such as opinion, advice, or criticism. Parents should attempt to respond with only what they notice of the child's feelings. Anything more or less may destroy the understanding that is being communicated. As an example of active listening, the child might comment, "I hate that baseball team. I'm never going back." The actively listening father might respond, "You're pretty mad at those guys?"

Son: "Yeah, they want me to play center field and I'd rather play catcher."

Father: "It's pretty disappointing not to tie down the catcher's spot."

Son: "It sure is, I really practiced hard for that spot. Oh, well, I guess it's a lot better than not playing at all." In this example the father pinpointed the son's feelings of anger and disappointment and reflected those feelings accurately back to the boy. The boy acknowledged his accuracy and supplied new information, including his ability to accept the setback and come to his own positive solution.

Often parents fear that their children will be unable to handle their feelings in such a situation and that the child will be unable to solve the problem. If parents allow their own fears to take hold they grab the initiative away from their children and begin supplying advice and solutions before the child has had the opportunity to work out his feelings and demonstrate that he can come up with an answer. Parents can learn to listen actively and to trust their children to work the feelings through to an acceptable solution.

Gordon (1970a) supplies several good reasons for employing active listening in interaction with children. First, emotional reactions to situations are often helped by talking them out with an interested, noncritical listener. Second, the act of sharing negative feelings with someone who understands but is not afraid of the feelings often serves to free the child of his concern about his feelings. The child learns that he can have those feelings without having to act upon them or without having to express them in a distorted way. Third, when parents take time to listen and accept the child's feelings as part of him, as he is right now, without demanding a change, the child begins to feel closer to and more affectionate with that parent. Fourth, when the child's needs are listened to he often feels free enough to look ahead to a solution to the problem. And fifth, parents who successfully practice active listening model good listening to their children. As a result, the children are often more willing and able to listen to the point-of-view held by the parents relative to any given situation or event. The work put forth in active listening is considerable. The E-P theorists feel that the gains described above will adequately repay parents who are willing to make the effort.

There are some cautions put forth for parents who might wish to use active listening to improve their relationships with their children. Parents must want to hear what their children are saying and feeling. Listening takes time. Parents must be willing to take the time or be honest enough to say that they haven't the time right now. Taking the time and being willing to listen should be accompanied by feelings of wanting to help and willingness to accept the child's feelings. When we do this and trust in the child we can expect that our attempts at active listening will be helpful. Listening has one interesting side effect that parents also need to be aware of. Parents may find that they receive new information about *their* phenomenal world, requiring changes in the way they as parents see the world and react to it.

Active listening is best used *when the child has a problem* and not when the child *is* a problem to the parents. For instance, if the child is crying, the crying may be irritating to the parents. At the same time the crying may be an attempt by the child to communicate a need to the parents. If the parents attempt to use active listening to get rid of the crying rather than to understand the child's feelings, they will really communicate lack of acceptance rather than acceptance. If this happens frequently, children begin to avoid communicating with their parents, for they feel they will not be understood. Gordon (1970a) says, "There is no better way to insure the failure of active listening than to use it to encourage a child to express his true feelings, after which the parent then moves in with evaluation, judgment, moralizing, and advice" (p. 87).

Active listening is not the only way parents can show acceptance of their children. Much understanding of children can be shown through nonverbal communication. A friendly hand on the shoulder, a pat on the back, or a smile also communicate love and understanding. Sometimes the most important thing a parent can do is to do or say nothing. Many children can benefit from the parents' not interfering in their activities (Gordon, 1970a). Rushing in to tie the shoelace of a child who can already tie his own communicates to the child that the parent does not accept him. As parents we often make this mistake when we are in a hurry. Allowing the child to do it himself, or try, and to even make mistakes in his trying can convey acceptance and trust to the child in a powerful nonverbal way.

Young children, obviously, will require more nonverbal communication than will older children. Parents of very young children need to become familiar with the child's peculiar body language so that they can respond to the child's needs. As we have noted above, the E-P theorists feel that the first three to five years are important in the formation of the child's guiding self-concept. Therefore, the parents must find nonverbal and verbal ways of helping the child know of their acceptance during this period. Gordon (1970a) emphasizes infants' need for their parents in that critical first few years of life. Being around is not enough, he says; it is more important that parents respond verbally and nonverbally to the child's needs.

The long-range goal of most parents is to help the child gradually become independent. This means allowing the child to assume more and more responsibility for solving his own problems. Of course, the younger the child, the more the parents will need to intervene in the problem-solving process. But as the child develops physically and mentally and as he is taught new skills, the parents must relinquish their hold over the child and allow him to find his own solutions. Parents who can genuinely accept the child and his feelings find this task easier than parents who are less accepting. Raskin and van der Veen (1970) suggest that parents' failure to consistently help the child feel positively valued as a capable person is at the heart of much psychological maladjustment.

Criticisms of the Existential-Phenomenological Approach

Rogers (1951; 1961) advocates an approach to child rearing that deemphasizes the exercise of control and puts the responsibility for self-actualization on the individual. However, this cannot occur without interaction with other people and the environment. The influence exerted by parents and others as part of the environment is a form of control, if it has any effect at all.

The existential-phenomenological theorists insist that change is the result of providing a noncontrolling atmosphere which is warm and empathic and which provides nonjudgmental feedback in the form of congruent responses from others. However, two of Rogers's associates (Traux and Mitchell, 1971) have shown that an alternative explanation is equally plausible. Traux and Mitchell found that Rogers significantly changed the behavior in five out of nine classes of client behavior by his selective attention to the words spoken by the client. There was a significant change in only one of the four classes of behavior which Rogers did not selectively reinforce. By use of techniques such as active listening, parents may selectively reinforce and thus change a part of their child's verbal behavior. Whether such other aspects of the child's behavior as his self-concept change because of these conversations is open to question.

Rogers (1961) and Maslow (1962a) have been criticized (Skinner, 1969) for emphasizing the individual's personal experience more than the accumulated experience of the culture they are a part of. The E-P theorists tend to prize behavior resulting from direct personal experience over behavior which is the result of following rules and prescriptions taught by others. Typically, rule-induced behavior allows the individual to respond to situations in a way which is likely to prove rewarding to himself and others, often without painful and time-consuming trial-and-error learning. It is difficult to see why experiential learning needs to be set above learning from the experiences of others.

Insistence upon experiential learning has led Rogers (1969) to a position which suggests that direct teaching is wrong. He continually emphasizes that experiencing and experiences are preferred to teaching. However, this poses a paradox, since it suggests that the techniques advocated by the E-P theorists are in a sense unteachable. This poses a dilemma for parents, too. If the socialization process must occur primarily through the process of direct experience, then the job for parents becomes one of exposing their children to as many varied experiences as possible. Because this approach to teaching is extremely time consuming, it places severe limitations on the total range of teaching parents may engage in. As a result, parents may be tempted to turn over much of their responsibility for child guidance to the child's experiencing, instead of attempting to provide direction and influence.

Rogers (1951) feels that turning over the child's development to the child's own experiencing is not only acceptable, but the right thing to do. This is so because Rogers assumes that the child is innately good (Nye, 1975, Raskin and van der Veen, 1970). Nye criticized this point-of-view in two ways. First, Rogers's assumption is based solely upon his hours of interviews with individual clients in therapy. Outside of the replication of this experience Rogers gives very little evidence to substantiate the reliability of his claims. Nye sees little reason to believe that this approach really reveals the complete nature of man. Nye's second criticism is really a question. If man is innately good, why aren't more people good? What has caused us to fail so frequently in our child rearing and cultural practices? It would appear that the innate qualities, if they exist, must be relatively weak in the face of environmental influences—otherwise they should be more in evidence.

Rogers's position has a great deal of appeal. His efforts have shown that the conditions of warm, empathic understanding and congruent feedback are important ingredients .of positive human interactions. These conditions have been shown to contribute to positive feelings between parents and their children. And, as Nye (1975) notes, Rogers sends us away with good feelings. Rogers's viewpoint is positive and optimistic. He sees man as struggling nobly to become the best he can be, and it is hard to argue against such an approach. Nonetheless, the evidence does not substantiate the strong claims often made by Rogers and his followers that they have discovered an answer to many of man's psychological problems (Koch, 1964).

The Behavioral
Approach

7

Undoubtedly the best-known behaviorist in the United States today is B. F. Skinner. Skinner's principles of operant conditioning have been applied widely in such institutional settings as mental health hospitals and homes for retarded children. More recently, his techniques have been applied in open systems such as the community (Tharp and Wetzel, 1969) and the schools (Haring and Phillips, 1972). The principles have also been specifically applied to discipline and guidance (Becker, 1971; Krumboltz and Krumboltz, 1972; Madsen and Madsen, 1972). While behavioral approaches have not yet circulated as widely as the developmental approach (*see* Chapter Three), the popularity of this method as applied to child rearing is growing.

Skinner (1953; 1974) starts with the basic premise that if we are to develop a science of human behavior we must assume that behavior is lawful and determined. If so, then we should find that how people behave is the result of conditions that can be made specific and which are, therefore, open to the observation of the trained observer, thus applying to psychology the basic premise of the physical sciences. According to Skinner (1953), it should not be assumed that human behavior differs in any peculiar ways which would require unique methods or special knowledge. The techniques of the physical sciences, applied to man, should reveal the specific conditions which lead to behavior, and once discovered these conditions should allow us to predict and to some degree control people's actions.

Behavior comes from a behaving organism (Skinner, 1953). Man, as a behaving organism, is the result of a long genetic history which predisposes him to differ in predictable ways from other species. Body structure is one obvious result of man's genetic history that sets him apart from other organisms. Man's ability to respond to verbal stimuli and the resulting verbal community is, to Skinner, another important result of man's peculiar genetic constitution.

Skinner (1953) cautions, however, that the appeal to heredity as the basis for behavior may lead us away from the relationship between external events and the behaving organism. Knowing that some part of behavior is the result of gross body type or genetic inheritance does not help a great deal. Such knowledge may help us to make better use of other techniques of control over behavior, but we cannot alter the genetic factor itself.

The appeal to heredity as an explanation of behavior is just one of several types of inner states which have been used to try to explain man's actions. The problem with using inner states as explanation is that they cannot be directly observed. Therefore, it is easy to ascribe qualities to them which may be unjustified, and since others are also unable to observe these inner states it becomes impossible to contradict or verify the influence of any given inner state upon behavior.*

---

*An amusing spoof of what can happen under these circumstances may be found in Haley's (1969) last chapter.

A thoroughly scientific view of man requires some method of at least theoretically observing inner states and detailing their influence on behavior. Skinner (1953; 1971; 1974) argues that until we can observe such events we may best proceed to understand man's behavior by sticking with variables that are describable in physical terms. Information about the inner state may shed light upon the nature of the relationship between behavior and the environment that influences it; but such information will not change the relationship (Skinner, 1953).

If we stay with the external variables that influence behavior we may find that there is a functional relationship between the external events and behavior. Such a functional relationship may not explain how an event causes an effect, but it does show that certain events generally occur together in a certain order (Skinner, 1953). When we can construct the relationships between behavior and the external events of which the behavior is a function, we will have constructed a scientific law. From Skinner's work over the past forty years, many of the relationships between the environment and human behavior are now known and can be used to predict behavior.

Wherever prediction is possible, it is also possible by the manipulation of influencing variables to control behavior. Control of human behavior in this sense does not mean forcible coercion. As Skinner (1973) explains we control diseases, not by physically wrestling with them, but by changing some of the conditions under which the disease may exist. Human behavior may be controlled in a similar way: by changing some of the variables which influence a given behavior, we can control the way the behavior exists or whether it exists.

Because parents are charged with the responsibility of socializing their children, they often guide, direct, or control their children's behavior (Blackham and Silberman, 1975). Therefore, understanding the principles of operant conditioning may help parents to teach their children.

The Behavioral View of the Nature of Man

According to Skinner's (1953; 1969; 1971) theory, biological structure and culture are man's twin inheritances. Our evolutionary history has produced an organism, man, capable of responding to a wide range of stimuli within his environment. Our responses to stimuli may in many cases have survival value. Reflexes are an obvious example of inherited characteristics with survival value. An eye blink is important in preventing damage to the eyes; quick removal of the hand from something hot may prevent a painful burn. Reflexes clearly have biological advantages and individuals who behave in these ways are most likely to survive long enough to pass on these adaptive characteristics.

Not all responses to environmental stimuli have so direct a connection to survival, however. Infants respond not only to food, but also to bright shiny objects, movements in their visual field, and a wide range of sounds. Skinner (1953) suggests that the ability to respond to a wide range of stimuli may have biological advantages inasmuch as it prepares the individual to manipulate his environment before he reaches a state of deprivation. The biological, genetic history of the species has prepared the individual to respond to his environment.

The responses we make to the environment are defined as behavior, and "behavior is a primary characteristic of living things" (Skinner, 1953, p. 45). Man is a behaving organism. But man does not behave in a vacuum. Man behaves in a social and nonsocial environment. By far the most important environment is the social one. Man has developed through biological evolution but he has also become what he is by means of the cultural evolution carried out by the species. Just as the biological structure of man has survival value, so does the culture man has devised. Cultures that succeed in helping men to get what they need and to avoid what is dangerous are more likely to survive and be transmitted to future generations (Skinner, 1971). To Skinner, the biological and cultural evolutions of man are very closely related. Man as we know him today is the product of both types of evolution.

According to Skinner (1971), the biological developments that made it possible for man to develop a culture have been critical in man's development. Once that evolutionary change took place culture began to influence man's behavior. The most important biological adaptation in the evolutionary process was undoubtedly the development of speech. Without communication all behavior would be unconscious. Conscious behavior is only possible in a verbal community. Having developed the capacity to speak, man could then begin to transmit to others important responses to the environment. In this way dangers could be avoided and members of the verbal community were more likely to survive.

Behavior, whether in the social or nonsocial environment, has consequences. The consequences of some behaviors feed back information to the organism. Depending on the nature of the feedback, that class of behavior is either more or less likely to happen again in similar circumstances. Skinner (1953) points out that it is not the same response which is repeated, but rather a similar response in the same *class* as the first. The class of events is called an *operant* by Skinner (1953); the word emphasizes the fact that the behavior *operates* on the environment to generate the consequences. A child's crying behavior is an *operant*. It can be described by such properties as how loudly or long the child cries, or whether the crying is accompanied by tears. In this sense, then, an operant may be defined in physical terms.

An operant is behavior that operates on the environment to generate consequences. What are the consequences of a child's crying? One frequent consequence is that someone picks the child up. Picking the child up when crying is *reinforcement* for crying. An operant can be defined in part by the things the child must do before receiving reinforcement, such as how loud and how long the child must cry to get picked up. Whether the tendency to cry increases (as it is likely to do if the child is picked up) or decreases is largely determined by the consequences that follow crying behavior. When such a change occurs we say the child has been *conditioned*.

Throughout most of our waking life we are interacting with the environment, and many of the consequences of our behavior are reinforcing. It is in this way that we learn to ride a bike, read a book, and fix a car. The principles of operant conditioning are as fundamental in the life of man as the law of gravity. Water runs downhill because of gravity, not because it wants to reach the ocean. According to behaviorists, man behaves because his behavior has consequences that are reinforcing, not because he wills it. The picture of man that develops from a strictly scientific analysis "is not of a body with a person inside, but of a body which *is* a person in the sense that it displays a complex repertoire of behavior" (Skinner, 1971, p. 199).

As Skinner earlier said, "The free inner man who is held responsible for the behavior of the external biological organism is only a prescientific substitute for the kinds of causes which are discovered in the course of a scientific analysis. All these alternative causes lie *outside* the individual. The biological substratum itself is determined by prior events in a genetic process. Other important events are found in the nonsocial environment and in the culture of the individual in the broadest possible sense" (Skinner, 1953, pp. 447-48).

But what of choice? Skinner suggests that even when we take the initiative to control the consequences of our own behavior in order to change that behavior we do so as a result of the culture that controls us. "The environment determines the individual even when he alters the environment" (Skinner, 1953, p.

448). Just as man has learned to use the laws which relate to gravity in order to fly, so too man must adapt to using the laws of conditioning to guide his own future development. Behaviorists consider environment responsible both for the evolution of the species and for the highly complex patterns of behavior displayed by the individual. And while the behavior of man is indeed complex, it is nonetheless lawful.

Skinner (1971) provides several examples of the environment controlling behavior rather than the free, inner, autonomous man: Aggression is reinforced by signs of damage to others. Blood, tears, running away may all signal defeat of a threatening enemy. Aggressive behavior may be part of the gene structure; presumably those who are best at defending themselves in a culture where aggression is common would survive and pass on to their offspring the propensity to aggress against others. However, as Skinner (1971) points out, other consequences often follow aggressive behavior. A child may push another child off the toy horse. Not only will he be reinforced by the other child's crying, but he will also take possession of the horse. The consequences which follow immediately after the behavior—that is, that are *contingent* upon the behavior—explain the aggressive act as well as it is explained by saying that the child wished to have the horse.

Skinner (1971) suggests the trait of industry as another example of environmental control replacing control by an inner man. He argues that although it appears to be well established that activity levels are genetically endowed, it is still true that individuals have personal ranges of activity. Therefore the individual will range between sleep and very vigorous activity, depending on the schedules he has been reinforced to follow. The explanation is then moved from an inner trait to the environmental history of reinforcement.

In arguing against the traditional view that man selects those events in his environment to which he gives his attention, Skinner theorizes that once again we can explain the behavior by determining external causes. For Skinner (1971), "The kinds of stimuli which break through by 'attracting attention' do so because they have been associated in the evolutionary history of the species or the personal history of the individual with important—e.g., dangerous—things" (p. 187). It could also be added that we attend to stimuli that have been associated with reinforcing events of any kind.

The advantage of the external explanation is that the contingencies are more open to observation and, therefore, more open to control. We observe the child push the other off the horse and then play with the horse. To reduce the likelihood of future pushing of children off horses we may take the horse from the aggressor. Parents have, of course, been doing this for years. What has been added is an explanation of why it works. Possession of the principle makes it possible for parents to persist when it appears necessary; and the principle makes it possible to apply similar techniques in other situations.

Skinner believes that his theory removes the need for internal explanations of man's behavior. He says that explanations of behavior which depend on the existence of an autonomous inner man lead us to the erroneous conclusion that behavior is uncaused (1971). It is his belief that all behavior is due to external influences explained by the principles of reinforcement. If this is so, then the activities once attributed to autonomous man are removed. The picture of man which emerges is that of man controlled by his environment. That environment is, however, largely manmade. Cultures have evolved in response to the needs of the individual members of those cultures, which means that man's behavior is largely controlled by man.

The Behavioral View of the Nature of Children

Behaviorists view children as born with individual genetic endowments. This unique endowment predisposes the child to behave in many individualistic ways. In addition, the infant begins immediately to develop patterns of behavior under the contingencies of reinforcement to which he is exposed. Because no two individuals are exposed to the same set or sets of contingencies, the uniqueness of the individual continues to grow throughout his lifetime. Most of the contingencies to which the child is exposed are arranged by other people: his parents, teachers, and peers. This is the process of socialization referred to in the introduction to this book. By the constant action of reinforcement the child is gradually taught the skills, knowledge, and attitudes which form part of his culture.

One important part of the contingencies the child is exposed to in his environment is his own body. The child's body is about the only part of the environment that stays with him and stays relatively the same from day to day. Even before he learns to speak he learns to differentiate himself from objects and other persons in his world. It is through this daily exchange with his world that the child comes to recognize "me" and "not me" and thus to develop his identity.*

According to Skinner (1971), the processes of reinforcement act upon the child through all his waking hours to build the basic patterns he will use to keep his balance, sit up, walk, talk, and take part in the life of his family. Changes happen, not because of the passage of time, but because of the reinforcements the child receives for his behavior while time is passing.† The size of the child's vocabulary, his ability to use numbers, and his ability to play complex games are, to Skinner, the result, not of the child's developmental age, but of the contingencies which have prevailed in his family and community. Grasp of the laws of gravity or the golden rule at any given age is due to the social and nonsocial contingencies of reinforcement which generate the behavior that we point to as evidence that the child has the concept. Skinner concludes his argument by stating, "The contingencies 'develop' as much as the behavior they generate" (p. 140). Developmental stages occur because the contingencies for a second stage are built upon the contingencies contained in the first stage. Within a given environment a child may acquire concepts in a developmental sequence, but the order is under control of a given set of contingencies, which may be changed.

Thus if the child's ability to master math or his vocabulary appears to grow, it is because we are focusing on the behavior and not attending to the contingencies. According to Skinner (1971), the behavior is always a function of the contingencies which give rise to it and maintain it.

Skinner's (1971) primary argument against the concept of growth as an explanation of behavior is that it emphasizes the final state without helping us to understand the processes necessary to reach the goal. To say that the child grows *toward* maturity or *in order to reach maturity* only indicates the end and does not tell us how to make progress toward that end.

The Relationship of the Individual to the Group

A group or a culture does not exist independent from the behavior of the individuals who make up the group (Skinner, 1971). It is always the members of

---

*The process for the infant is not dissimilar to the explanation given by Freud (Chapter Two) and Piaget (Chapter Five).

†This is a major point of dispute between the developmentalists, Freud, Gesell, and Piaget (chapters Two, Three, and Five) and Skinner's brand of behaviorism.

a family who maintain the social contingencies which are the characteristic family ways of behaving. Family practices, like genetic traits, are passed from parents to children. Successful family behaviors are learned by the individual members of the family and are then passed on to their children.

The individual is the focal point of many lines of development (Skinner, 1971). The uniqueness of the individual is above question. Each cell of his body is distinctly unique in its genetic inheritance. And even in the most strict and controlling family, every member of the family has a unique personal history.

Attempts by parents to make their children into carbon copies of themselves are unlikely to succeed. Influences by others outside the family, including teachers and the child's peers, as well as differential patterns of reinforcement from the nonsocial environment, shape each child into a unique individual. Skinner notes (1971; 1973) that to try to make all the members of a group alike is a poor design for a group, for it would eliminate the diversity necessary to meet unforeseen environmental events. Such a family or culture would be developing the seeds of its own demise rather than its survival.

Skinner (1971) has stated that group practices that lead the individual to work for the good of others may further the survival of all. Thus if parents are reinforced for sacrificing immediate reinforcement so that their children may have reinforcers, the children will be more likely to survive and pass on the practices of their parents. Within any group, certain values are designed to generate behavior that will have such deferred consequences. "The culture 'makes the future important' by analyzing contingencies, by extracting rules from them, by reinforcing people when they follow the rules, and so on" (Skinner, 1973, p. 262). The individual who makes the best use of the rules extracted by others increases both his own and his group's probability of survival.

While it is always the individual who acts or behaves, it is the group which has the most powerful effect. Group action increases the power of the individual to receive reinforcers. Cooperative behavior often leads to increased reinforcement for each of the individuals involved (Skinner, 1953; Marwell and Schmitt, 1975). This explains group behavior for both pro-social groups such as church organizations and anti-social groups such as delinquent gangs. According to Skinner the reinforcement generated by the group easily exceeds the sums of the consequences which could be generated by any individual acting alone. The total reinforcing effect is greatly increased for each member of the unit, and the action is conditioned.

Group membership has still other ways to "pay off" individual members. Imitation of others, as well as cooperation with others, increases the likelihood of reinforcement (Skinner, 1953). Observation of others behaving and receiving consequences which would be reinforcing to the child increases the probability of the child responding with similar behaviors (Bandura and Walters, 1963).

Social behavior, then, occurs because people are important to other people as part of the social environment. Many kinds of reinforcement occur only in the presence of other people. While some forms of sexual and aggressive behavior require others only as objects, most forms of social reinforcement depend upon others as mediating units (Skinner, 1953; 1957). The statement "bread and jam, please" brings no response from the nonsocial environment. However, in the appropriate social environment it may lead to a primary reinforcer.

Skinner (1953) suggests that behavior which is reinforced through the mediation of others differs markedly from behavior reinforced by the mechanical environment. Social reinforcement is apt to change from time to time, depending upon the state of the reinforcing individual. The child may make several different responses, all of which receive the same effect, while at other times the child's apparently identical behaviors achieve different effects. The child may ask for a drink, something to eat, and permission to go to the bathroom, all of which have been reinforced before; but the parent, who is deeply engrossed in reading a novel, ignores him. At another time the child may ask for a drink three times and receive water, milk, and root beer, depending upon mother's state at the time of asking. The variation in effects following responses which are mediated by others leads, according to Skinner (1953), to a more extensive repertoire of social behaviors. Social behavior may also become more flexible under these circumstances, since the child will shift much more readily from one form of response to another when his behavior is not effective.

The social environment is clearly man-made. It shapes the language a person speaks, the customs he adheres to, and his responses to religion, government, ethics, education, and economics. Just as the individual controls himself by manipulating the world in which he lives, so does the culture man has created act to control the behavior of its members. The culture is in a sense a huge exercise in self-control, for "the man that man has made is the product of the culture man has devised" (Skinner, 1971, p. 208).

Having concluded that the social environment controls the individual's behavior more than the individual controls his environment, Skinner (1953) reasons that it will be far more effective to change the culture to bring about desired changes in human behavior than to change individuals. This is so because any change effected within the individual's behavior will be lost at his death. Changes in the culture tend to have much more enduring effects, since cultures tend to survive for longer periods. Skinner suggests that we might do well to begin to look to a philosophy which places more emphasis on the survival of the group and less emphasis on the individual (1953, 1971). For families this would mean more emphasis upon doing things for and with the family and for the good of the family. Members of the family would be reinforced more strongly for cooperative acts and for sacrificing self-goals if it means attaining family goals. If survival of the family culture is valued highly, then that survival could best be assured by placing the family good above the good of the individual. This can only be accomplished if the individual members of the family are encouraged to behave in this way by proper reinforcement, as families are created by individual actions and survive only through the behavior of individuals (Skinner, 1953).

If, as Skinner's (1953, 1971) analysis would lead us to believe, man's behavior is shaped by the society in which he lives, little actual control is left to the individual. Why then should parents teach their children self-control, and if they decide to teach it what is it that they are teaching?

Self-awareness and Self-control

Skinner defines a self as "a repertoire of behavior appropriate to a given set of contingencies" (1971, p. 199).* Thus the patterned set of behaviors one emits when his parents are around make up his self as known to his parents. The patterns one uses with one's friends may be similar to those exhibited in the presence of parents or they may differ markedly. In this way the individual may have numerous selves, each generated by different sets of contingencies.

Skinner (1971) suggests that self-knowledge and self-control are two selves in this sense. That is, they are two repertoires of behaviors which are appropriate for two sets of contingencies. The self that is known and the self which does the knowing and the controlling come from differing sources. The self that is known is most likely the genetic self, the biological organism that Freud referred to as

---

*Compare Skinner's description of self with the description given by the existential-phenomenologists (Chapter Six).

the id. The knowing and controlling self stems from the social environment and corresponds to Freud's superego, or what many refer to as the conscience.

We "know" ourselves to the extent that we can observe our own behavior. What is known is our responses to various stimuli and the stimuli themselves. We know our responses, whether they are external, such as writing one's name in the blank where it says "Name," or whether they are internal, such as thinking of one of our favorite things. Writing and thinking are both responses to stimuli. The stimuli, like the responses, may be internal or external; the processes remain the same.

Distinguishing between the controlled self and the controlling self, even when they are contained within the same skin, helps us to understand how changing the culture is an exercise in self-control. As Skinner (1971) states, "When a person changes his physical or social environment 'intentionally'—that is, in order to change human behavior, possibly including his own—he plays two roles: one as a controller, as the designer of a controlling culture, and another as the controlled, as the product of a culture" (pp. 206-7). Skinner (1953) also said, "A man may spend a great deal of time designing his own life—he may choose the circumstances in which he is to live with great care, and he may manipulate his daily environment on an extensive scale. Such activity appears to exemplify a high order of self-determination. But it is also behavior, and we account for it in terms of other variables in the environment and history of the individual. It is these variables which provide the ultimate control" (p. 240).

Utilizing internal variables as guides to behavior is extremely difficult. Although we are very close to our own body states it is very difficult to discriminate one state from another. The problem of helping a child discriminate between fear and anger is increased because parents have little access to the internal states of the child which might serve to help us to help the child discriminate. While it is a fairly easy problem to help a child discriminate between circles and squares by reinforcing verbal responses in the presence of various shapes, we cannot follow the same procedures in teaching him the difference between two emotional states. It is impossible to have the two emotions at the same time for comparison: "this half of you is experiencing fear, and that half is anger."

Much more typically we approach the problem of emotional states through external behaviors. Aggression, whether verbal or nonverbal, is usually attributed to anger, although at times we fight when we are afraid and do not wish to show it. Loving acts, such as kind, soft words, caresses, and thoughtful acts for others, are usually attributed to feelings of affection. When we see the child behaving in these ways we may attach verbal meanings to the internal states, which we only *assume* accompany these acts. For example, "When you bite and hit your friend you must be very angry" and "You must love your sister very much to share your cookies with her like that." In this way it becomes evident that self-knowledge and self-management are derived from social interaction. The contingencies which give rise to responses such as "I love you" or "I'm really angry right now" require a verbal community (Skinner, 1973).

Self-awareness is one type of adaptation to the environment. Such awareness may help to solve problems if a person takes effective remedial action. In some cases self-awareness may interfere with the correct behavior. Skinner (1971) gives the example of the concert pianist. His skilled movements would be disrupted should he make a conscious effort to be aware of them. Skinner concludes, "The extent to which a man *should* be aware of himself depends upon the importance of self-observation for effective behavior. Self-knowledge is valuable only to the extent that it helps to meet the contingencies under which it has arisen" (Skinner, 1971, p. 193).

We can conclude from the discussion of the individual and the group that Skinner sees the two as inseparable. Man as an individual does not really exist as we know him outside of his meaningful social groups. The culture, though it is designed and acted out by men, also controls the behavior of man the individual through the ordering of contingencies. In some ways this is close to Freud's concepts of man and the group. Freud felt (*see* Chapter Two) that the culture served to hold the biological instinctive behavior of man in check. And while Skinner does not postulate that diabolical drives are held back by cultural practice, he does agree that culture serves as control over the behavior of the individual. Skinner's analysis of the contingencies helps us to see the relationships between the individual's behavior and the behavior of others in the social group.

How Children Acquire Behavior

The behavioral approach has become highly technical as research into the nature of behavior develops. In the discussion which follows a number of the key technical ideas will be discussed and their implications for child rearing indicated.

Skinner (1953) reserves the term *learning* for the process of re-sorting responses in complex situations. He uses the term *reinforcement* for events which strengthen behavior and *conditioning* for all the resulting changes in behavior. The two cases of reinforcement available are the *classical conditioning* model first discovered by Pavlov and the *operant conditioning model*.

Classical conditioning. In the Pavlovian model a stimulus is presented *with* a reinforcer. The change in behavior follows these events; for example, the child may be presented with a Halloween mask (stimulus) at the same time someone slams a door (reinforcer). Young children often cry in response to loud noises and show other reflex behaviors, such as the typical startle pattern. The child will show evidence of conditioning if when presented with the mask at a later time he also shows some of the fear reactions. Fear reactions are often found to be associated with cases of classical conditioning. The important factors to be noted about classical conditioning are that the stimulus and the reinforcer are *paired*— that is, they occur together—and that the behavior which is to be conditioned *follows* the stimulus and reinforcing events.

Operant conditioning. In the operant conditioning model the sequence of events differs markedly. The child is presented with a stimulus to which he responds with some behavior. Following his response he is presented with a reinforcer. These three events define a contingency: a stimulus, followed by a response, followed by reinforcement. The infant lying in the crib may observe a mobile (stimulus) over his head. He swings his arm and strikes the mobile (response), whereupon the mobile spins and bounces (reinforcer). If the child swings his arm in the direction of the mobile more frequently following this series of events we take that increase in frequency as evidence of conditioning having taken place. The term *operant* emphasizes the fact that it is the child's behavior which operates upon the environment to produce consequences. Some of those consequences feed back to the child (he sees the mobile spin and dance) in such a way that they increase the likelihood of repetition of the class of behaviors which produced the effect. The importance of feedback is clear. The child must be stimulated by the consequences of his behavior for conditioning to occur.

The sequence in operant conditioning is stimulus, response, and reinforcement. The important property of the contingency is temporal. Behavior is followed by reinforcement. It does not matter to the child how the reinforcement (movement of the mobile) occurs; as long as it follows arm swinging, arm swinging is likely to be increased. "Operants grow strong because they are followed by important consequences in the life of the *individual*" (Skinner, 1953, p. 90).

As our understanding of the effects of contingencies increases, we can more often predict what the child will do. The more accurate our observation of the contingencies, the more accurate our predictions. Furthermore, by arranging contingencies we can increase the probability that a child will respond in a given way.

Some Descriptive Properties of Reinforcers.*

	Presentation	Withdrawal	Withhold all
Positive Reinforcer	A. Positive reinforcement; increases behavior.	B. Punishment; reduces behavior.	C. Extinction; reduces behavior.
Negative Reinforcer	D. Punishment; decreases behavior.	E. Negative reinforcement; increases behavior	

Properties of reinforcement. Reinforcers have a number of important properties (*see* accompanying diagram). Skinner (1953) begins by defining a positive reinforcer as "any stimulus the *presentation* of which strengthens the behavior upon which it is made contingent. . . . A negative reinforcer (an aversive stimulus) is any stimulus the *withdrawal* of which strengthens the behavior." Note that both of these conditions serve to reinforce or strengthen the response they follow. It is important to note that in the case of a negative reinforcer it is the absence after presence of the stimulus which reinforces. As shown in the diagram, presentation of a positive reinforcer or removal of a negative reinforcer are similar to rewards, while their opposites are punishments. The effect of removing a positive reinforcer is to somewhat reduce the likelihood of repetition of the class of behavior which preceded it. Presenting a negative reinforcer has a similar effect. Parents sometimes "ground" a child by restricting him to the home or to his room following some misbehavior. Withholding a child's freedom is an example of removing a positive reinforcer. Spanking a child for a misdeed is a common example of presenting a negative reinforcer.

Individuals differ in the kinds of events that reinforce them. Different children often respond very differently, as most parents will readily attest. The only way to tell exactly what is reinforcing for a given child at a given time is to make a test: the parents observe the child and count the number of times he performs the behavior they are interested in seeing increase or decrease. After they have collected this "baseline" information, they make what they believe will be a reinforcing event contingent upon the behavior (if they wish to increase it) and continue to count the frequency of occurrence. If the frequency increases, they know that the event is reinforcing to the child at that time. For example, if the parents wish to increase the incidence of the child's saying "please" and "thank you," they would count the number of times he says "please" and "thank you" appropriately during the week. Following this they praise the child lavishly each time he says "please" and "thank you." If they do this for a week or two and

---

*From *The Analysis of Behavior* by Holland and Skinner. Copyright 1961, by McGraw Hill Book Company. Used with permission of McGraw Hill Book Company.

continue to keep count of the times the child responds correctly, they will be able to tell if their praise is indeed reinforcing the desired behavior. If the behavior increases, the praise is reinforcing for the child, at this time.

What is reinforcing for an individual at any particular time largely depends on the history of reinforcement and conditioning he has received (Skinner, 1953). Of course, response to *primary* reinforcers—food, water, sleep, sexual contact—is undoubtedly due to hereditary survival qualities carried in the individual's genetic history. "Food, water, and sexual contact, as well as escape from injurious conditions are obviously connected with the well-being of the organism. An individual who is readily reinforced by such events will acquire highly efficient behavior" (Skinner, 1953, p. 83).

Many events come to be reinforcing because of their association with primary reinforcers. These are *conditioned* reinforcers. Children often get very excited when placed in their high chairs because of the anticipation of eating, even though there was originally nothing inherently reinforcing about sitting in the chair. The high chair is a conditioned reinforcer. Events which lead up to pleasant experiences often gain reinforcing properties. Thus planning for a vacation can often be as pleasant as the trip. Children behave well before Christmas or other special holidays when parents make their participation in the events contingent upon good behavior.

Many conditioned reinforcers such as holidays and special events have become *generalized* reinforcers. Generalized reinforcers usually gain their power to reinforce by first being associated with more than one primary reinforcer. Praise, for example, comes to be a generalized reinforcer after it has been frequently paired with several primary reinforcers such as being fed by mother and father or being held (physical contact). If parents have paired praise with these acts frequently, we might reasonably expect praise to act as a reinforcer for saying "please" and "thank you" at appropriate times.

Some events, such as attention, are important and become generalized reinforcers because they help the child to receive other reinforcers. The child is not likely to receive a drink of water by asking unless he first has a parent's attention. Attention may therefore be used as a reinforcer. Some mothers become "deaf" to a child's requests unless they first hear the word "please." In this way asking preceded by saying "please" is reinforced.

Attention may not be enough, according to Skinner (1953). Often to gain reinforcement from others we must also have their approval. In this way any sign of approval from others may gain reinforcing properties. A smile or the words "that's good" or "you're doing fine," become generalized reinforcers because they have often been paired with primary reinforcers of one type or another.

In a similar manner, affectionate acts become generalized reinforcers. People who act affectionately toward children often dispense other rewards as well. Therefore, according to Skinner, the child learns to respond to those people who are affectionate toward him just as he learns to respond to other generalized reinforcers. Often just being around persons who have shown us affection is reinforcing. Parents sometimes condition certain behaviors in this way. For example, the father who says to his son, "If you complete your math homework assignments each night this week I'll take you fishing Saturday," is using the reinforcer of fishing plus his presence to increase the probability of math homework being done during the week.

Generalized reinforcers recognized because of their physical specifications are *tokens*. The most common token is money. Money comes to have great reinforcing value because it can be exchanged for many kinds of primary reinforcers. Like the other generalized reinforcers, it can often be reinforcing at times when a primary reinforcer would not be effective. One may not be inclined to work for a second steak dinner if it could only be consumed immediately following the first. The individual is satiated on food when he has eaten to his satisfaction. The food-satiated organism is not easily reinforced by food. However, that same individual may work for money which he will later use to purchase another steak.

Parents sometimes set up token systems to reinforce children's behaviors in the home. Picking up the clothes off one's bedroom floor may be worth two blue chips, dusting may be worth three, and ironing a shirt one. At the end of the week blue chips may be redeemed for candy, a shopping trip with mother, or a trip to the ice cream store with dad for a banana split. Having a variety of things one might trade one's chips for increases the likelihood of the chips remaining as generalized reinforcers. Having only one thing they may be used for may fail to reinforce because the child becomes satiated on that reinforcer during the week.

Extinction. When reinforcement is withheld following a response, the response becomes less and less frequent. The process of reducing the frequency of a response by withholding all reinforcement is called *operant extinction.* If we turn the key of the car and the car won't start, we eventually stop turning the key. If parents totally ignore tantrum behavior, tantrums slowly subside.

Extinction is an effective way of removing operant behavior. However, some of the properties of extinction should be understood by parents. First, extinction is the result of the conditioning which has built the behavior. If the child has been reinforced for only a few responses then the behavior may extinguish very quickly. The longer the history of reinforcement, the longer the extinction process. Thus the child who has only "gotten his way" (i.e., been reinforced) for a few tantrums will quickly extinguish tantrums if parents completely ignore the tantrum behavior. On the other hand, if the child has been rewarded for tantrums over a long period of time, extinction takes considerably longer.

There are emotional side effects, however: the extinction process is often accompanied by displays of frustration and rage. When accustomed reinforcers are no longer forthcoming, organisms often react emotionally. On finding that the car won't start we often pump the gas pedal furiously, twist the key back and forth violently, cuss a little, and possibly hit the dashboard. The child who is not getting a response to his tantrum may increase the violence of his arm and leg flailing, scream louder, and cry more and longer. Parents need to be aware that things may get worse before they get better when extinction procedures are used. Not being aware of the emotional response to extinction may lead parents to accidently reinforce the behavior in an even more disturbing form. In one case a child accidently hit his head against a closet door during a tantrum his mother was attempting to ignore. The resulting loud bang brought such a sudden and active response from mother that from then on whenever he had a tantrum he managed to bang his head against a door. When emotion accompanies extinction we often find that the behavior increases in frequency or strength for a period of time and then begins to fall away. There may be several periods of increase in emotion as tension builds up and then fades. If parents are prepared for these occasional flare-ups they can better wait them out while extinguishing the behavior.

Shaping. Children learn complex skills, attitudes, and value patterns by the slow processes of conditioning and extinction. Skinner (1953) suggests that operant conditioning shapes behavior in much the same way a sculptor shapes a lump of clay. After much work the sculptor seems to have created a completely novel design. However, we can always go back to each of the small successive steps which led to the final effect. We may follow this process back to the original undifferentiated lump, if we wish. The final product may appear unique but the processes which created it did not create it "whole." The same thing may be said for complex behavior such as riding a bike. Complex behavior is the result of continuous *shaping* by the environment.*

Learning to walk, to speak, to read, and to do complex equations in math—all are accomplished by gradual shaping through reinforcement and extinction. Incorrect behavior is extinguished or punished, and correct behavior rewarded. Thus as the child mispronounces a word, such as saying "ripte" for "ripe," we say, "No, that's not right" (mild punishment). "The word is ripe" (cueing the correct pronunciation). We then reward the child, when he does it right, by praise and affection. "Ripte" is a close approximation which leads to the correct response—but only through reinforcement procedures.

Correct behavior is built up a small step at a time. To help a child learn a difficult skill parents are most successful if they break the process down into the smallest steps possible and then reinforce each of the correct steps as the child progresses. Because they overlook the small steps done correctly, parents often fail to take advantage of the child's doing part of the job right. (*See* the discussion of improving the self-concept in Chapter Six.) In this way they miss an opportunity to reinforce the part the child did right, and when they punish the child for not doing it completely right, the child responds as if being punished for doing it all wrong. The result is that the parent weakens the tendency to respond.

Maintaining Behavior

According to Skinner's (1953; 1971) analysis, behavior takes place in the present. Conditioning in the history of the individual and the variables in the present environment are responsible for the behavior in the current situation, and they also determine the behavior in future situations. Behaviorists predict future events, not from cause to effect, but rather from effect to effect (1953). Predictions of the child's future behavior are based on what the parents see him do right now in response to a given set of stimuli, and based on his present rates of response, which are a function of his conditioning history. If the event in the future is similar to a present event in its stimulus values; if the individual is in a similar state of deprivation; and if there have been no marked changes in his reinforcement history, then we might expect that he will respond with a similar class of operants—that is, effects will be similar. Thus the effects in the present situation are used to predict the effects in the future situation.

The principles of reinforcement may help us to understand how skilled responses which have been generated by relatively precise contingencies may survive in the human organism for half a lifetime. Early experiences may determine later behavior, if they are well reinforced and if they have not been extinguished.

Forgetting. Forgetting, according to Skinner (1953) should not be confused with extinction. In forgetting the effect of conditioning is simply lost as time passes. Lacking opportunity to practice an operant is not the same as producing the operant and not receiving reinforcement following the response. Extinction requires that the response be emitted and not reinforced. Thus behavior which has been strongly reinforced but which has not been used for some time may return to full force relatively quickly. The adult who has not ridden a bike for years may have the opportunity to ride and find that he quickly regains his previous skill.

Early conditioning builds through gradual shaping the complex sets of

---

*When the material to be taught is highly specialized or technical, parents often turn the teaching over to specialists in schools, religious institutions, and various vocational preparation institutions from apprenticeships to professional schools.

probabilities of response which we speak of as thinking, creativity, and planning for the future. It is through the shaping process, in which some behaviors are reinforced and others extinguished, that the individual's early experiences place their mark on the future. There are no dark and mysterious forces which work to bring out the behavior. This is in contrast to Freud's explanation (*see* Chapter Two) of how early experience works on the adult. According to the behaviorists, if we know the history of the individual and his current schedule of reinforcement, then we can predict fairly well his future behavior in similar circumstances.

Reinforcement schedules. Reinforcement can follow a response in a number of ways. If a response is reinforced every time it is emitted, it is said to be on a *continuous reinforcement* schedule. Continuous reinforcement is most useful in strengthening a particular operant or training a new one. For example, if the child can say "thank you" but does not do it very often, the parents may build up the frequency by reinforcing the child every time he says "thank you." However, if we wish the child to continue to say "thank you," we must change from continuous reinforcement to some other schedule, since one of the principle weaknesses of the continuous reinforcement schedule is that it is relatively easily extinguished.

In addition to continuous reinforcement there are two general patterns which may also be used: *interval* and *ratio* reinforcement schedules. When a given amount of time must elapse after the last reinforcement before another reinforcement occurs we speak of it as interval reinforcement. In a fixed-interval schedule, the time between reinforcements is definite, as in the time between paydays for people on wages or salary. Or an interval schedule may be set to vary from a few seconds to five minutes, with an average time lapse of two and one-half minutes. This type of schedule is known as a variable-interval schedule.

Fixed-interval schedules produce positively accelerated patterns of response (Ferster and Skinner, 1957; Holland and Skinner, 1961; Thompson and Grabowski, 1972). That is, the number of responses increases as the next time for reinforcement approaches. Parents often see the same patterns when they use fixed-interval reinforcement. For example, "I'll give you fifteen minutes to clean up that bedroom" often results in ten minutes of "lollygagging" and five minutes of cleaning up the bedroom.

Variable-interval reinforcement produces a moderate but rather steady output of responses. The wavelike quality of the fixed-interval schedule is not apparent. A parent might produce this type of schedule by looking in every once in awhile on a child who is doing his homework, reinforcing him if he is studying. For some children, the parent's merely looking in will constitute a reinforcement. For others something more concrete is necessary.

It should be recalled that operants, such as studying behaviors, grow strong (increase in frequency) when followed by important consequences. What is an important consequence for one child may not be for another.

In addition to interval schedules, reinforcement can be dispensed on ratio schedules, which means that a number of responses occur without reinforcement before a response is again reinforced. Fixed-ratio schedules require a fixed number of responses to be emitted between reinforcements. Fixed-ratio schedules typically generate high rates of response with little or no pausing after reinforcement (Ferster and Skinner, 1957; Holland and Skinner, 1961; Thompson and Grabowski, 1972). Parents sometimes contract with their children to reinforce behavior on a fixed-ratio schedule: for example, "I'll give you five cents for every ten pages you read for your English class." By slowly increasing the number of responses required for reinforcement as the child's skill picks up, large numbers of responses can be established and maintained. A pigeon on a fixed-ratio schedule of nine hundred responses to one reinforcement gave 73,000 responses in the first 4½ hours following termination of reinforcement (Holland and Skinner, 1961).

Variable-ratio schedules may also be established. Variable-ratio schedules generate rather high rates of response and are highly resistant to extinction. Many forms of gambling are established on a variable-ratio schedule. Slot machines are carefully programmed to pay off (reinforce) the players on a variable ratio. On variable-ratio schedules reinforcement may come on the next response following a reinforcement, or it may take many responses before another reinforcement occurs. Usually the schedule is designed to reinforce on an average number of responses, say five or ten or fifteen, with some upper and lower limits set.

Returning to our earlier example of teaching the child to be consistent and persistent in saying "thank you": resistance to extinction is developed by changing from a continuous reinforcement schedule to a variable schedule. The transition is important. Reinforcement should be frequent at first, with the ratio only slowly widened. In addition, the ratio must become more and more unpredictable as time goes on. Once the child is saying "thank you" consistently, we may begin to reinforce only every other time, then sometimes every second time and other times every third time, then occasionally going as long as five times.

The observing parent or student will note that the variable pattern is not uncommon. We tend to be somewhat unreliable in dispensing reinforcement, and as a result our children are frequently reinforced, for good or ill, on variable schedules. For example, the child who seeks to get his mother's attention while she is on the phone or talking to a neighbor is successful sometimes on the first try, sometimes on the third, and sometimes on the tenth. Because he has been reinforced on a variable-ratio schedule, such attention-seeking behavior is very difficult to extinguish once it has been established.

Schedules of reinforcement are important for the maintenance of behavior, whether it be good behavior or misbehavior. When parents wish to have a behavior persist, they should see that the behavior is placed on a variable schedule with frequent enough reinforcement to keep it going at the level they desire. It is important that we recognize that the behavior *will not* stay in force without reinforcement. If the behavior is not emitted, forgetting will occur. If the behavior is frequently emitted without reinforcement, extinction will occur and the response will slowly fade from the child's repertoire.

Application of Behavioral Theory to Child Rearing

Parents are an important part of the child's world. Therefore changes in the parents' behavior will change the child's environment significantly, especially if the parents shift from punishment to reinforcement of desirable behaviors (Rozynko, Swift, Swift, and Boggs, 1973). Persons who reinforce others become generalized reinforcers. Their attention is rewarding as well as their approval. Positive reinforcement is seen by children as loving behavior (Madsen and Madsen, 1972). Increasing positive reinforcement may be seen, therefore, as increasing the affection between parents and children.

If such positive results are likely to occur, what prevents parents from taking action? In family life it is often difficult to identify who is responsible for actions and even which actions are responsible for the behavior which occurs. The family is a system of exchanges of reinforcement and punishment. Frequently such systems serve to protect parents and other members of the family from criticism, while at the same time the system prevents anyone from taking any effective action (Rozynko, et al., 1973). Family members often feel that if the other person would only change in the desired direction then everything would be resolved. For example, the parents may be heard to comment that "if only the kids would do this or that, then everything would get better around here." Everyone wants the other person to change first (Stuart, 1969; Watzlawick, et al., 1967). However, according to behaviorists, if parents wish to make changes in their child's behavior they must make significant changes in their child's environment. And since parents are one of the most significant aspects of the child's environment, they must make changes in their own behavior.

Why parents punish. At present, parents frequently resort to punishment as a corrective device. Why do parents continue to use punishment despite the admonitions of child development experts over the past fifty years? The explanation is in the functional relationship of punishing the child to the parents' behavior: punishing behavior gets reinforced. When the child is punished for an annoying behavior the child temporarily stops. The terminating of the annoying behavior is highly reinforcing to the parent. This withdrawing of a negative reinforcer has the rewarding effects described earlier in this chapter. As a result, the next time the child presents the annoying behavior the parents will be more likely to apply punishment.

Effects of punishment. Skinner (1953; 1971) has spoken out strongly against punishment as a child-rearing technique. Though punishment is a most effective technique in eliminating a response (Skinner, 1953; Azrin and Holz, 1966), the change in behavior is achieved at tremendous cost. One of the principal disadvantages in the use of punishment is that the punished child is driven away from the punishing parent. The close interpersonal relationship so necessary between parent and child may be destroyed if the most frequent form of interaction between the two is punishing. (Compare this with the discussion of effects of punishment on self-concept in Chapter Six.)

Punishment weakens a response because any behavior that ends the punishment is rewarded by the end of the punishment. If a child escapes from his father's spanking by running away, he is negatively reinforced for running away. He is more likely to try to run away the next time his father corrects his behavior by spanking. One response to punishment is, therefore, *escape* behavior.

At the same time the child is receiving a spanking, he is associating the punishment with all manner of cues related to the spanking. The parent hopes that he is associating the misbehavior with the spanking so that as he approaches the forbidden deed he will recall the punishment and avoid the misbehavior. *Avoidance* is another response to punishment. However, it is often difficult to control the cues the child attaches to the punishment. As the father is closer in time to the punishment than is the misbehavior, it is probable that the child sees father as the cue that punishment is about to follow. Should this be the case, the child is just as likely to avoid father as to avoid the misbehavior. Skinner states (1953) that the first effect of the aversive stimuli used in punishment is confined to the immediate situation. It need not be followed by any change in behavior in later situations.

When punished behavior is strong it also brings about reflexes characteristic of fear, anxiety, and other emotions. Rage or frustration may result from real or imagined restraint. The result may be *counteraggression.*

Escape, avoidance, and counteraggression are the most common responses to punishing stimuli or situations (Skinner, 1973). Counteraggression can be directed toward the punishing parent or, if that is too dangerous because of the risk of further punishment from the parent, the child may turn his aggressive feelings on others nearby. Siblings are the most frequent recipients of redirected counteraggression. Azrin and Holz (1966) note that both avoidance and counteraggression are disruptive of the important social relations in well-functioning families.

Furthermore, Skinner (1953) has noted that if the child is punishing himself through guilt feelings or other avoidance techniques the rage and frustration the child feels cannot be escaped by normal means. The behaviors which result may appear strange and bizarre. Indeed, this is one explanation for "psychosomatic" illness. Certainly such behaviors will interfere with the normal effective behaviors required by the individual in his daily living.

Why punishment is ineffective in changing behavior. Punishment does not permanently weaken responses (Skinner, 1953). It suppresses the behavior temporarily by substitution of an emotional reaction. If the emotional reaction serves to prevent the child from performing the act, but the behavior still has strong reinforcement qualities for the child, the child will continue to approach. Approaching without getting punished extinguishes the punishment (negative reinforcer). The avoiding behavior is then less and less strongly reinforced (avoidance is escape from punishment: no punishment means no avoidance). Therefore the punished behavior slowly emerges. If punishment is discontinued the behavior may emerge in full strength. If the child occasionally performs the misbehavior without punishment and is reinforced for the act he is on an intermittent reinforcement schedule which makes the behavior even more persistent.

Alternatives to punishment. One alternative to punishment is extinction. Extinction requires that the behavior be emitted by the child and that it not be followed by any reinforcer. For example, to eliminate a child's whining behavior, *every* time the child whines the parents would have to ignore the child and his behavior. When the child is not whining, the parents should give him attention and approval for positive behavior. Persistence in this behavior should reduce the whining over a reasonable period of time.

Some behaviors may be weakened by the passage of time. If the occasions that elicit the behavior are avoided, forgetting takes place. The problem with this approach is the necessity to avoid occasions for the behavior and the slowness of the desired change.

A third method available to parents for reducing undesirable behavior is to condition, by positive reinforcement, an acceptable behavior which will interfere with the undesirable behavior. The process of reinforcing an *incompatible behavior* has several advantages. First, it prevents the undesirable behavior from occurring, thus preventing it from being strengthened by further reinforcement. Second, the relationship between the parent and the child improves because the parent is busy looking for opportunities to reinforce the positive behavior rather than trying to catch the child in misbehavior. And third, the parent is teaching the child a new, more socially useful behavior.

An example of treating an undesirable behavior through strengthening an incompatible behavior may be taken from the following case history. As time approached for a school party several of the teachers became concerned. One little girl was in the habit of pinching the other little girls to the point of making them cry. The teachers were concerned that the party would be ruined if this happened. After consulting with the author the teachers decided to ask the girl to pass the pickles, or whatever else was close at hand, any time she appeared about to pinch someone. Obviously she couldn't be pinching and passing the pickles at the same time. In addition, the teachers could reward her with praise and smiles for performing the positive act of pickle passing. The teachers followed through on this and everyone enjoyed the party.

In some cases, undesirable behavior may be eliminated by use of the satiation principle (Krumboltz and Krumboltz, 1972). In this case the parents either allow or require the child to repeat the behavior without reinforcement until the child tires of it. A spitting child may be handed a small eight-ounce paper cup and be directed to fill it up. Some cautions to be observed in this technique include avoiding accidental reinforcement of the misbehavior. Removing the child from the sight and sound of other children who might cheer the child on is important. It is also important that the actual behavior to be removed is satiated. Writing one hundred times "I will not talk back" will satiate writing, but will probably do little about the talking back (Krumboltz and Krumboltz, 1972).

A final advantage of parents' seeking positive alternatives to punishment will be a more positive self-image for the child. As Rozynko and others (1973) point out, when we live in communities that verbally punish behavior we learn to behave similarly: we punish others and ourselves verbally. If, on the other hand, we live in communities that verbally reinforce positive behavior we learn to reinforce our own positive behavior with verbal reinforcement. If the child has positive words to describe himself he will build a positive self-image. In this way, too, children may learn to be internally motivated. If we tell the child that he must feel good inside when he shares with his sisters or others, then he will learn to tell himself that he feels good when he shares. As Becker (1971) puts it, parents should practice "catching the children being good."

Criticisms of the Behavioral Approach

The most frequently criticized aspects of the behavioral approach are Skinner's arguments related to free will and freedom of choice, the nature of control in human behavior, the use of punishment, and the extent to which the findings of behaviorism may be extended from the laboratory into the more complex fields of human interaction.

The issue of determinism and freedom of choice is perhaps the most criticized concept in Skinner's radical behaviorism (Nye, 1975). Skinner (1953; 1971; 1974) has taken the position that all behavior is determined by environmental and hereditary influences and that free will or free choice is an illusion built upon our cultural conditioning. Rogers (1964) and others (Mahoney, 1974; Novak, 1973; Platt, 1973; and Ritchie-Calder, 1973) have criticized this position. The critics argue that man can and must make subjective choices which cannot be predicted. The existential-phenomenological theorists argue against Skinner's rather rigid determinism on the basis of statistical randomness and the complexity of the human organism (Platt, 1973; Ritchie-Calder, 1973; Rosen, 1973). Mahoney (1974) argues against total determinism on the basis of evidence he has accumulated about the functions of cognitive processes. Mahoney believes that cognitive processes mediate the individual's behavior in ways which are not explained by strict conditioning laws. Malcolm (1964) notes that the issues have a long and emotional history in philosophy and it is clear that Skinner's arguments have not resolved the issues.

Behaviorism's insistence on determinism has frequently raised the spectre of a world in which all behavior is controlled by big brother. Skinner has argued that control, through the exchange of reinforcements, exists at all levels of behavioral interaction regardless of whether it is deliberate or not. The issue of control in human interaction became especially heated following Skinner's publication of *Beyond Freedom and Dignity* (1971). Many people seem willing to allow considerable control to be exercised over the behavior of prisoners, mental patients, and retarded individuals. Many people are willing also for considerable control to be exercised over children at school and at home. However, with serious contention that adult behavior is under the control of others, either deliberately or indirectly, the debate begins. Rogers (1956) and others (Black, 1973; Perelman, 1973) ask who will control the controllers. None of these critics find Skinner's (1971; 1973) suggestion that we develop "effective counter-control [by bringing] some important consequences to bear on the behavior of the controller" (1971; p. 171) very reassuring.

Another frequent criticism of Skinner's work is that he treats human beings as objects to be controlled and manipulated (Nye, 1975). Deliberate control of human behavior has frequently been denounced as devaluing human individuality. Perelman (1973), for example, takes strong exception to Skinner's position, suggesting that all forms of control are subject to corruption. Therefore control by conditioning is also subject to corruption.

Recently Skinner's position on punishment has come under criticism (Nye, 1975). According to Nye there is a growing body of research which indicates that punishment works. That is, under certain conditions punishment may lead to rather permanent changes in behavior without the counterproductive side effects suggested by Skinner (1953). Further research may shed light on this important issue, which is so central to the efforts of many parents in socializing their children.

The last criticism of behaviorism is the issue of generalization. The question is how far the basic laboratory findings can be generalized to the complex issues of human functioning. Skinner (1953; 1971; 1974) has frequently suggested the need to apply the methods of science, by which he means behaviorism, to issues of education, politics, and community living. Many have criticized him on this issue. Nye (1975) suggests that the tenets of behaviorism may be too narrow, too limited to be applied to all areas of human behavior; that while behavioral techniques have been found to be effective in limited closed environments such as schools, hospitals, and institutions, there is no evidence that they will prove effective in resolving such complex problems of human behavior as are found, for example, in the political arena.

Skinner's work has been criticized largely in terms of his theoretical or metaphysical concepts. The research which describes the nature of reinforcement and the relationship of stimuli to behavior remains relatively unchallenged. The issue appears to be whether or not *all* behavior can be reduced to the basic elements of discriminative stimuli, responses, and reinforcing stimuli. And this continues to be an open question.

Epilogue

It is interesting that all the theories reviewed regard the spirit of enquiry and contribution to the good of others as the desirable result of child rearing. That message comes through in psychoanalysis as part of the ego ideal in the super-ego. In Gesell's developmental-maturational approach it is seen as innate and to be fostered by the "democratic family." Adler makes a good point of "social interest" and Piaget sees the culminating point of adolescence as the development of a sense of oneness with all mankind. The existential-phenomenological theorists emphasize the inherent potential for including others as one becomes self-actualized. Skinner believes that any culture which does not condition those values into its members will not long survive.

Many of the problems parents face daily in their child-rearing practices could undoubtedly be helped by answers to the questions raised in the several theories found in this book. Until the answers are found, the work of socializing our children must continue. Wise parents will use the best information available today combined with love and understanding. Hopefully they will instill or keep alive within their children a spirit of enquiry and a willingness to contribute to the good of all mankind.

Appendix

TO: Swan and Oregon Staffs
FROM: Jimmy Hymes

DATE: June 4, 1945
SUBJECT: Just Something to
Think About # 4

SUB-TITLE: The Child on the Pot Has His Personality in a Pliable Position

"All I do is toilet kids. I never teach them anything. . . ." "In the early morning we have our creative activities. But with large groups so much of the rest of the day is taken up with routines. . . ." Have you ever heard it?

What do we mean by routines? An activity that occurs many times a day, and day after day after day? Toileting does, so maybe "routine" is a good name for it. Or do we mean something that is done routinely? A job we do to get it over with, with no thinking involved, no skill, no planing necessary, no particular results expected, nothing important to the child bound up with it? Toileting is not a routine. (Nor are eating, washing, sleeping. . . .)

You have to get some perspective on it. A child is born. He urinates and defecates. He doesn't need any teaching. He makes out all right, but when he is still very young, something new is added. We decide he has to learn, not how to urinate, because he knows that, but how to do it in the way our society thinks is nice . . . and when we think it is nice . . . and where . . . and with what attitudes . . . and what words.

Is it teaching? Is it education? Well . . . the mother says "No" to the child. It is one of the first times he bumps into discipline. The mother says, "That's right. In the pot." It is one of the first times he bumps into right and wrong, appropriate and in-appropriate. (At the college level we call it "Ethics" and give a Ph.D. for it.) The mother says, "Good boy, Johnny." And Johnny, for one of the first times, begins thinking and feeling about the kind of person he is. She says, "Bad. Bad." And little Johnny learns something about success and failure. Mother makes a face. Baby learns that some things are considered clean and some dirty. Mama says, "Mustn't touch," and sex rears its ugly head for one of the first times. Johnny doesn't wet his diaper; Mother looks pleased and maybe gives him an extra hug. Johnny gets a lesson in affection. He wets and he wets and he wets. He just can't help it because his little bladder hasn't grown enough. But mother doesn't like it and Johnny learns that it is a hard world, with tough high standards.

Success, failure, adequacy, inadequacy, clean, dirty, right, wrong, love, rejection, sex, acceptance, shame. . . . My goodness. And it all happens in the bathroom.

And it happens day after day after day, and many times a day. So that all kinds of very important feelings and attitudes get tied up with it and pretty well established even before Johnny comes to our eighteen-month-old group—to say nothing of what has happened by the time he is ready for the fives. Some attitudes are good and we can try to build on them. And some are not so good. We could try, skillfully, to change them slowly and to give them a new start in a right direction. The setting is

127

right. Bathrooms are small, intimate. We can talk with children and laugh with them, starting conversations; we can interpret to them, assist them, or let them help themselves or give just the right amount of aid.

But then . . . "I like to teach. I like to be on the play court. There the kids are doing something. They're learning. . . ." Still . . . the child on the pot does have his personality in a pliable position.*

*Used with permission of James L. Hymes, Jr., Ed.D., Carmel, Calif., formerly Director, Kaiser Child Service Department, Portland, Ore.

References

Adler, A. *Social interest*. New York: Capricorn Books, 1964.

Allport, G. W. *Becoming*. New Haven: Yale University Press, 1955.

Allport, G. W. Psychological models for guidance. In J. F. Rosenblith and W. Allinsmith (Eds.). *The causes of behavior II: Readings in child development and educational psychology*. Boston: Allyn and Bacon, 1966.

Allred, G. H. *Mission for mother: Guiding the child*. Salt Lake City: Bookcraft, 1968.

Ansbacher, H. L., and Ansbacher, R. R. (Eds.). *The individual psychology of Alfred Adler*. New York: Harper Torchbook, 1956.

Aronfreed, J. *Conduct and conscience: The socialization of internalized control over behavior*. New York: Academic Press, 1968.

Axline, V. *Play therapy*. Boston: Houghton Mifflin, 1947.

Azrin, N. H., and Holz, W. C. Punishment. In W. K. Honig (Ed.). *Operant behavior: Areas of research and application*. New York: Appleton-Century-Crofts, 1966.

Baer, D. M., and Wright, J. C. Developmental psychology, *Annual review of psychology* (Vol. 25). Palo Alto, Calif.: Annual Reviews, 1974.

Bandura, A., and Walters, R. H. *Social learning and personality development*. New York: Holt, Rinehart, and Winston, 1963.

Bardis, P. D. Family forms and variations historically considered. In H. T. Christensen (Ed.). *Handbook of marriage and the family*. Chicago: Rand McNally, 1964.

Becker, W. C. Consequences of different kinds of parental discipline. In M. L. Hoffman, and L. W. Hoffman (Eds.). *Review of child development research*. New York: Russell Sage Foundation, 1964.

Becker, W. C. *Parents are teachers*. Champaign, Ill.: Research Press, 1971.

Berger, L., and McGaugh, J. L. Critique and reformulation of "learning-theory" approaches to psychotherapy and neurosis. In T. Millon (Ed.). *Theories of psychopathology*. Philadelphia: W. B. Saunders, 1967.

Berkowitz, L. *The development of motives and values in the child*. New York: Basic Books, 1964.

Birns, B., and Golden, M. The implications of Piaget's theories for contemporary infancy research and education. In M. Schwebel, and J. Raph (Eds.). *Piaget in the classroom*. New York: Basic Books, 1973.

Black, M. Some aversive responses to a would-be reinforcer. In H. Wheeler (Ed.). *Beyond the punitive society*. San Francisco: W. H. Freeman, 1973.

Blackham, G. J., and Silberman, A. *Modification of child behavior*. Belmont, Calif.: Wadsworth, 1971.

Brill, A. A. Introductory remarks. In Freud, S. *The basic writings of Sigmund Freud* (A. A. Brill, Ed. and trans.). New York: Modern Library, 1938.

Brim, O. G., Jr. *Education for child rearing*. New York: Russell Sage Foundation, 1959.

Brown, R. *Social psychology*. New York: The Free Press, 1965.

Burr, W. R. Role transitions: A reformulation of theory. *Journal of Marriage and the Family*, 1972, 34: 407-16.

Burr, W. R. *Theory construction and the sociology of the family*. New York: Wiley, 1973.

Burr, W. R., Mead, D. E., and Rollins, B. C. A model for the application of research findings by the educator and counselor: Research to theory to practice. *Family Coordinator*, 1973, 22: 285-90.

Caldwell, B. M. The effects of infant care. In M. L. Hoffman, and L. W. Hoffman (Eds.).

Review of child development research. New York: Russell Sage Foundation, 1964.

Campbell, J. D. Peer relations in childhood. In M. L. Hoffman, and L. W. Hoffman (Eds.). *Review of child development research.* New York: Russell Sage Foundation, 1964.

Christensen, H. T., and Carpenter, G. W. Value-behavior discrepancies regarding pre-marital coitus in three Western cultures. *American Sociological Review,* 1962, 27: 66-74.

Combs, A. W. A perceptual view of the adequate personality. In A. W. Combs (Ed.). *Perceiving, behaving, becoming: A new focus for education.* Washington, D.C.: National Education Association, 1962.

Dinkmeyer, D., and Dreikurs, R. *Encouraging children to learn: The encouragement process.* Englewood Cliffs, N. J.: Prentice-Hall, 1963.

Dreikurs, R. *Psychology in the classroom* (2nd ed.). New York: Harper & Row, 1968.

Dreikurs, R., and Solz, V. *The challenge of parenthood.* New York: Duell, Sloan, and Pearce, 1958.

Duckworth, E. Language and thought. In M. Schwebel and J. Raph (Eds.). *Piaget in the classroom.* New York: Basic Books, 1973.

Duckworth, E. The having of wonderful ideas. In M. Schwebel and J. Raph (Eds.). *Piaget in the classroom.* New York: Basic Books, 1973.

Erickson, E. H. *Childhood and society* (2nd ed.). New York: W. W. Norton, 1963.

Eysenck, H. J., and Wilson, G. D. *The experimental study of Freudian theories.* London: Methuen, 1973.

Ferster, C. B., and Skinner, B. F. *Schedules of reinforcement.* New York: Appleton-Century-Crofts, 1957.

Flavell, J. H. *The developmental psychology of Jean Piaget.* Princeton, N. J.: Van Nostrand, 1963.

Ford, D. H., and Urban, H. B. *Systems of psychotherapy: A comparative study.* New York: Wiley, 1963.

Fraiberg, S. H. *The magic years.* New York: Scribner's, 1959.

Frank, R. W., Jr., and Meserole, H. (Eds.). *The responsible man: The insights of the humanities.* New York: Doubleday, 1965.

Freud, A. *Psychoanalysis for teachers and parents.* Boston: Beacon Press, 1935.

Freud, A. *The writings of Anna Freud* (Vol. 4). New York: International Universities Press, 1968.

Freud, S. *The basic writings of Sigmund Freud* (A. A. Brill, Ed. and trans.). New York: Modern Library, 1938.

Freud, S. *Civilization and its discontents.* New York: W. W. Norton, 1961.

Fromm, E. *Man for himself.* New York: Holt, Rinehart, and Winston, 1947.

Furth, H. G. *Piaget for teachers.* Englewood Cliffs, N. J.: Prentice-Hall, 1970.

Furth, H. G., and Wachs, H. *Thinking goes to school.* New York: Oxford University Press, 1975.

Gesell, A. *Infant development.* London: Hamish Hamilton, 1952.

Gesell, A., and Amatruda, C. S. *Developmental diagnosis: Normal and abnormal child development.* New York: Harper, 1941.

Gesell, A., and Amatruda, C. S. *The embryology of behavior.* Westport, Conn.: Greenwood Press, 1945.

Gesell, A., and Ilg, F. L. *Infant and child in the culture of today.* New York: Harper and Brothers, 1943.

Gesell, A., and Ilg, F. L. *The child from five to ten.* New York: Harper, 1946.

Gesell, A., and Ilg, F. L. *Child development: An introduction to the study of human growth.* New York: Harper, 1949.

Gesell, A., Ilg, F. L., and Ames, L. B. *Youth: The years from ten to sixteen.* New York: Harper and Brothers, 1956.

Gesell, A., and Thompson, H. Learning and growth in identical twin infants. *Genetic Psychology Monographs.* 1929, 6: 1-124.

Gewirtz, J. L. Mechanisms of social learning: Some roles of stimulation and behavior in early human development. In D. A. Goslin (Ed.). *Handbook of socialization theory and research.* Chicago: Rand McNally, 1969.

Gollin, E. S., and Moody, M. Developmental psychology. *Annual review of psychology* (Vol. 24). Palo Alto, Calif.: Annual Reviews, 1973.

Gordon, T. Group-centered leadership and administration. In C. R. Rogers (Ed.). *Client-centered therapy.* Boston: Houghton Mifflin, 1951.

Gordon, T. *Parent effectiveness training.* New York: Peter H. Wyden, 1970. (a)

Gordon, T. A theory of healthy relationships and a program of parent effectiveness training. In J. T. Hart, and T. M. Tomlinson (Eds.). *New directions in client-centered therapy.* Boston: Houghton Mifflin, 1970. (b)

Goslin, D. A. (Ed.). *Handbook of socialization theory and research.* Chicago: Rand McNally, 1969.

Haring, N. G., and Phillips, E. L. *Analysis and modification of classroom behavior.* Englewood Cliffs, N. J.: Prentice-Hall, 1972.

Hartmann, H. Psychoanalysis as a scientific theory. In T. Millon (Ed.). *Theories of psychopathology.* Philadelphia: W. B. Saunders, 1967.

Haley, J. *Strategies of psychotherapy.* New York: Grune and Stratton, 1969.

Hilgard, E. R. *Theories of learning.* (2nd ed.). New York: Appleton-Century-Crofts, 1956.

Hill, R., and Aldous, J. Socialization for marriage and parenthood. In D. A. Goslin (Ed.). *Handbook of socialization theory and research.* Chicago: Rand McNally, 1969.

Hitt, W. D. Two models of man. *American Psychologist,* 1969, 24: 651-58.

Holland, J. G., and Skinner, B. F. *The analysis of behavior.* New York: McGraw-Hill, 1961.

Hollingshead, A. B. *Elmtown's youth.* New York: Wiley, 1949.

Hymes, J. Unpublished memo, Oregon State University, 1945.

Ilg, F. L., and Ames, L. B. *Child behavior.* New York: Harper and Row, 1953.

Inhelder, B., and Piaget, J. *The growth of logical thinking from childhood to adolescence.* New York: Basic Books, 1958.

Jensen, M. R. Empathy and power in sibling relationships. Unpublished thesis, Brigham Young University, 1971.

Kagan, J. Acquisition and significance of sex typing and sex role identity. In M. L. Hoffman, and L. W. Hoffman (Eds.). *Review of child development research.* New York: Russell Sage Foundation, 1964.

Kagan, J., and Klein, R. E. Cross-cultural perspectives on early development. *American Psychologist,* 1973, 28: 947-61.

Kamii, C. Piaget's interactionism and the process of teaching young children. In M. Schwebel, and J. Raph (Eds.). *Piaget in the classroom.* New York: Basic Books, 1973.

Kelly, E. C. The fully functioning self. In A. W. Combs (Ed.). *Perceiving, behaving, becoming: A new focus for education.* Washington, D.C.: National Education Association, 1962.

Kline, P. *Fact and fantasy in Freudian theory.* London: Methuen, 1972.

Koch, H. L. The relationship of "primary mental abilities" in five- and six-year-olds to sex of child and characteristics of his sibling. *Child Development,* 1954, 25: 209-23.

Koch, S. Psychology and emerging conceptions of knowledge as unitary. In T. W. Wann (Ed.). *Behaviorism and phenomenology.* Chicago: University of Chicago Press, 1964.

Kohlberg, L. Development of moral character and moral idealogy. In M. L. Hoffman, and L. W. Hoffman (Eds.). *Review of child development research.* New York: Russell Sage Foundation, 1964.

Kohn, M. L. Social class and parental values. *American Journal of Sociology,* 1959, 64: 337-51.

Krumboltz, J. D., and Krumboltz, H. B. *Changing children's behavior.* Englewood Cliffs, N. J.: Prentice-Hall, 1972.

Kuhn, T. S. The structure of scientific revolutions (2nd ed.). Chicago: University of Chicago Press, 1970.

LeMasters, E. E. *Parents in modern America: A sociological analysis.* Homewood, Ill.: The Dorsey Press, 1970.

Lipsitt, L. P., and Eimas, P. D. Developmental psychology. *Annual review of psychology* (Vol. 23). Palo Alto, Calif.: Annual Reviews, 1972.

Maccoby, E. E., and Masters, J. C. Attachment and dependency. In P. H. Mussen (Ed.). *Carmichael's manual of child psychology* (3rd ed.). New York: Wiley, 1970.

Madsen, C. K., and Madsen, C. H., Jr. *Parents/children/discipline.* Boston: Allyn and Bacon, 1972.

Mahoney, M. J. *Cognition and behavior modification.* Cambridge, Mass.: Ballinger, 1974.

Malcolm, N. Behaviorism as a philosophy of psychology. In T. W. Wann (Ed.). *Behaviorism and phenomenology.* Chicago: University of Chicago Press, 1964.

Marwell, G., and Schmitt, D. R. *Cooperation: An experimental analysis.* New York: Academic Press, 1975.

Maslow, A. H. *Toward a psychology of being.* Princeton, N. J.: Van Nostrand, 1962. (a)

Maslow, A. H. Some basic propositions of a growth and self-actualization psychology. In A. W. Combs (Ed.). *Perceiving, behaving, becoming: A new focus for education.* Washington, D.C.: National Education Association, 1962. (b)

Medinnus, G. R., and Johnson, R. C. *Child psychology: Behavior and development.* New York: Wiley, 1965.

Merton, R. K. *Social theory and social structure.* Glencoe, Ill.: The Free Press, 1957.

Millon, T. (Ed.). *Theories of psychopathology.* Philadelphia: W. B. Saunders, 1967.

Novak, M. Is he really a grand inquisitor? In H. Wheeler (Ed.). *Beyond the punitive society.* San Francisco: W. H. Freeman, 1973.

Nye, R. D. *Three views of man.* Monterey, Calif.: Brooks/Cole, 1975.

Pearlin, L. I., and Kohn, M. L. Social class, occupation, and parental values: A cross-national study. *American Sociological Review,* 1966, 31:466-79.

Perelman, C. Behaviorism's enlightened despotism. In H. Wheeler (Ed.). *Beyond the punitive society.* San Francisco: W. H. Freeman, 1973.

Phillips, J. L., Jr. *The origins of intellect: Piaget's theory.* San Francisco: W. H. Freeman, 1969.

Piaget, J. *The construction of reality in the child.* New York: Basic Books, 1954.

Piaget, J. *Science of education and the psychology of the child.* New York: Orion Press, 1970.

Piaget, J., and Inhelder, B. *The psychology of the child.* New York: Basic Books, 1969.

Platt, J. R. The Skinnerian revolution. In H. Wheeler (Ed.). *Beyond the punitive society.* San Francisco: W. H. Freeman, 1973.

Raskin, N. J., and van der Veen, F. Client-centered family therapy: Some clinical and research perspectives. In J. T. Hart, and T. M. Tomlinson (Eds.). *New directions in client-centered therapy.* Boston: Houghton Mifflin, 1970.

Ritchie-Calder, L. Beyond B. F. Skinner. In H. Wheeler (Ed.). *Beyond the punitive society.* San Francisco: W. H. Freeman, 1973.

Rogers, C. R. *Client-centered therapy.* Boston: Houghton Mifflin, 1951.

Rogers, C. R. *On becoming a person: A therapist's view of psychotherapy.* Boston: Houghton Mifflin, 1961.

Rogers, C. R. Toward becoming a fully functioning person. In A. W. Combs (Ed.). *Perceiving, behaving, becoming: A new focus for education.* Washington, D.C.: National Education Association, 1962.

Rogers, C. R. *Freedom to learn.* Columbus, Ohio: Charles E. Merrill, 1969.

Rosen, R. Can any behavior be conditioned? In H. Wheeler (Ed.). *Beyond the punitive society.* San Francisco: W. H. Freeman, 1973.

Rosenthal, R. *Experimenter effects in behavioral research.* New York: Appleton-Century-Crofts, 1966.

Rozynko, V., Swift, K., Swift, J., and Boggs, L. J. Controlled environments for social change. In H. Wheeler (Ed.). *Beyond the punitive society.* San Francisco: W. H. Freeman, 1973.

Sameroff, A. J. Learning and adaptation in infancy: A comparison of models. In H. W. Reese (Ed.). *Advances in child development and behavior* (Vol. 7). New York: Academic Press, 1972.

Sampson, E. E. The study of ordinal position: Antecedents and outcomes. In B. A. Maher (Ed.). *Progress in experimental personality research* (Vol. 2). New York: Academic Press, 1965.

Schachter, S. Birth order, eminence and higher education. *American Sociological Review,* 1963, 28: 757-67.

Schooler, C. Birth order effects: Not here, now now! *Psychological Bulletin,* 1972, 78: 161-75.

Schooler, C. Birth order effects: A reply to Breland. *Psychological Bulletin,* 1973, 80:213-14.

Schwab, J. J. A quiver of queries. In H. Wheeler (Ed.). *Beyond the punitive society.* San Francisco: W. H. Freeman, 1973.

Schwebel, M., and Raph, J. (Eds.). *Piaget in the classroom.* New York: Basic Books, 1973.

Sinclair, H. From preoperational to concrete thinking and parallel development of symbolization. In M. Schwebel, and J. Raph (Eds.). *Piaget in the classroom.* New York: Basic Books, 1973.

Skinner, B. F. *Science and human behavior.* New York: Free Press, 1953.

Skinner, B. F. *Verbal behavior.* New York: Appleton-Century-Crofts, 1957.

Skinner, B. F. *Contingencies of reinforcement: A theoretical analysis.* New York: Appleton-Century-Crofts, 1969.

Skinner, B. F. *Beyond freedom and dignity.* New York: Knopf, 1971.

Skinner, B. F. Answers for my critics. In H. Wheeler (Ed.). *Beyond the punitive society.* San Francisco: W. H. Freeman, 1973.

Skinner, B. F. *About behaviorism.* New York: Knopf, 1974.

Stolz, L. M. Youth: The Gesell institute and its latest study. *Contemporary Psychology,* 1958, 3: 10-15.

Stuart, R. B. Operant-interpersonal treatment for marital discord. *Journal of Consulting and Clinical Psychology,* 1969, 33:675-82.

Sullivan, H. S. *The interpersonal theory of psychiatry.* New York: W. W. Norton, 1953.

Tharp, R. G., and Wetzel, R. J. *Behavior modification in the natural environment.* New York: Academic Press, 1969.

Thompson, T., and Grabowski, J. G. *Reinforcement schedules and multioperant analysis.* New York: Appleton-Century-Crofts, 1972.

Truax, C. B., and Mitchell, K. M. Research on certain therapist interpersonal skills in relation to process and outcome. In A. E. Bergin, and S. L. Garfield (Eds.). *Handbook of psychotherapy and behavior change.* New York: Wiley, 1971.

Voyat, G. The development of operations: A theoretical and practical matter. In M. Schwebel, and J. Raph (Eds.). *Piaget in the classroom.* New York: Basic Books, 1973.

Watzlawick, P., Beavin, J. H., and Jackson, D. D. *Pragmatics of human communication.* New York: W. W. Norton, 1967.

Way, L. *Adler's place in psychology: An exposition of individual psychology.* New York: Collier Books, 1962.

Wheeler, H. (Ed.). *Beyond the punitive society.* San Francisco: W. H. Freeman, 1973.

Wolberg, L. R. Technique of reconstructive therapy. In T. Millon (Ed.). *Theories of psychopathology.* Philadelphia: W. B. Saunders, 1967.

Yarrow, M. R., Campbell, J. D., and Burton, R. V. *Child rearing: An inquiry into research and methods.* San Francisco: Jossey-Bass, 1968.

Yates, A. J. *Theory and practice in behavior therapy.* New York: Wiley, 1975.

Zigler, E., and Child, I. L. *Socialization and personality development.* Reading, Mass.: Addison-Wesley, 1973.

Index

About the Author

D. Eugene Mead is an associate professor of child development and family relationships at Brigham Young University. He is a member of the American Psychological Association and the American Association of Marriage and Family Counselors. His work has been in the areas of parent education and counseling, family communication and behavior, and marital and family counseling. Dr. Mead has been a consultant in family counseling for parents and teachers in numerous institutions in the United States and Canada. He has also written many articles on child rearing for parents and for professionals. His educational degrees include a doctorate from the University of Oregon in counseling-psychology, a master's from San Jose State College in psychology, and a bachelor's from the University of Oregon in psychology.